Why Those Who Shovel Are Silent

Why Those Who Shovel
Are Silent

A History of Local Archaeological
Knowledge and Labor

Allison Mickel

UNIVERSITY PRESS OF COLORADO

Louisville

Published by University Press of Colorado
245 Century Circle, Suite 202
Louisville, Colorado 80027

 The University Press of Colorado is a proud member of the Association of University Presses.

The University Press of Colorado is a cooperative publishing enterprise supported, in part, by Adams State University, Colorado State University, Fort Lewis College, Metropolitan State University of Denver, Regis University, University of Colorado, University of Northern Colorado, University of Wyoming, Utah State University, and Western Colorado University.

∞ This paper meets the requirements of the ANSI/NISO Z39.48–1992 (Permanence of Paper).

ISBN: 978-1-64642-114-5 (hardcover)
ISBN: 978-1-64642-126-8 (paperback)
ISBN: 978-1-64642-115-2 (ebook)
https://doi.org/10.5876/9781646421152

Library of Congress Cataloging-in-Publication Data

Names: Mickel, Allison, author. ·
Title: Why those who shovel are silent : a history of local archaeological knowledge and labor / Allison Mickel.
Description: Louisville, CO : University Press of Colorado, 2021. | Includes bibliographical references and index. | Summary: "Years of ethnographic work with current and former workers at two Middle Eastern archaeological sites combined with archival research. Describes the knowledge that locally-hired laborers possess about artifacts, excavation methods, and interpretation, showing that archaeological workers are experts—and are paid by archaeologists to pretend to be less knowledgeable"— Provided by publisher.
Identifiers: LCCN 2020051278 (print) | LCCN 2020051279 (ebook) | ISBN 9781646421145 (hardcover) | ISBN 9781646421268 (paperback) | ISBN 9781646421152 (ebook)
Subjects: LCSH: Community archaeology—Jordan—Petra (Extinct city) | Community archaeology—Turkey—Çatal Mound. | Archaeology—Methodology. | Archaeology—Social aspects—Jordan—Petra (Extinct city) | Archaeology—Social aspects—Turkey—Çatal Mound. | Excavations (Archaeology)—Jordan—Petra (Extinct city) | Excavations (Archaeology)—Turkey—Çatal Mound.
Classification: LCC CC77.C66 M53 2021 (print) | LCC CC77.C66 (ebook) | DDC 930.1—dc23
LC record available at https://lccn.loc.gov/2020051278
LC ebook record available at https://lccn.loc.gov/2020051279

Cover photograph by Allison Mickel

To my parents, Elaine and Steve

To my partner, Jon

To all the people and places
whose perspectives made this possible.

Look. There's been a lot of work in excavation. We've led it. We know it.

—Arbayah Juma'a Eid al-Faqir
Petra, Jordan
November 2014

Contents

Figures

Acknowledgments

For the warm welcomes in family homes, for the openness and trust, for the willingness to share memories, laughs, regrets, and criticisms with me, and for all the tea, apricots, *pide, mansaf, maqluba,* cookies, and candy, I want to thank the current and former site workers of the Temple of the Winged Lions in Petra, Jordan, and of Çatalhöyük, Turkey. The endless hospitality extended to me by the communities of Umm Sayhoun, Wadi Musa, Beidha, and Küçükköy created not only an incredible research environment but also a wonderful home for the months I spent in these places. Thank you to my found family, Suleman (Abu Raneen) Samahin, Ahmed al-Faqeer, and Atullah al-Mowasa, for the introductions made and doors opened, especially your own.

The connections created and interviews conducted over the course of this project would not have been possible without Eman Abdessalam's assistance navigating the houses and neighborhoods of Petra or the generously volunteered time and translation abilities of Numan Arslan, Cansu Kurt, Duygu Ertemin, and Tunç İlada. I cannot adequately express how appreciative I am for you helping me in all the many ways you have, from setting aside your other work and responsibilities to walking or driving with me for miles and miles to offering new ideas and thoughtful feedback on my ideas as they first emerged. I hope you can see the impact of your contributions in the completed work.

Thank you to the directors of the projects at the Temple of the Winged Lions in Petra and at Çatalhöyük, who not only provided essential logistical support for this research but, more important, allowed me to look closely and critically at their archives and practices. I learned so much during this project, not only about labor relations and knowledge production in Middle Eastern archaeology but also about what good, reflexive scholarship and leadership looks like from all our conversations and collaborations. To Dr. Christopher Tuttle, Dr. Glenn Corbett, and Maria Elena Ronza of the Temple of the Winged Lions Cultural Resource Management Initiative, along with Dr. Barbara A. Porter of the American Center of Oriental Research, I am so grateful for everything you made possible for me in Petra. Dr. Ian Hodder, thank you for all of this but not only for this—I have much more to thank you for.

The five years of fieldwork that culminated in this project were funded by a number of scholarly organizations: primarily the Fulbright Program, as well as the American Schools of Oriental Research, the Stanford Archaeology Center, the Abbasi Program in Islamic Studies, and the Biblical Archaeology Society. Writing retreats at Lehigh University, funded by the Humanities Center and the ADVANCE Center for Women STEM Faculty, were essential in completing the final stages of this project. The amount and quality of research that all these organizations support is astonishing, and I am honored to contribute to that body of work.

This book has been shaped and undeniably improved by the invaluable critical feedback of my four dissertation committee members. Dr. Michael Shanks, thank you for pushing me to keep asking "so what?" Dr. Benjamin Porter, thank you for giving me something new to think about after every conversation in both northern California and southern Jordan. Dr. Barbara Voss, thank you for pointing me to the next questions to ask, the next places to go, the next approaches to pursue to make an intervention that is new and important. Finally, to my adviser, Dr. Ian Hodder, thank you for the work that first inspired me to study archaeology when I was eighteen years old, thank you for accepting me onto the Çatalhöyük project so long ago based on a very eager e-mail, thank you for that phone call in February 2011 telling me I was accepted to Stanford's PhD program, and thank you for five years of constant mentorship, guidance, and encouragement.

I have also been lifted up by a phenomenal community of mentors and colleagues who have shaped my thinking on this subject of archaeological labor in crucial ways. The American Center of Oriental Research in Amman, Jordan, provides an essential hub for archaeologists and anthropologists working in Jordan. In particular, thank you to Barbara Porter and Jack Green for your questions, insights, and the opportunities you make possible for so many scholars. I have a memory of a conversation with Leigh-Ann Bedal in the seating area at ACOR when this project was emerging that shaped the questions I asked and has led to so many more thoughtful conversations. Morag Kersel's support for early career researchers is unmatched in the field, in my view. Thank you for asking "where's the book" so many times over the last few years. Åsa Berggren, at Çatalhöyük (and beyond), has also been a force in pushing this book forward and further.

Thank you to the team at the University Press of Colorado who have shepherded this book from prospectus to proofs to pages: to Darrin, to Dan, to Laura, and to Cheryl. I am grateful for the feedback from the three anonymous reviewers whose feedback pointed out the gaps and weaknesses in early drafts; any remaining flaws, of course, remain my own. I also cannot express sufficient gratitude to Randall McGuire for his early and enthusiastic support for this work. Most of all, to my editor, Charlotte Steinhardt, thank you forever for believing in this project and taking care of it—and me—through all the inevitable obstacles and hard-earned celebrations. Your recognition of the scholarly stakes of this work and simultaneously the emotion wrapped up in the act of authorship made the publication process so seamless and rewarding.

Lastly, I want to express my most sincere love and appreciation for all of the boundless support I received from my family and friends. Every one of your e-mails, postcards, text messages, and social media posts cheering me on helped me to keep thinking, keep typing, and keep remembering that I benefit from an unbreakable network of support. Emma Horton, I will always have a spare bed and freshly baked brownies waiting for you. To Elaine, Stephen, and Scott Mickel and Jon Irons, thank you and I love you, for everything.

Why Those Who Shovel Are Silent

The stories in this account link together Nabataean idols, carbonized brains, winged lions, Neolithic pregnancies, figurines, obsidian daggers, Roman coins, and beads. These stories draw into view heavy buckets full of soil and the splintering wooden handles of picks used to loosen cobbles and compacted earth. They hint at connections between the answers to questions about the origins of settled life, the construction strategies for monumental religious buildings, the dietary and subsistence practices of societies who lived 9,000 years ago, and the reasons why impressive ancient sites and structures were destroyed and abandoned.

The stories come from two groups of archaeological experts who have participated in research projects for decades handling artifacts, sorting out stratigraphy, and engaging in critical interpretive conversations. Both groups are made up of people who possess comprehensive, detailed expertise about all of these objects and ideas; people who, despite this expertise, have never documented their archaeological knowledge of these objects and topics.

The two groups come from the local communities at Petra, Jordan, and Çatalhöyük, Turkey—two archaeological sites separated by more than 520 miles and five millennia. Petra, located in what is now southern Jordan, was the capital city of the Nabataean kingdom, which flourished primarily between the fourth century BCE and AD 106, when it was annexed by the Roman Empire.[1] Çatalhöyük, in southern Anatolia, was a

DOI: 10.5876/9781646421152.c000

Neolithic and Chalcolithic settlement from about 7400 BCE to 5600 BCE.[2] In terms of their locations, time periods, and archaeological assemblages, these sites have little in common.

They have both, however, been excavated for more than 50 years. Picks and shovels have churned through the earth at both sites nearly constantly, throughout dramatic transformations in the discipline of archaeology. So much has changed in archaeologists' research questions, methodologies, tools, and knowledge production practices since the summer of 1961 when two archaeological projects—coincidentally—began: one at Çatalhöyük and one in Petra. Through all this change, local community members from these two sites were employed to hold picks and shovels, to push wheelbarrows, to sift the excavated soil and pull out sherds of pottery or shards of glass.

In this book I ask: What effect have those 50 years of change in archaeological practice had on the role local community members at these two sites played in the archaeological research process?

I ask: *Have they had any effect at all?*

This was not the initial question I had in mind when I began my research in 2011. At that time, my goal was to build on the work of others who had pointed out a long-standing problem in archaeology wherein local laborers dig but do not document (Berggren and Hodder 2003; McAnany and Rowe 2015; Steele 2005). I wanted to provide evidence that information had been lost as a result of this arrangement—to show that site workers in archaeology possess knowledge about the archaeological past and excavation strategy that disappears as projects end or as these people pass away. I went to Çatalhöyük and Petra to accomplish this because of their long histories of excavation and because this loss of knowledge was particularly urgent at these two sites.

When I began this project, for instance, only two elderly men from Küçükköy, the small village next to Çatalhöyük, still survived who had worked on excavations there in the 1960s. Beyond their memories, there is no way of ascertaining what site workers did, saw, or knew about the excavations at Çatalhöyük during this time period, since James Mellaart (1967), the archaeologist, does not mention them outside of four names in the acknowledgments in his monograph. Between 1961 and 1963 when he dug at Çatalhöyük, he hired dozens of men from Küçükköy and Beycesultan, another nearby town, but their names and contributions are almost entirely absent from his publications on his excavations.

This is certainly unjust. It is, at the same time, not unusual for the era. Mid-twentieth-century archaeology, especially in the Middle East but also elsewhere, was characterized by hierarchical and militaristic excavation strategies. During this time period, archaeologists hired enormous work-forces to move massive volumes of earth as quickly as possible for wages that were as low as possible. These resident laborers' work was character-ized as unskilled manual labor, so site workers' names—let alone their con-tributions—were rarely recorded. Philip C. Hammond, who began dig-ging in Petra in 1961, exemplified these practices. His first archaeological excavation involved removing 4,500 m³ of sand (the equivalent of nearly two full Olympic-size swimming pools) out of the amphitheatre in Petra. He hired so many men from the local Bedouin community that it only took a few months in total for them to complete this monumental project (Hammond 1965).

Hammond (1996) continued to excavate in Petra for the next 44 years, hir-ing between 20 and 40 workers each season. I estimate that over the course of Hammond's 44 years of excavations, more than 300 Jordanian men resid-ing in the area worked for him, as well as a few women who did the cleaning and laundry and sometimes the cooking for the project. Despite this turn-over in workforce, Hammond employed only two foremen across nearly a half-century—first a man named Abu Shahir, who has since passed away, and later, Dachlallah Qublan al-Faqir.

Each year, when Hammond and his team of student archaeologists arrived at Petra, he would tell the foreman how many workers he needed on the proj-ect. The foreman was then given latitude in terms of who to hire. According to Dachlallah, he made the decisions based on "who needed the work." He said in an interview, "You have all these people who say 'I want to work. I want to work.' Some from the Ammarin, some from Bedul, some from Sayyidin, some from Wadi Musa [different tribes and communities in the Petra area]. I mean, all of the people ask and ask. So I take some from here, some from here, some from here. Just the good ones."

It is apparent, though, after searching for Hammond's former workers throughout the Petra area, that both Dachlallah and Abu Shahir showed a strong preference for hiring members of their families. One woman who washed pottery for Hammond's project, for example, said in an interview that she "only worked on this excavation because Abu Shahir wanted to hire his family." Like Mellaart and other contemporary archaeologists, Hammond did not systematically record the names of the workers anywhere.

Once hired, the local diggers would stand in a line so Hammond could assess them and make assignments to specific trenches. From there, both the student excavator supervising that trench and the foreman were responsible for keeping track of workers' arrival times each day and the quality of their work. The students' field notebooks represented my main initial lead for finding Hammond's former workers, since they noted the first names or nicknames of workers who arrived late, who failed to follow directions, or whose work was especially impressive. One of the most experienced students, who went on to earn his PhD while working on the project, was placed in charge of the payroll for the project, giving out the weekly salary. According to the former participants in Hammond's project, they were paid less than 1 Jordanian dinar (JD)[3] for a day of work in the early years of the project, eventually raised to 10 JD per day (the national minimum wage for archaeological work) by the end of the project in 2005. The workers could be fired at any time by the foreman or by Hammond because they showed up late, took too many breaks, had been drinking alcohol, behaved in an overly familiarly way with women members of the project, and, as I will show, for asking too many questions or challenging excavation methodology.

These early archaeological projects at Petra and Çatalhöyük epitomize the distanced relationships that existed between foreign archaeologists and local workers in the Middle East through the mid-twentieth century. Workers were not considered crucial participants in the scholarly work of archaeology. Their work was characterized as bodily, not brainy. This belief in the separation of manual and intellectual work, of unskilled versus skilled labor in archaeology, created the crisis I sought to illustrate ethnographically: that after 50 years of excavations, two communities of archaeological experts had developed who were never fully involved in the production of archaeological knowledge about the past. I wanted to show that this represented a loss to science and history.

I believed this would be uniquely possible to do at Petra and Çatalhöyük because of the current community archaeology projects at both sites. While there are many sites in the Middle East and around the world that have been excavated for 50 years or longer, there are not as many that have been involved in the recent turn toward public engagement in archaeology. Since the early 1990s, archaeologists worldwide have increasingly recognized the importance of engaging stakeholder groups in all dimensions of the archaeological process, including intellectual and decision-making activities. Archaeologists working in contexts around the globe have developed public education programs, supported tourism initiatives, and worked to involve local and descendant communities in setting research goals and plans (Atalay 2012; Colwell-Chanthaphonh and Ferguson 2008; Merriman 2002, 2004; Silliman 2008; Stottman 2010). Public and community archaeology has emerged as an identifiable subfield of archaeology, which has influenced the broader discipline to become more aware of the political impact of archaeological work and how it affects descendant groups, resident communities, and other stakeholder populations. This disciplinary shift transformed excavation practice at both Petra and Çatalhöyük. Philip Hammond concluded his research in Petra in 2005, having excavated the Temple of the Winged Lions for decades, and in 2009 a new archaeological project started at the site when Christopher A. Tuttle formed the Temple of the Winged Lions Cultural Resource Management initiative (TWLCRM). The emphases of TWLCRM were thorough documentation, responsible conservation, and local community involvement in every step of the process (Tuttle 2013). TWLCRM created a core team of five local community members from the Bedouin village of Umm Sayhoun in Jordan who held supervisory roles over the excavation, conservation, and documentation of the site. TWLCRM also hired larger teams of local community members for a few weeks at a time, rotating the members of this team to include and train as many people from the area as possible. Each iteration of the larger teams was designed to include members from a mix of tribes and families and prioritized giving employment opportunities to families in need. They sought as well to hire and train women in archaeological skills for the first time in Petra. TWLCRM is an example of the movement toward an archaeology that promotes community participation instead of the traditional relations between archaeologists and local communities.

This same shift began somewhat earlier at Çatalhöyük, where excavations were renewed in 1993. During this time, Ian Hodder's Çatalhöyük Research Project (ÇRP) established itself as a site for progressive methodologies—in terms of adaptable and democratized recording, integration of computerized technologies, sampling strategies, and community involvement (Atalay 2010, 2012; Bartu 2000; Berggren et al. 2015; Hodder 2000). Instead of a colossal army of a local labor force, ÇRP each year hired a group of five to fifteen site workers from the local village of Küçükköy, approximately 1.2 km away from the Neolithic mound. The strategy for hiring, too, differed from earlier projects in the region.

In the earliest years of the project, Hodder attempted the model of asking a foreman to hire laborers but quickly recognized that only members of the foreman's family were receiving work opportunities. Hodder then hired a different foreman and made it an explicit priority to offer employment to individuals from multiple different families. Over the years, the project re-hired those who had worked on the project in the past, allowing these individuals to build on their previous training and take on jobs with increased responsibility. Hodder (2000) also deliberately hired women, a decision that elicited vehement resistance at first from the conservative and patriarchal local community but which Hodder has defended as essential to engaging and uplifting the local community as a whole, not just the men. Indeed, the Çatalhöyük model of recruiting and employing women for archaeological work was an inspiration for the TWLCRM's decision to do the same.

Instead of setting a daily wage in advance or adhering strictly to the national standard, project leadership and workers together negotiated the workers' salary at Çatalhöyük. These negotiations also included the terms of employment, such as normal working hours and agreements around Ramadan and Bayram,[4] when religious and familial obligations conflicted with work expectations. Furthermore, to engage locally hired individuals and their communities in the project's activities, ÇRP brought on social anthropologists who met with residents of nearby towns to discuss what Çatalhöyük meant to them and ultimately had a team dedicated to Community-Based Participatory Research (Atalay 2010; Bartu 2000; Shankland 1999a, 1999b; see chapter 1).

My goal of seeking and engaging community members' expertise therefore aligned with the broader inclusive priorities of the contemporary excavations at these two sites. Not only would I be able to build on the positive relationships the new projects had developed with local communities, but I also saw an opportunity to collaborate with the project directors on altering excavation practice so that local expertise would be invited and included—resulting, I hoped, in more diverse, complex, and nuanced knowledge about the past.

In 2011, I joined the Çatalhöyük project as an excavator, and in 2012, I became the TWLCRM project anthropologist. In both roles, I participated in onsite digging and conservation work, which allowed me to not only observe but also experience the organization of these teams, their methods, and the crystallization of ideas into facts as information moved through the archaeological project. I worked at each site for two to three months every summer until 2016, in addition to living in Petra for a complete year in 2014–2015. During this time, I lived at the houses affiliated with the archaeological projects. Each workday, I would go to the excavations at each site and work with the locally hired laborers. At Çatalhöyük, I directed excavations, both supervising and working with site workers to set up our equipment, dig, sieve, sort artifacts, and clean up at the end of the day. Throughout these activities, I spoke with workers about their thoughts and interpretations of the remains being uncovered. On the TWLCRM project, local team members led the excavation work, and my onsite role was much more documentary in nature. I photographed the work as it proceeded but also participated in sieving, pottery washing, artifact sorting, labeling, and tent raising. I attended weekly team meetings and participated in all team-related events, including celebrations of work progress and visits to the site by local schoolchildren and students from Amman.

In total, I spent approximately 12 full months at Çatalhöyük and 14 months in Petra. Dedicating this amount of time to living in each research location is a rarity in archaeology, which tends to involve short-term, periodic engagements. Archaeologists infrequently gain emic insight into the heterogeneity of the communities among whom we live and work. The sustained nature of my fieldwork meant that I experienced the interacting, sometimes competing scales of society and watched communities fracture and come together in often surprising ways. I was in Turkey, for instance, as nationalist sentiment escalated, affecting foreign-led archaeological projects and everyday life even in small villages like Küçükköy, just outside Çatalhöyük. I experienced this at the level of state policy, when in my final season of fieldwork I was barred from entering Küçükköy or conducting any more interviews. I also experienced these changes at a local level: during one field season, as tens of thousands of protestors speaking out against Erdoğan's leadership were being teargassed by Turkish police in Istanbul 750 km away, in our area police had to step in to protect protestors from the incensed, stick-wielding groups of Erdoğan and Adalet ve Kalkınma Partisi (AKP) supporters who outnumbered the protestors (Burch 2013).

I was in Petra when the Jordanian government cracked down on a long-term money laundering scheme, with drastic financial repercussions for families across southern Jordan as hundreds of vehicles, numerous flocks of sheep and goats, and nearly $60 million were seized (JT 2016). The communities living around Petra, in response, shut down the gates of Petra and the surrounding highways. I watched as these tribes and families—who most often emphasize their differences (Bille 2012; Kooring and Simms 1996; Russell 1993)—came together to collectively claim power over this archaeological site and use it as leverage to make (ultimately unsuccessful) demands for the return of their property. The timing of my research, in terms of both length and moment, put me in a position to recognize that communities who identify at times as collectives may disassociate under different circumstances and might coalesce under others, motivated by issues related to both economy and cultural heritage.

Partly on this basis, I spent my time forging deep relationships with both local community members and archaeologists, a process that made clear how diverse these groups are. Primarily on weekends and during evenings, I went to the homes and workplaces of current and former workers from the two sites to interview them about their expertise in archaeology. I interviewed them in their own languages, unless they requested otherwise (some men in Petra in particular are fluent in English from working in the tourism industry).[5] The site workers I grew to know included men of all ages, from those whose toddlers sat in my lap during our conversation to the grandfathers who offered me armfuls of apricots, harvested from the orchards they had spent their lives cultivating. I even spent time with a few women who had worked at these sites, hired for highly specific tasks like washing pottery, cooking, doing laundry, and sorting residue. These individuals possessed different nationalities, kin affiliations, socioeconomic backgrounds, marital statuses, gender identities, and education levels, as well as experience in archaeological work. Some had worked for decades in archaeology; others, only a few seasons. Some had carried out only the physical work of earth moving, while others had taken on more specialized tasks.

Despite these differences, across both contexts, these diverse former site workers seemed to agree on one thing: they had no expertise in archaeology.

This book explains how this is possible—not that locally hired laborers lack expertise in archaeology (on the contrary, the longest chapter is dedicated to demonstrating the expertise they *do* have) but rather that they would make the decision to maintain that they lack expertise. I define "expertise" broadly, to refer to the full range of specialized knowledge and skills—explicitly stated and tacitly embodied—locally hired laborers have developed in archaeology by virtue of their long-term participation in excavation and which supports the production of knowledge about the human past. Defining and searching for this flexible concept of expertise, I thought, would allow me to demonstrate the hidden forms of expertise site workers possess. I wanted to be able to demonstrate to fellow archaeologists that for generations we have dug alongside site workers whose insights and abilities have escaped our view but would be legible to our community once pointed out.

I approached this project anticipating that site workers would argue that they had access to privileged information and had perfected methodologies previous archaeological project directors had never recognized. I was a member of the projects employing them, after all, and my stated goal was to collaborate with project directors to shift the excavation design. If anything, I thought site workers might even exaggerate their knowledge and skill set in hopes of getting a wage increase or a preferred job. But I kept encountering just the opposite. Whether I asked about classic forms of archaeological expertise, like identifying forms of pottery, or more amorphous and alternative forms, like listening to the sound of the soil against a spade, the site workers explicitly denied having any such expertise.

This finding begins to make sense in the context of the development of archaeology in the Middle East, which I analyze in chapter 1. I focus on the 200-year history of labor management on excavations in the Middle East, and I illustrate what has changed in archaeological labor management strategies and, most crucially, what has not. Recognizing the degree to which the colonial and economic origins of Middle Eastern archaeological practice continue to inform how we excavate today is the first essential insight to understand why career archaeological site workers routinely choose to claim a lack of knowledge about the excavation process.

The historical review in chapter 1 contextualizes the accounts of the site workers and excavators from the projects under study and lays the groundwork for understanding what about the experience and structure of archaeological projects in the Middle East is region-specific. I also situate archaeology as a scientific practice, with similarities between excavation and laboratory labor. I therefore look to science studies for theoretical and methodological approaches that can offer analytical purchase on the links between labor and knowledge production practices in archaeology—and vice versa.

Chapter 2 then establishes that site workers' claims of a lack of expertise do not represent the knowledge and skills they actually do possess. In this chapter, I use Hammond's excavations in Petra (1963–2005) as a window into earlier approaches to labor management and Hodder's excavations at Çatalhöyük (1993–2018) as a window into labor management after the recent turn toward community engagement. These two projects serve as representative case studies of disparate priorities, programs, and paradigms for the labor relations in place in archaeological research settings. Viewing them side by side allows for a comparison of how divergent strategies for scientific labor management impact site workers' ability to develop expertise and participate in knowledge production on an excavation.

To examine site workers' experiences and expertise, I compare the memories they shared during our conversations to the archival materials from each of these projects, showing the ways the records both corroborate and complement each other. I use social network analysis to make a quantitative and visual comparison between the site archives and the oral histories of site workers and to illustrate that the knowledge site workers possess is structural, not anecdotal. This analysis reveals that site workers on projects both before and after the shift toward community engagement in archaeology developed measurable insights into archaeological finds and methods. Even though these projects were managed according to contrasting principles and priorities and even though educating and training local excavation participants is a stated goal of community-oriented projects like TWLCRM and ÇRP, locally hired laborers working were learning about the research process and site assemblages before the implementation of such community engagement strategies.

Does this mean that earlier projects weren't as exclusive as they have been characterized by proponents of public archaeology? Or does it mean that community engagement efforts have not been as transformational from an educational standpoint as one might hope?

Chapter 3 addresses these possibilities. I demonstrate that despite their extensive knowledge of archaeological assemblages and methods, locally hired laborers across the sites and contexts lack insight into the interpretations of the findings from the projects on which they have worked. I identify a number of long-standing barriers that continue to prevent local laborers on many archaeological projects from acquiring knowledge about interpretation and analysis in archaeology, even on projects that emphasize public engagement. I argue that these barriers block the transfer of ideas in both directions, preventing archaeologists from benefiting from the archaeological expertise site workers possess. Many of these barriers stem from the ways archaeological excavations have been organized and run since the beginning of the discipline. These are inherited stoppages with colonial origins that community archaeology has not yet sufficiently addressed, which prevent locally hired laborers from gaining insight into the analytical processes and outcomes of archaeological research.

But site workers habitually deny knowledge not just of research questions and conclusions. In fact, they very often deny knowing anything about artifacts or methodologies that they have already described in detail.

I argue that this is because the disciplinary legacies outlined in chapter 1 go far beyond the inherited barriers named in chapter 3 that limit site workers' access to participating in the analysis of archaeological assemblages. Specifically, the underlying labor structures in Middle Eastern archaeology—regardless of whether community engagement is a priority—have not transformed even as so much else has changed in the discipline. The ways archaeologists have made decisions about hiring and firing local workforces have not been overturned through community archaeology. Instead, opportunities for paid work have consistently been made available for excavation workers who downplay their scientific knowledge, emphasizing instead their traditionalism and simplicity. I call this phenomenon "lucrative non-knowledge," and it is the subject of chapter 4.

I then ask what about lucrative non-knowledge can be identified in archaeological contexts outside the Middle East, which may lack the specific colonial and Orientalist origins but still retain the predominance of foreign-led archaeological projects. In chapter 5, I examine the piecemeal ethnographic and historical literature on archaeological labor to discern the economic dynamics at sites in India, sub-Saharan Africa, Latin America, and elsewhere. I attempt as well to understand what locally hired site workers in these areas are paid to do—and, more important, what working identities they are paid to perform. Like a network, I connect these disparate studies to one another through a commonality: that most often it is not their archaeological expertise for which most practiced excavation workers are economically rewarded but rather a performance of docility, submission, or an exaggerated "traditional" identity. The effect for archaeology is that the discipline produces less inclusive, less nuanced knowledge as site workers contribute their expertise only in subtle, implicit, tacit ways. To produce more dynamic understandings of the archaeological record, the economic structures of excavation must be sufficiently overturned so that site workers are paid for the explicit expression of their archaeological expertise and not for hiding it.

My aim in this book, though, is not merely to offer critique without hope. The shift toward reflexivity in archaeology has led to a multi-strand, multi-decade amassing of literature on the discipline's need to decolonize and to critically examine its aims, methods, and theoretical approaches. These calls have been necessary and important. More recently, though, there is an emerging and more optimistic discussion of how exactly archaeologists might reimagine their work, whether through an enchantment-led approach (Perry 2019), through archaeologies of care (Caraher 2019), or through an archaeology of heart (Lyons et al. 2019; Lyons and Supernant 2019). Forward-looking frameworks like these are sprouting, budding, blossoming out of the substantive critique of archaeology's failures in equity, inclusion, and justice. Concepts like these do not purport to "solve" archaeology, instead offering something like trail markers pointing to potential ways forward but making no promises about the difficulty of the journey.

In chapter 6, I, too, offer a trail marker—one limited in scope but which orients this book toward the future, not simply the past. I argue that if site workers were included in the documentation efforts of the archaeological endeavor—and were paid for it—the interpretations reached over the course of the excavation could incorporate their particular perspectives and insights. I examine other projects that have used ethnographic interviews, sketching, video, crafting, and collaborative exhibit design toward this end, assessing their potential to transform the economic dynamics of archaeological labor that have created the phenomenon of lucrative non-knowledge. I also present the results of experiments I conducted in which I asked site workers at Petra and Çatalhöyük to create photographs illustrating their experiences and insights into their work. In these experiments, I found that each participant developed an individual style of photography and that the photographs presented a willingness to play with the canonical types of photos from archaeological excavations, often lacking an identifiable main subject or taking photos of objects and places traditionally underrepresented in archaeological photographic archives. Of course, multimedia recording technologies such as photography and video aid in creating a comprehensive, multidimensional vision of the research process. But more important, these technologies redefine the politics and economics of representation so that locally hired laborers are both recognized and rewarded for their role as creative co-producers of archaeological knowledge.

After this anticipative discussion of how recording can be made more inclusive and more capable of engaging the specific observations and interpretations site workers have to offer, I expand the focus even further and suggest what this research reveals not just about archaeology but about science in general. Although there is a great deal of discussion about the management of people in scientific research contexts, along with the nature of their expertise and practices (e.g., Barley and Bechky 1993; Blok and Downey 2003; Doing 2004, 2008), "work" and "labor"—in both their physical and fiscal senses—remain underexamined (Vann 2004; Vann and Bowker 2006; Wouters et al. 2008). Archaeology is sweaty work, archaeology is an industry; accordingly, I address both body and economy. The conclusions I offer delineate what about this research is specific to excavation in the Middle East—with its particular colonial legacy—and, in contrast, what ties a man pushing a wheelbarrow across a grassy mound in 1962 to the knowledge production processes ongoing in libraries, laboratories, and other locations around the world.

Through the course of investigating, measuring, and engaging the expertise site workers possess in Petra and at Çatalhöyük, objects like bucrania, bracelets, and copper rings; methods such as sieving and brushing; and hypotheses regarding topics like bodily ornamentation and regional trade connections are drawn together and come into view. Using a diverse set of complementary methods, tacking among quantitative evidence, visual tools, thick description, and vivid imagery, I trace the connections between these disparate elements of the archaeological process to elucidate the perspective and roles of people who experience and see all these things, who connect them through their physical work and interpretive processes. As in archaeological excavation itself, I collect all of these disparate objects, practices, and ideas together and examine how they unite, in an attempt to understand the labor relations and epistemological processes that hum at the center of the archaeological research endeavor, connecting all of these objects, ideas, and activities together. The networked analysis I present thereby brings into focus the entangled economics of expertise enabling facts to form from the fragmentary material record of the past.

1

Local Communities,
Labor, and Laboratories

In 1929, a twenty-seven-year-old named Seton Howard Frederick Lloyd—who later became president of the British School of Archaeology in Iraq—traveled to Iraq for the first time. With several seasons of experience supervising excavations in Egypt on his résumé, he was chosen to participate in the Oriental Institute expedition to Khorsabad. But Lloyd (1963) himself admits that the expertise he had developed in Egypt proved to be of little help when he arrived to Iraq. At Khorsabad, several generations of looting and destruction had added to the obfuscation of mud brick stratigraphy, making the site challenging to excavate systematically. After chipping away at the earth for days, the team eventually realized that their first trench, so carefully planned and tenaciously dug, was actually drilling into a solid mud brick wall.

The Oriental Institute excavations, though, are remembered for their contributions to knowledge about Assyrian architecture and town planning, not their destruction of it (see Frankfort 1950; Loud 1936; Loud and Altman 1938). Soon after this initial mishap, the American team members were taught how to identify and trace the walls by a group of Arab men from a village called Sherqat, who years before had learned precise excavation strategies from German archaeologists Walter Andrae, Robert Koldewey, and others. These Sherqati excavators, moreover, had improved upon the techniques they had been

DOI: 10.5876/9781646421152.c001

taught, inventing their own specialized digging equipment. Ultimately, they so perfected the craft of exposing ancient mud brick walls that footprints and hoof marks could be discerned in the bricks of the buildings they excavated impeccably (Lloyd 1963: 38). Lloyd (1963: 46) refers to them as "our invaluable Sherqati experts," revealing the level of his admiration for their abilities and professionalism.

Yet only five years earlier, James Henry Breasted, the director of the Oriental Institute (the sponsoring institution of the excavations at Khorsabad), secured a $10 million grant from John D. Rockefeller to build a state-of-the-art archaeological research center and museum in Cairo, Egypt. His goal in establishing these institutions was to staff them with Americans and Europeans, who would then be the natural choices for any open positions in the Egyptian antiquities department rather than up-and-coming Egyptian Egyptologists (Goode 2007). Breasted hoped to forestall the training of Egyptian students who might otherwise take control of the antiquities department and impose restrictions on how foreign projects could operate in the country. In a letter to Rockefeller's wife, Breasted called his enormous financial expenditure and political maneuvering "the price one had to pay to save these people from themselves" (cited in Goode 2007: 11).

How could such different views on the local populations coexist at the same time—and at the same institution? Do they reflect idiosyncratic differences between the individual standpoints of Lloyd versus Breasted or of the specific conditions in Iraq versus Egypt?

I argue that they do not. Instead, by considering these examples in context, significant trends emerge throughout the history of archaeology: first, a persistent cognitive dissonance among archaeologists regarding the communities they have encountered during the course of their work, and second, an imagined distinction between the manual labor of fieldwork and the scholarly activity of recording, analyzing, and publishing the archaeological record. As Lloyd's memoirs illustrate, local communities have long been involved in the physical activities of excavation. They are conspicuously absent, however, from documentation and publication, sometimes blocked from participating by the same archaeologists who praise their abilities with a trowel or a spade.

When and how did the work of locally hired laborers in the Middle East become so disentangled from the rest of the archaeological process? Are manual labor and scholarship as separate in archaeological contexts in other parts of the world? In other scientific disciplines? And, most important, how can ethnography begin to weave them back together?

INTERACTIONS BETWEEN ARCHAEOLOGISTS AND COMMUNITIES IN THE MIDDLE EAST

NINETEENTH-CENTURY SCIENTIFIC EXPEDITIONS AND COLONIALISM

The roots of contemporary archaeologists' relationships with locally hired laborers lie in nineteenth-century scientific expeditions by European travelers, aimed at mapping out ancient sites and monuments. The diaries, letters, and publications surviving from these expeditions convey an overwhelming fear of the Arab world. These Western explorers report dressing up in costumes to blend in with the communities they encountered in an effort to gain respect or safe passage. For instance, the legends surrounding Johann Ludwig Burckhardt, who in 1812 became the first European traveler to visit Petra, paint a picture of a man who spent two years steeping himself in Syrian culture, at which point he was declared an authority on Islamic law by scholars of the Qur'an (see Albright 1954; Bliss 1906; Fagan 2004). He then took on the name Sheikh Ibrahim ibn Abdullah, allowing him to pass unchallenged through Jordan and on to Saudi Arabia and Egypt. One tale from his memoirs describes how he "pretended to have made a vow to slaughter a goat in honour of Haroun (Aaron)" so he could gain peaceful access to the valley of Wadi Musa in modern-day Jordan (Burckhardt 1822: 419). This narrative is often recounted to exemplify how successful and clever Burckhardt was at slipping into these foreign societies undetected.

Across the board, in fact, guidebooks for Westerners who wanted to travel to the Middle East in the nineteenth century recommended broadly that their readers pose as Arabs or Turks. Recent histories of archaeology have challenged the underlying assumptions of this practice. Brian Fagan (2004), for example, maintains that these behaviors and disguises were a means of associating oneself with the local aristocracy and keeping apart from the middle or lower classes except to acquire servants or concubines (see also Graham 1989; Moscrop 2000; Reid 2002). Hiding one's identity in anticipation of encountering Middle Eastern groups implies that there is truth to the stereotype of despotic and dangerous Arabs. The need to trick local inhabitants and sneak past them only makes sense if one presumes that attack is inevitable and imminent.

Furthermore, the latent notion that any adventurous European traveler has the right to cross through another community's territory without confrontation only makes sense in the context of nineteenth-century European imperialism. Many of these early ventures served a double purpose: not only to advance scientific knowledge but also to lay the groundwork for later military occupations or conquests. Early European explorers of the Middle East produced maps that were often used by the armed forces of their home nations; in fact, the funding for these archaeological expeditions routinely came from the army. Later, digging tools employed for archaeological excavations were frequently reused implements of trench warfare.

While the discipline was in these ways closely intertwined intellectually and materially with the aims of European expansion, archaeologists on the ground often acted as effective political agents of these same interests. Their interactions with local Middle Eastern residents often therefore exhibit not only fear but a hard-handed diplomacy, an abrasive attempt to win the hearts and minds of the various groups of people living in these territories. The memoirs of Austen Henry Layard (1849, 1853, 1887)—one of archaeology's first excavators—exemplify this. Layard transcribed a speech by one of his most skilled workmen, Abd-ur-rahman, in which Abd-ur-rahman expresses wonder at how accurately archaeologists can predict the location of buried monumental ruins and asks Layard how they do it. In response, Layard (1849: 316) "seized this opportunity to give him [Abd-ur-rahman] a short lecture upon the advantages of civilization and of knowledge . . . All I could accomplish was, to give the Arab Sheikh an exalted idea of the wisdom and power of the Franks." Rather than respond to Abd-ur-rahman's methodological questions, Layard perceived an opening to pontificate about the superiority of Western society.

Establishing a cultural distinction between the Occident and the Orient was, after all, a project to which nineteenth-century archaeology contributed integrally. Travelers' and excavators' portrayals of Middle Eastern societies overflow with descriptions of what the authors perceived as cultural degeneration. Faith in Islam and nomadic pastoral subsistence practices, together with Orientalist conceptualizations of the Middle East as lawless and licentious, suggested to Christian researchers that those living Middle Eastern communities had somehow replaced or devolved from the ancient biblical characters credited with building glorious monuments and thriving cities.

This imagined schism between the glorious ancient past and the miserable present justified colonial interest in the region by suggesting that the people currently living in the Middle East were unable to care for a land or a cultural heritage that was eminently not their own (Abu El-Haj 2001; Bahrani 1998; Bernhardsson 2005; Colla 2007; Corbett 2014). Because occupants were seen as culturally distanced from the archaeological remains, villages on or near archaeological sites were viewed as a threat to antiquities, adding to the sense of a moral imperative on the part of European and American researchers to protect historical treasures by removing the objects from the country and removing apathetic or destructive denizens from the sites. Given this pervasive belief, it is unsurprising that when a school of Egyptology was opened in 1870, designed to educate native Egyptians in archaeology and cultural resource management, it was shut down only four years later by Auguste Mariette, the French director of antiquities in khedival Egypt. Mariette also committed himself to preventing university-educated Egyptians from achieving positions in the antiquities service. From his point of view, because Western civilization represented the cultural inheritor of Pharaonic Egypt, Westerners should accordingly take responsibility for the protection and investigation of Egyptian monuments and artifacts (Colla 2007; Doyon 2014; Reid 2002; Wynn 2007).

There is no evidence to support the notion that local Middle Eastern communities did not or could not appreciate archaeological remains. On the contrary, a close reading of legends in the history of Middle Eastern archaeology reveals how invested these communities were in the antiquities in their territories. In 1881, after Mariette's own hasty forty-eight-hour clearance of a newly discovered tomb in Deir el-Bahri, villagers from the local settlement of Qurna followed the steamer carrying the tomb contents down the banks of Luxor, firing shots and ululating to lament the loss (Ceram 1968; Fagan 2004). This hardly seems like the behavior of a population ignorant of the importance of archaeological remains.

Furthermore, archaeologists' own activities and descriptions of the men they employed belie the idea that local community members posed a threat to archaeological remains. Layard himself—orator on the superiority of Western civilization—habitually led multiple excavations at far-flung sites simultaneously between 1845 and 1851. The workers digging in his absence demonstrated their proficiency in careful earth removal, artifact recovery, and excavation decision-making (Larsen 1996). It seems that Layard recognized this; when he went to investigate mounds outside of Baghdad, approximately 250 miles from Nimrud, he brought thirty of the workers from Nimrud with him, setting them to work on several different mounds at once.

Famed archaeologist William Matthew Flinders Petrie, digging in Egypt from 1890, employed men from the village of Quft, who also became well-known in the archaeological community as a reliable pool of capable archaeological laborers. In his diaries, Petrie admires the Quftis' proficiency at recovering small finds, as well as their in-depth knowledge about the local terrain and resources (Quirke 2010). Petrie even entrusted workers with recording tasks as specialized as drawing scale plans. He occasionally mentions the names of the workers who discovered remarkable finds—an extremely rare practice in the history of archaeology and an indication of Petrie's regard for these men's capabilities. Later, he brought the Qufti workers to conduct the labor for his excavations outside of Egypt. In fact, today, New York University's excavation at Abydos hires the living trainees of the Quftis taught originally by Petrie (O'Connor 2011).

More than 150 years ago, then, archaeologists were recognizing and attesting to the expertise of locally hired laborers—both in practice and in text. And yet, the predominant narrative of the archaeological literature from this time period espouses apathy on the part of local communities regarding Middle Eastern cultural heritage. Explaining this requires illuminating how the entanglement of colonialism and archaeology material impacted the way foreign researchers hired and organized native workers during excavations. Some early archaeologists were explicit about the ways they intentionally alienated local populations from the archaeological remains they lived near. Petrie, for example, deliberately brought workers from villages distant from the archaeological site to minimize the likelihood that they would assert claims over the interpretation or export of artifacts (Quirke 2010). Jacques de Morgan, working at the same time at Susa, described how he never paid more than a pittance to reward workers for recovering exceptional finds in order to "leave the workmen in ignorance about what they find" (cited in Dyson 1968: 31).

Starting with Lady Hester Lucy Stanhope's 1810 dig at Ashkelon, archaeological projects throughout the nineteenth century including those at Thebes, Telloh, Nineveh, Nippur, and Susa hired hundreds and frequently thousands of men to execute the manual labor. Mariette, for example, routinely conscripted upward of 7,000 Egyptians to move earth. Donald Malcolm Reid (2002) argues that this practice would have been associated with the digging of the Suez Canal—an undertaking notorious for its exploitative and cruel treatment of Egyptians. More generally, employing and managing thousands of workers required a military-style team organization that mimicked, amplified, and concretized the global power relations between European and Middle Eastern polities.

The workers subject to this labor management strategy were distanced from a claim to both the physical artifacts and the scientific information produced through the excavation. It is here, in nineteenth-century archaeology, that the first intentional untethering of digging from interpretation is apparent. Such unbraiding is perhaps most directly evinced in Petrie's instructional text, *Methods and Aims in Archaeology* (1904), in which "the excavator" and "the labourers" are two separate chapters. Petrie's perfect excavator possesses a wide range of personality traits and abilities, including knowledge of history, organization, and expert pattern recognition. By contrast, his section on the ideal laborer sounds like shopping for livestock:

The Egyptian is good at steady work, but the Syrian is very different, and it took some weeks at Tell Hesy to educate men into continuous regular digging. They would jump out of their holes every few minutes, and squat on the edge for a talk with the next man; and only a steady weeding out of about a third of them every week, gradually brought up the best of them into tolerable efficiency. In Greece such difficulties are even greater, and rational regular hard work cannot be reckoned upon, as in Egypt. The best age for diggers is about 15 to 20 years. After that many turn stupid, and only a small proportion are worth having between 20 and 40. After 40 very few are of any use, though some robust men will continue to about 50. The Egyptian ages early; and men of 45 would be supposed to be 65 in England. The boys are of use for carrying from about 10 years old; and they generally look mere boys till over 20. The ornamental man with a good beard is quite useless and lazy; and the best workers are the scraggy under-sized youths, with wizened wiry faces, though sometimes a well-favoured lad with pleasing face will turn out very good. In choosing boys the broad face and square chin are necessary tokens of stamina; and the narrow feminine faces are seldom worth much. (Petrie 1904: 20–21)

One does not have to search hard to find evidence that workers were not just regarded but also treated as livestock. In 1847, when Layard (1849) set about bringing a massive stone-carved winged lion from Nimrud to the British Museum, he soon realized that the load was too heavy for the buffalo he had yoked for the task and instead hired an army of Iraqi men to pull the cart. Naturally, they struggled with the task and tried a number of methods to make headway, including forcing one of the least popular Iraqi men to lie down in front of the cart until the wheels were on top of him. What is most astonishing about this anecdote is not even the sequence of events itself but that in retelling the story more than 100 years later, Curt W. Ceram (1968: 295) describes it as "the Arabs having the time of their lives," evoking a sort of Iraqi Sambo image rather than acknowledging the certain violence of the scene.

It is not only in storytelling from the twentieth century where the continued legacy of nineteenth-century colonialism is apparent. Through the twentieth century, the archaeological site continued to function as a microcosm in which broader global politics played out in the interactions between archaeologists and local communities, where intellectual labor and physical effort would be increasingly segregated from one another.

The Middle East was an arena for one bloody conflict after another during the twentieth century—and with each war, archaeological fieldwork largely ceased. World War I, two Egyptian Revolutions, armed conflict between Iraqis and Kurds, the Syrian revolt, Iraqi Shia revolts, World War II, the Arab-Israeli conflict, the Iranian coup d'état, the Six-Day War, Black September, the Lebanese Civil War, the Iranian Revolution, the Iran-Iraq War, the Turkey–Partîya Karkerên Kurdistanê (PKK) conflict, and the Gulf War all forestalled archaeological work in the areas where fighting was taking place. The story of twentieth-century Middle Eastern archaeology is one of excavations stopping and starting, of ending unexpectedly, and of government transformations allowing new groups of Middle Eastern nationals to participate in archaeological research and cultural resource management. Declarations of independence and freshly ratified constitutions enabled greater control over antiquities trade and the establishment of national repositories for artifacts while antiquities departments were emptied of foreigners, filled instead by citizens of the country in question. Still, even as some Middle Eastern nations achieved independence and asserted greater control over their own archaeological resources—passing antiquities legislation, constructing national museums—the very borders of the independent states of the Middle East were often negotiated and determined by colonial powers in view of the archaeological remains they contained. This was the case, for instance, with mandatory Iraq, Palestine, and Jordan (Bernhardsson 2005; Corbett 2014).

It was during this time period—and as an outcome of these wars—that the contemporary boundaries of both Jordan and Turkey were drawn. Both nations achieved independence in the twentieth century—Turkey in 1923 from the Allied occupation of the defeated Ottoman Empire and Jordan in 1946 with the Treaty of London, which ended the British Mandate period. Before independence, both the Ottoman Empire and the British protectorate of Transjordan had antiquities departments and antiquities laws governing the issuance of excavation permits and export policies. But in these countries as in others in the region, independence gave Jordan and Turkish nationals unprecedented control of the archaeology conducted within their borders. In Jordan, this opportunity was seized eagerly; remaining foreigners were purged from the Department of Antiquities, including Gerald Lancaster Harding who had been the department's director for decades and had overseen the construction of the Jordan Archaeological Museum on Amman's Citadel (Corbett 2014). Suddenly, Jordan and Turkish archaeologists and administrators—and the nationals of other Middle Eastern states, in their respective countries—were the ones making decisions about the archaeology taking place within their newly defined borders.

Much has been written about how Middle Eastern states have used archaeology intentionally to define their national identities and ideologies, in Jordan (Corbett 2014; Fleming 2015; Massad 2001), in Turkey (Atakuman 2008; Özdoğan 1998), in Israel (Abu El-Haj 2001; Ben-Yehuda 2002; Galor 2017; Yahya 2005), in Iraq (Abdi 2008; Bernhardsson 2005), in Persia/Iran (Abdi 2001; Ansari 2012), in Egypt (Reid 2002; Wynn 2008), and elsewhere. The archaeology conducted in service of establishing ancient national origins and of rewriting the histories of these communities was frequently focused on particular regions or time periods. Projects serving this interest were, moreover, led by members of the upper classes of the newly formed nations. Mehmet Özdoğan (1998), for example, describes how archaeology had been an elitist venture since the Ottoman Empire and how the influx of German archaeologists fleeing the Nazi regime during World War II led to a high standard of teaching and professionalism in Turkey. Becoming an archaeologist in Jordan, Turkey, and many other Middle Eastern countries involves earning a university degree and competing for one of a very few, highly selective positions in government departments or, if one holds a PhD, in the academy.

Accordingly, for several reasons, even after independence and even as the number of archaeologists from the countries under discussion grew, foreigners continued to lead most archaeological projects. The young states were often most interested in sponsoring or supporting excavation and conservation work on sites that fit into their national narratives. In addition, archaeology remained an elite and often exclusive sector in these nations. Meanwhile, issuing foreign excavation permits often reaped fiscal and diplomatic rewards.[1] While the real financial impact of archaeological projects has been debated (Douglas 2014; Majd 2003), foreign excavators did and do pay for excavation permits, along with visas, airfare, accommodations, equipment, food, and labor. Excavation permits, the export of antiquities, and investment in heritage conservation and development have all also played crucial roles in the negotiation of global soft power (Goode 2007; Luke and Kersel 2013).

For all these reasons, foreigners continued to dominate excavations in the Middle East throughout the twentieth century. Their interactions and relationships with Middle Eastern communities over this time period exhibited more continuity with the nineteenth century than difference. For instance, even in countries that had achieved independence from colonial authorities, foreign archaeologists continued to bring back a substantial amount of the objects recovered for museums in their home countries. This practice, called *partage*,[2] continued well into the twentieth century in most Middle Eastern countries that hosted large-scale foreign-led archaeological projects, ending in Egypt only in the 1980s. The persistence of *partage* signifies a continuation of the Orientalist idea that Western nations represent the cultural inheritors of ancient Middle Eastern societies rather than a recognition of local communities' ability and desire to maintain control over the archaeological resources in their territories.

The conditions of labor at twentieth-century archaeological projects in the Middle East also changed little from the nineteenth century. The tradition of employing hundreds of workers to dig in militaristic style under the supervision of one or two foremen continued on projects including Persepolis, Medinet Habu, Gezer, and many other sites in Mandate Palestine (see Davies 1988; Majd 2003; Masry 1981; Moorey 1991; O'Connor 1996). Not only does this practice lead to a high incidence of mistakes and diminished quality of recording, but it also alienates workers from the physical archaeological remains and the intangible knowledge that can be gained from them. Leonard Woolley, for instance, working at Ur between 1922 and 1934, never employed more than 5 supervisors for 250 workers. Although he entrusted his Syrian foreman Sheikh Hamoudi Ibrahim and Ibrahim's three sons with a variety of tasks (including all of the photography for the site), Woolley never shared the purpose, progress, hypotheses, or conclusions with any of the assistants he hired (Lloyd 1963).

There are also stories in twentieth-century archaeological accounts describing expert local laborers. In William Foxwell Albright's (1954: 18) recommendations for archaeologists working in Palestine, he states: "It is very important to have good native foremen, either Palestinian or Egyptian; Egyptian foremen from Quft (Coptus), trained directly or indirectly by Reisner, are the best as a group." George Reisner worked at Coptos from 1900 to 1904 and even fifty years later, the workmen he trained—or the workers those workmen had trained—were recognized as the best by one of the most influential archaeologists working in the Middle East. Reisner employed local draftsmen, publication secretaries, and photographers at Coptos (Brovarski 1996; Kendall 1996). When he left Coptos, he brought his trained workforce with him, suggesting a level of trust and even dependence. Reisner trusted his foreman, Said Ahmed, enough that when beginning a new excavation, Said Ahmed would arrive first and direct the excavation of the first few levels (Davis 2004; Kendall 1996). Perhaps the greatest indication of how professional and well-known these men from Coptos became is that one element of the Fisher-Reisner method—the prevailing scientific excavation methodology prior to the invention of the Wheeler-Kenyon method—entailed hiring individuals trained by Reisner or his workers (Davis 2004). The people and the particular expertise they had (not even the training methods used to develop that expertise) were integral elements of twentieth-century scientific archaeology.

But Reisner—along with Petrie, Layard, de Morgan, and countless other archaeologists before him—limited the aspects of archaeological fieldwork in which he trained the workers from Coptos. His letters home exemplify his contempt toward Egyptians, saying "the native brutality of a half-civilized people is still alive in the hearts of the Egyptians" (Reisner 1919). Even though Reisner did hire Egyptian photographers and taught his foreman to keep his own excavation diary in Arabic, the majority of the recording—and all of the analysis as well as publication—was performed by the other American excavation team members (Thomas 1996). Reisner and the archaeologists working in the Middle East who followed his influential methodology accordingly inherited the disciplinary dissonance between relying on local communities' archaeological skills and preventing their total involvement in all aspects of the process.

Furthermore, as problematic as interactions were between the nineteenth-century pioneers of Middle Eastern archaeology and local communities, their Orientalist interest in documenting all aspects of the places and people they encountered resulted in a great deal of vivid description of the local workers they hired to excavate. Laborers are, by contrast, largely absent from the published records of twentieth-century archaeology. The earth seems to dig itself, with emphasis instead placed on the importance of analysis performed on the assemblages once collected and cleaned or on the stratigraphy once exposed. The contemporary context of archaeological sites appears to have mattered little in the archaeological work performed in the Middle East during the previous century.

RECENT COMMUNITY ENGAGEMENT

The invisibility of local laborers changed somewhat during the late 1980s and the 1990s as proponents of emerging post-processualist, feminist, queer, and Marxist archaeologies in Europe and the United States advocated for greater reflexivity in archaeological work. They argued that better archaeological research would only be possible with a greater awareness of how archaeologists' subjectivity and positionality influence the knowledge production process. Archaeologists increasingly challenged their own authoritative claims to the interpretation of the past, recognizing that history and heritage have different—and often conflicting—meanings to various stakeholder groups.

Feminist and queer archaeologies had a particular impact on perceptions and treatment of gender in the discipline, including in archaeological practice. One of the most iconic and incisive treatments of the topic came from Joan M. Gero (1994, 1996), who recounted her personal experience and ethnographic observations of a specific archaeological project, illustrating gender-based differences in how men and women physically dig and present what they find. Her account contributed a personal and humanistic component to a larger movement during the 1980s and 1990s to take stock of the role of gender in archaeology—in terms of both analytical foci and representation in the discipline (Claassen 1994; Nelson et al. 1994; Woodall and Perricone 1981). Gender has indeed been a preeminent focus of research by philosopher of archaeology Alison Wylie (2001, 2003), who has examined archaeological epistemology and demonstrated how marginal actors—especially women—are often discredited as epistemic agents in the archaeological knowledge production process.

Since these early accounts and studies, women archaeologists have continued to track gender-based representation in the field. In 2003, Margaret W. Conkey (2003: 877) reflected that feminism had "absolutely" changed archaeology but that "who can be a knower in the discipline" was still contested territory. Stephanie Moser (2007) challenged the stereotypes, rhetoric, and circulating images reinforcing the notion that archaeological fieldwork is a masculine enterprise. All of this discussion has had an effect on gender equity in archaeology; more women than ever are directing field projects (Schlegel 2014), becoming professional archaeologists (Lazar et al. 2014), applying for and earning pre-doctoral National Science Foundation (NSF) fellowships (Goldstein et al. 2017), and completing graduate programs (Goldstein et al. 2017; Zeder 1997).

Nearly all feminist critiques of archaeology have focused on academic and professional archaeologists rather than locally hired laborers. This may be attributed to the fact that historically, local women have been hired for domestic work and not onsite fieldwork. The armies of site workers in the Middle East described above, for instance, were made up of men,[3] and before the contemporary excavations at Çatalhöyük and the Temple of the Winged Lions in Petra, no projects at these sites had explicitly and intentionally hired more than one or two women for household jobs.

Although they have almost never focused particularly on site workers, the attention feminist and other post-processual archaeologists have brought to issues of equity, representation, and situated knowledge in archaeology catalyzed a shift in the discipline toward being concerned with the politics of archaeological practice and of the past. Increasingly, archaeologists are aware that both their findings and their procedures have consequences for local communities, descendant populations, and other interested interlocutors. Many archaeologists today are concerned with redressing how archaeological fieldwork has been exclusive or even exploitative in the past. This global movement in archaeology has led to a proliferation of projects involving social engagement components, particularly in the United States, England, and Australia. Although the practice of public archaeology remains more widespread in these countries than in the Middle East, there has also been an increase in publicly oriented projects in the Middle East since the beginning of the twenty-first century. But have they challenged or changed the structural conditions for archaeological workers in the Middle East?

This is a difficult question to answer, as the increased attention on local communities has resulted in extremely different, hyper-local community engagement initiatives across the Middle East. The belief underlying this diversity has been eloquently expressed by Laurent Dissard, Melissa Rosenzweig, and Timothy Matney (2011: 69): "Ethical archaeology on the ground is best defined as a set of unwritten rules, negotiable and malleable on a daily basis, negotiated within a dialogue between archaeological team members, local communities, and the wider public, and not beholden to any universal set of abstract ethical principles."

The authors' self-assessment of their own community engagement work in southeastern Turkey focuses primarily on specific issues of access to the site for the inhabitants of the local village—illustrating their very argument that not every socially engaged or ethical archaeology project will have the same problems or solutions. Indeed, the problem of access is not particularly relevant for considering archaeologists' relationships with and responsibilities to site workers.

Other archaeologists have taken a different stance from the pursuit of hyper-local and dissimilar approaches, instead aiming to refine a set of best practices that could be adapted to other sites in the Middle East or even worldwide. One example of this is the project at Quseir, Egypt, run by Stephanie Moser and a large group of collaborators since 1999. Moser and her colleagues produced seven recommendations for how archaeological projects could and should engage community members. These recommendations consisted of "communication and collaboration, employment and training, public presentation, interviews and oral history, educational resources, photographic and video archive, and community-controlled merchandising" (Moser et al. 2002: 229). Combining all of these strategies, in their view, functions as "a methodology for ensuring effective community involvement in the study of the archaeological resource" (Moser et al. 2002: 220), a suite of best practices or at the very least a tested model that could provide some broadly applicable guidelines for other projects aiming to include stakeholder communities. Still, though, they do not name labor management practices as a methodological component requiring alteration in the pursuit of community engagement.

Other community engagement initiatives extend well beyond the activities normally encapsulated within the archaeological endeavor, such as the multi-strand initiatives led by Sonya Atalay (2010, 2012) at Çatalhöyük in Turkey. Motivated primarily by ethical concerns, Atalay has forged multiple avenues of engaging the local village inhabitants at Çatalhöyük by creating a children's theater program, a newsletter, and an annual festival for sharing the project's methods and findings. The work Atalay performed at Çatalhöyük represents another category of community engagement by archaeologists in the Middle East, one that is about building relationships and following the community's lead in finding creative means to transcend the ordinary parameters of archaeological work. Atalay's approach further exemplifies the diversity among archaeological endeavors that share the broad aim of involving Middle Eastern communities in archaeological work but which, again, are not specifically concerned with locally hired laborers.

So there is not yet—and may never be—the sort of established best practices for community archaeology in the Middle East that Moser and her colleagues (2002) started working toward almost two decades ago. Each of the projects mentioned here has achieved successes in its particular context with regard to its site-specific goals. But in spite of the diversity in the design and execution of community engagement in contemporary Middle Eastern archaeology, the fundamental issue of local laborers as a "community" seems to have eluded close examination. Aside from occasional remarks recognizing that archaeological projects continue to provide employment opportunities, there is a lack of critical attention to labor relations in archaeology or how local labor contributes to the production of archaeological knowledge in discussions of public archaeology in the Middle East. In fact, on the whole, projects aiming to engage non-specialist interlocutors around the world have not identified site workers as a particularly important discrete group of people to involve in archaeology. In accepting the political implications of archaeological work and the wider ramifications archaeological research can have for local, regional, and national communities, archaeologists have tended to overlook those individuals with whom we have most closely interacted since the inception of the discipline.

LOCAL LABOR IN GLOBAL PUBLIC ARCHAEOLOGY?

Local labor has been mostly missing from public archaeology discourse around the world, not just in the Middle East. This makes sense, perhaps, within the subgroup of public archaeologists who identify as advocates for a public archaeology in which archaeologists use their training and their particular perspectives on the past to advocate for change in the present (see Larsson 2013; Little and Zimmerman 2010; Sabloff 2009; Sayej 2013). M. Jay Stottman (2010: 9) articulates this vision for public archaeology:

> I want to emphasize that archaeology can be used as an agent for change to
> benefit society directly. In order to accomplish this task, archaeologists must
> reconceptualize and broaden their view and use of archaeology. Archaeology is
> not just a tool to pursue the past but something that can be used to change the
> present and future. Archaeologists as activists can intentionally use their skills
> and research to advocate for the communities in which they conduct research.

This last sentence makes clear that in this form of public archaeology, the professional expertise archaeologists uniquely possess should guide their interactions with non-archaeologists. For those advocating this approach, the scientific authority of archaeologists enables them to support just causes. Their ability to assess how well claims about the past fit with real, material evidence in an empirical way is a key power to mobilize in emancipatory archaeological practice. As Randall H. McGuire (2008: 230) has said, "Archaeologists need to retain some authority over the production of knowledge in order to assess correspondence . . . If we wield politically convenient falsehoods to support the cause, we lose any authority in the struggle." In this vision, archaeologists should embrace their particular education, skills, and academic authority and occupy activist spaces that are out of reach to public communities in order to support their interests. They can use their privileged knowledge and empowered positions as scientists and intellectuals to speak and act on behalf of well-informed policy changes, media attention, and legal decisions.

In my view, there is room for site workers to participate in an activist archaeology centered on putting expertise to work for social justice. Since they are at once members of communities most often affected by injustice in cultural heritage management and—as the historical accounts presented above reveal—knowledgeable contributors to excavation, they are uniquely positioned to use archaeology in service of equity.

But in the history of archaeology, their expertise has been consistently explained and treated as distinct from the scholarly knowledge archaeologists possess. Even when they have been recognized as valuable to the archaeological endeavor, this has been for their physical ability to dig without damaging archaeological remains or their awareness of where potential sites lie. In this context, site workers are unlikely to emerge as identifiably valuable participants in a public archaeology practice that privileges archaeologists' scientific authority in public discourse and action.

One might rather expect to find the topic of engaging and relating differently to site workers in the forms of public archaeology that advocate instead *de*-centering archaeologists' scientific authority in favor of consulting with interested publics at all stages of research—from the mere decision to begin an investigation to choosing particular methodologies to the final conservation and presentation of the site. This approach is perhaps best illustrated by Community-Based Participatory Research (CBPR), which is defined as a research model in which scientists and community members partner together to share equitably in contributing expertise and making decisions about all aspects of the research process. CBPR has been practiced by a number of archaeological scholars, including Sonya Atalay (2012), whose work at Çatalhöyük I describe above; Julie Hollowell and George P. Nicholas (2009; Nicholas 2008), who use CBPR to explore intellectual property–related issues in archaeological contexts; and Kent G. Lightfoot (2006, 2008), who consults with native Californian communities to design archaeological field methods that respect their beliefs and desires. Proponents of CBPR argue that consequential public engagement requires flexibility in all dimensions of the research process and even in defining what is relevant to archaeological work. For them, real community archaeology demands surrendering at least some authority over the total research endeavor.

CBPR and similar approaches that de-center archaeological authority have been used to advocate for the rights of descendant communities, local residents, and other underrepresented groups frequently left out of the decision-making processes around archaeological sites. But site workers are very rarely singled out for their position as a specialist sector of the lay "public" to whom archaeologists should cede their control over research planning and execution. This may be because in a sense, they already have some representation in the research process. Site workers have proximity to the artifacts recovered and access to the site that is in contrast to the types of exclusion CBPR works to end. Even if site workers may be members of the communities CBPR advocates for including, they occupy a liminal position between the community and the archaeological team that puts them outside the purview of this form of public archaeology.

And so site workers fall within the interstices of the strands of community-engaged archaeology that have developed over recent decades. They do not possess the requisite archaeological education or training to serve as activists in academic, legal, and journalistic spaces in pursuit of social justice. At the same time, site workers are too small and specific a community, and one that is too close to the archaeological endeavor, to earn dedicated attention from public archaeologists who seek to de-prioritize archaeological expertise. These trends form a major part of the reason site workers' role in the archaeological process has not changed even as perspectives on archaeologists' obligations to non-specialists have transformed. Site workers are not, in a strict sense, non-specialists. But they are also not archaeologists.

Instead, their position is clear from their title—site *workers*. They are laborers in the scientific project in archaeology. Their experience is similar to that of laborers in other scientific contexts, whose knowledge and abilities are similarly hidden by their structural positions in the research enterprise. Archaeological site workers, laboratory technicians, and medical assistants share an experience of disjuncture among the expertise they possess, their power to act on it, and the rewards they gain from it. These gaps, I argue, are precisely the conditions that lead to the scientific workers' experience of Marxian alienation.

LABORERS IN THE LABORATORY

In both the archaeological and laboratory contexts, parallel organizations of labor and comparable hierarchies preclude recognition of the intellectual contributions of those who perform the physical work that enables scientific research to proceed. In fact, this gap between the existence of expertise and the recognition of it has been a research concern across the field of science and technology studies (STS), where knowledge is explicitly viewed as something that must be "manufactured" (Knorr Cetina 1981; see also Knorr Cetina 1999; Latour 1987; Latour and Woolgar 1979). Steven Shapin has located the roots of denying the scientific knowledge of research support staff as early as the seventeenth century, when the chemist and natural philosopher Robert Boyle employed a veritable army of men as chemical assistants to carry out experiments in his laboratory. Their involvement "was usually deemed to involve physical effort or manual skill, but, with few exceptions, little knowledgeability" (Shapin 1989: 554). Meanwhile, however, Boyle's own hands infrequently touched his experimental equipment, his eyesight was too poor to make his own scientific observations, and he was known to travel for extended periods of time, leaving the experiments entirely in the hands of the technicians who are only mentioned indirectly in Boyle's notes (for instance, as "'lusty and dexterous' assistants" [Shapin 1989: 557]). In the earliest days of systematic experimentation and the origins of the scientific method, technical expertise and tacit knowledge were rendered invisible. And while "it is tempting to make a clear distinction between seventeenth-century arrangements and the life of the modern laboratory" (Shapin 1989: 562), contemporary science studies demonstrate continuity between past and present.[4] Stephen Barley and Beth Bechky (1993) have revealed how today's laboratory technicians—because of their intimate familiarity with the laboratory's tools and machines—pride themselves on being able to see anomalies and make observations the scientists ranked above them cannot. The authors have transcribed conversations between directors and support staff in scientific and engineering settings that illustrate how the technicians' contextual knowledge and past experience are often critical in research and design processes but go unrecognized.

Indeed, while science studies has illustrated the idiosyncratic and locally contingent nature of scientific knowledge production,[5] ethnographers and historians of science have equally demonstrated that the denial of expertise held by certain participants in the research process is a common characteristic of scientific practice across disciplines and applications. Annemarie Mol and John Law (1994), looking at doctors diagnosing and treating anemia in tropical settings; Regula Valérie Burri and Joseph Dumit (2008), studying the performance of scientific imagery; Park Doing (2004), conducting ethnography in a physics laboratory; and Sheila Jasanoff (1998), writing about interpreting DNA evidence for criminal trials, have all convincingly revealed discrepancies between who possesses the know-how to perform certain scientific activities versus who is legally or normatively permitted to perform those activities. Across contexts, students and assistants often know best how to operate devices or read printouts and images. The students and assistants with these capabilities, meanwhile, are not in positions that allow them to offer diagnoses or scientific interpretations. Despite their often greater experience and abilities, technicians and students in diverse scientific settings—like locally hired laborers in archaeology—are not the ones to give the final interpretive word on a test or an experiment. Nick Russell and colleagues (2000: 239–240) neatly summarize this seeming universal: "The craftsman has become a technician . . . his or her skill at manipulating complex technical equipment [is] now informed by scientific knowledge. But the role of such technical experts does not seem to be recognized in pay, status, or job satisfaction." The devaluation of expertise, in other words, is a phenomenon that pervades scientific practice across disparate disciplines.

Science studies scholars have offered several compelling reasons as to why this problem persists—all of which have relevance to archaeological knowledge production. For one, there is the "lone wolf" concept of the scientist or archaeologist in which the teamwork, dialogue, and debate essential to knowledge production are effaced (Russell et al. 2000; Shapin 1989; see Hodder 1999 for a discussion of how this happens in archaeology). In addition, the formation of facts in science—including archaeology—has always been shaped by historical and social determinations regarding who is a trustworthy observer. Steven Shapin and Simon Schaffer (1985: 69) have called "the matter of fact . . . a social as well as an intellectual category," referring to the emphasis on *who* had witnessed a given experiment for determining whether findings were valid. Class, race, gender, and other identity categories are all crucial in determining who in the research process receives credit and in what form. Related to this, a third proposed reason for the invisibility of assistants and technicians in scientific research has been the stringent hierarchies of the scientific enterprise (Barley and Bechky 1993). Promoting greater egalitarianism in the laboratory or excavation could be a way of making the unseen scientific labor more visible. There is, however, another possible reason why the contributions of scientific workers remain hidden and un-credited, one that lacks a clear solution. As Russell and his colleagues (2000: 240) have stated, "The combination of manual with mental activities in technical work is itself anomalous."

The incongruity of physical and intellectual labor is apparent in the history of archaeology, as shown above. Park Doing (2004) experienced this same phenomenon during his ethnography in a physics laboratory. He describes how the scientists in the laboratory did not see the embodied knowledge operators possessed as expertise because they believed it to be innate or inborn rather than trained or taught. Significantly, the scientists included in Doing's study often expressed the same sort of cognitive dissonance regarding technicians that archaeologists have historically evinced regarding site workers, as the scientists routinely expressed appreciation for operators' "lab hands." But surprisingly, the operators in Doing's study did not argue for greater recognition of their cognitive capabilities. Instead, even Doing (2004: 310) himself, when he was an operator, "felt flattered that the scientist would stake future actions on a declaration from me, but I also felt the sting . . . To the operators, the compliments from the scientists were backhanded slights to their real abilities." His findings raise an important question for examining archaeological labor in the Middle East: How do locally hired laborers experience a similar phenomenon of being praised for their physical abilities alone, if their contributions are recognized at all?

In this, archaeology and other sciences are comparable to other industries. The production of knowledge and the labor structures used in scientific research are not so different from the production of material goods. Both rely on entrenched hierarchies for their continued functioning. Robert Paynter (1983) has in fact previously made this case for commercial archaeology specifically, where archaeological projects are forced to take on the same corporate labor structures and management practices employed in more profit-seeking endeavors. In the interest of both efficiency and control, it is necessary for each participant on an archaeological excavation to specialize in particular tasks (like a factory worker) rather than having a wide base of skills and knowledge.

Michael Shanks and Randall H. McGuire (1996) extend this critique to academic archaeology by virtue of the fact that universities are in the business of training professionals who will serve society. They argue that the most apt classification for the work archaeologists of all kinds perform is "craft." This term, they claim, appropriately brings together the thinking, doing, and feeling entailed in archaeological work. Like Paynter, Shanks and McGuire compare archaeological labor management to that utilized in factory production, where workers take on repetitive, fragmentary tasks and have little to no access to the final analysis or knowledge their work enables. Their description hums resonantly with Karl Marx's (2012 [1844]) concept of alienation, or *entfremdung*, though Marx himself might protest this application of his ideas. In his writings on labor and science, Marx (1906; Marx and Engels 1848) argues that technological innovations, including industrial agriculture and machinery, facilitated the emergence of both surplus value and capitalism. Science and industry thus became inextricably tangled with one another, and science was "press[ed] into the service of capital" (Marx 1906, 391). For Marx, this meant that the intellectual activity of science remained distinct from the physical, material activities of proletarian workers and laborers (see also Marx and Engels 1998 [1845]). The work accomplished by STS scholars has already illustrated that imagining such a distinct separation does not hold up to scrutiny; in fact, laboratory studies have demonstrated that intellectual activities in the lab enable and in turn are enabled by physical action such as seeing, hearing, smelling, lifting, weighing, and moving.

Still, in his explanation of alienation, Marx (2012 [1844]) argues that the organization of labor associated with capitalism construes the worker as an instrument rather than a person—a device used to maximize profits and fulfill the goals of the bourgeois social classes. Alienation then proceeds in three successive steps. The first is the alienation of the worker from the product of his own labor, as the worker participates in neither the design nor consumption of the goods and services he is laboring to produce. In exchange for supposedly unskilled labor, the worker is given wages that provide the greatest possible return for the upper classes who control the labor system, causing the worker to feel increasingly divested not only from the product of his labor but also from the work activities themselves. This is the second step of alienation Marx discusses—alienation from the act of producing. As the worker is unable to exercise any control over the valuation of his abilities or contributions, he is equally unable to enjoy any personal fulfillment from the productive activities in which he is engaging. The final stage of alienation Marx outlines is alienation from one's *Gattungswesen*, translated to "species-essence," which encapsulates broad, abstract concepts including consciousness, self-determinism, and free will.

The first stage of alienation stands out as especially relevant to the situation of archaeological labor, since locally hired site workers rarely, if ever, enjoy benefit from the knowledge products that come out of the digging they have performed. They do not gain any portion of the academic prestige or indirect monetary profit that comes from peer-reviewed publications. In this sense, even coauthoring publications—the process of working together to formulate the finalized narratives that will circulate about an archaeological assemblage and the act of explicitly sharing credit for creating this knowledge—represents an unsatisfying method of redressing the inequalities and alienation of the excavation process, since local laborers are unlikely to enjoy the benefits of academic authorship. They are not, after all, applying for university positions or vying for tenure. In many settings, the communities site workers come from may be illiterate or not fluent in English, and in these situations, even the social capital they might be expected to accrue as a result of archaeological coauthorship is definitively limited. The site workers themselves are frequently unable to read (or to read the language of an archaeological publication), preventing them from reading the content of archaeological texts.

I am not arguing that site workers desire access to these products of the archaeological research project. That gap, however, between who is making the knowledge and who gains from it once it is made and distributed bears an uncomfortable resemblance to the industrial conditions out of which Marx's critique was born. Neither the factory worker nor the site worker has the means to enjoy the products of their labor.

The monetary rewards for both the factory worker and the site worker are, furthermore, minimal. I have described how in the past, archaeologists intentionally limited the salaries of site workers so as not to suggest that the artifacts uncovered were valuable. Today, with funding difficult to secure and project budgets as tight as they are, wages for site workers remain low. Not all countries where archaeologists work have minimum wage laws that apply to excavation laborers, and even when they do, the seasonality and temporary nature of excavation work means there is little financial benefit to be gained from working on an excavation. In fact, this has been a frequent complaint of many site workers, both Turkish and Jordanians, I have met. They also mentioned that archaeological work frequently has health impacts—from back strain to inhalation of dust—that harms them physically and costs a great deal of money to treat, which archaeological employers do not cover.

Alternatively, tourism and the development of heritage sites have frequently been suggested in the past as a promising means for local communities to benefit economically from archaeological excavation. However, archaeologists and heritage practitioners drawing on global case studies have overwhelmingly demonstrated that tourism is most often too unstable and centrally controlled to be a reliable, profitable resource for communities living on or near archaeological remains (Alhasanat 2010; Baram and Rowan 2004; Brand 2000; Comer 2012; Doan 2006; Giraudo and Porter 2010; Gray 1998; Hazbun 2008, 2010; Meskell 2005b). Therefore, none of the direct outcomes of archaeological work—nothing that the site workers are laboring to produce—provides a reliable benefit they can enjoy. Excavation workers are excluded from the actual products of their labor *and* do not receive the kinds of benefits or advantages they explicitly desire in return for their labor.

The degree to which workers are consciously aware of this disparity and the degree to which it leads to the subsequent forms of alienation proposed by Marx (from the act of producing and from sense of self) requires ethnographic engagement with the workers themselves to determine. I therefore apply the methodology of the laboratory study to view the operation of the labor-epistemology dynamic on the archaeological site and follow Russell and colleagues' (2000: 238) assertion that oral history is "the only feasible way to fill this gap in the historical record" on science's invisible technicians. In so doing, I contribute a perspective on site workers to both science studies and, more specifically, the rapidly expanding body of ethnographic research conducted by archaeologists as part of the literature collectively referred to as "ethnography of archaeology."

ETHNOGRAPHY OF ARCHAEOLOGY

The term *ethnography of archaeology* encompasses a variety of projects with very different goals. This is immediately apparent in discussions of the multitude of ways ethnography has been applied to archaeology as a research process, referred to by a set of overlapping terms like *ethnoarchaeology, ethnographic archaeology*, *anthropology of archaeology*, and *archaeological ethnography*, which have been inconsistently applied to describe both similar and dissimilar research frameworks (see Edgeworth 2003, 2006; Hollowell and Nicholas 2008). Despite attempts to draw clear boundaries between these methods and perspectives (e.g., Castañeda 2008; Meskell 2005a), many archaeologists have instead settled on fluid definitions of "ethnography." For Lisa C. Breglia (2006: 174), the word refers to "an eminently ethical engagement between archaeologists, ethnographers, and local communities," which asserts no specific research methods or theoretical questions, while Yannis Hamilakis and Aris Anagnostopoulos (2009: 73) define it as "a transcultural space for engagement, dialogue, and critique, centered upon the material traces of various times and involving researchers and other participants who are normally kept apart to coexist, share information and ideas, engage in common practices, but also disagree and clash."

A few comprehensive reviews of the different recent ethnographic approaches to understanding various aspects of archaeology have been published (cf. Castañeda 2008; Edgeworth 2006; Hamilakis 2011; Hollowell and Nicholas 2008). This book dialogues with those ethnographic studies that contribute to the ongoing conversation on epistemology in archaeology. These studies, by and large, have not yet closely examined the character of the knowledge possessed by site workers but have provided more general insight into how hierarchies form within archaeological projects. Matt Edgeworth (2006), Carolyn Hamilton (2000), and Blythe E. Roveland (2006) describe how excavation participants who succeed in establishing themselves as experts often gain more insight into emerging ideas at a site and, as a result, later demonstrate a greater willingness to share their own developing hypotheses. This cycle reproduces the status quo governing whose perspectives become cemented and disseminated as archaeological knowledge.

Moreover, many ethnographers of archaeology debate about what the ethnographic evidence suggests in terms of how to change problematic and long-standing disciplinary dynamics. On one side of this debate, Richard Handler (2008) describes how quickly any reflexive method as practiced by archaeologists becomes rote and perfunctory and suggests—along with Quetzil E. Castañeda (1996), David Shankland (1999b), and Larry J. Zimmerman (2008)—that to avoid such habituation, non-archaeologists should be the ones to critique archaeology rather than the practitioners of the discipline. These scholars argue that when perspectives from within the discipline are the only ones considered about the discipline, it leads to misunderstanding and continued disempowerment of the people affected by our research practices.

Not everyone shares this view. Lynn Meskell (2005a), for example, argues that the insider expertise and experiential understanding archaeologists possess grants a unique ethnographic perspective on fieldwork and disciplinary practices that others cannot achieve. For Mark P. Leone (2008) as well, archaeologists have an unmatched capability to launch a critique of their own field because archaeology's greatest success has always been in disrupting dominant discourses about the past. Furthermore, archaeologists are not incidental to the archaeological process; they possess a privileged, emic perspective on the scientific work they conduct, which has the potential to challenge and change the discipline. The insider experience of these archaeologists and, moreover, their expertise in analyzing the ways humans and objects assemble together and interact increases the possibility of designing new approaches to excavation practice that take into account the totality of people and things that enables research to proceed.

Once all of these factors are taken into account—the power politics that have created disproportionate representation and also disproportionate access to knowledge, the need to overturn the status quos in both archaeological practice and discourse, the need to fill many different kinds of gaps in the literature on archaeological epistemology—it is clear that neither non-specialists nor archaeologists alone have the capacity to study and critique the archaeological enterprise in a way that leads toward these goals. Instead, collaborative methodologies are needed, along with research that joins the privileged, professional, analytical expertise of an archaeologist with the necessary but historically excluded etic perspectives diverse public interlocutors offer.

I aim to do just that, to seek out the voices of local laborers while also preserving the analytical approaches engendered by my own professionalization as an archaeologist and anthropologist. This means examining changes and continuities in practices, beliefs, and behaviors over time, analyzing transition and stability diachronically. It means taking memories and oral histories as seriously as documentary sources and physical objects. It means making full use of both qualitative and statistical modes of inquiry. It means digging in, metaphorically more than physically, to other people, perspectives, places, and times and being willing to be surprised by what one encounters. In chapter 2, I assess how closely the expertise of site workers correlates with that of foreign excavation teams—and I begin in one of those moments of surprise, sitting on a rug sharing tea and *ful*[6] with a Bedouin man and listening to his recollections of his time working at the Temple of the Winged Lions in Petra, Jordan.

2

Site Workers as Specialists, Site Workers as Supporters

"He found a lot of things, you know."[1] *Nawaf*[2] *ripped off another piece of pita and scooped it in the stewed beans steaming in the pan between us. He slipped the beans and bread into his mouth, tasting the salt and spices added during the last half hour as he shared vivid memories with me, transporting us both back in time to Philip C. Hammond's 1983 excavations in the Temple of the Winged Lions in Petra. "I remember one time, you know, he found, like, an eagle from bronze and a statue and . . ." He trailed off, taking a sip from the ornate glass brimming with dark amber tea on the floor in front of him.*

In the course of juggling my pen, notebook, tea, pita, and beans, I was certain I had misheard him. What could he mean by "an eagle from bronze?" He had mentioned with nonchalance what would surely have been an incredible find. Moreover, I didn't remember anything about a bronze eagle from my hours spent poring over Hammond's archive. I glanced at my phone to ensure it was still recording so I would be able to transcribe his exact words later, and I attempted to clarify. "Do you remember anything special? Like a particular thing?"

"Yeah, yeah," Nawaf replied, looking at me. "The big, uh . . . big falcon, you know. Very big."

"Oh!" I realized that I hadn't misheard after all. "Really? Was it like a sculpture?"

"Yeah. It's like this." He searched on his iPhone for a photo of a falcon to confirm that I understood. Turning the screen to face me, he explained that the photograph was taken in the Wadi Arabah desert north of Petra. In

DOI: 10.5876/9781646421152.c002

the photo, his friend had a large falcon perched on his arm, about 20 inches tall, with brown spots on its wings and a vicious black beak. "You know, big falcon. From the roof. It's like this one. Big. With wings, you know?"

"Complete or broken?" I asked.

"No, it's complete. Bronze."

"Oh . . . Wow." I was especially surprised to hear this detail, since I could not recall seeing any mention in the archives about an object like what Nawaf was describing, a nearly 2-foot-tall intact bronze falcon statue. How could I have missed it?

Late that night, I caught a ride in a pickup truck from the Bedouin village back to the house in the nearby town where I was living. I turned on my computer and opened all the site notebook PDFs from Hammond's 1983 excavations at the Temple of the Winged Lions, intrigued by what Nawaf recalled but skeptical about being able to find any confirmation in the surviving documentation from the archaeological team.

But on page 18 of Andrew Jones's notebook recording the excavation procedures and findings from trench II_1W, I found this line (figure 2.1):

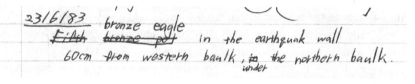

Figure 2.1. *Andrew Jones's documentation of the bronze eagle from Stratigraphic Unit 3 in trench II_1W at the Temple of the Winged Lions in Petra, Jordan. It reads:*
"23/6/83 ~~Fifth bronze pot~~ bronze eagle in the earthquak [*sic*] wall 60cm from western baulk, ~~in~~ under the northern baulk." Philip C. Hammond/American Expedition to Petra Archive. Courtesy, American Center of Oriental Research, Amman, Jordan.

Seeing this, I could hardly feel surprised that I did not recall this record immediately when Nawaf mentioned a bronze eagle. The fourteen words documenting this object are buried in a lengthy, detail-laden list of bronze bowls, pieces of irons, and plaster flakes found in the same Stratigraphic Unit (SU), and there is no language conveying the uniqueness of this find (although it is assuredly the only bronze eagle recorded in any of the site notebooks).

As with any archive, the site notebooks from the first Temple of the Winged Lions excavation are inherently partial, recording certain aspects of the scientific process but not others. They emphasize the color and texture of the soil, dates of excavation, and a quick listing of the finds recovered from each SU, including an expedient pottery analysis. Even when certain special finds occasion a small sketch or some measurements, the treatment is brief.

Many site workers, in contrast, remember the moment a particular statue was exposed or what it depicted or what hypotheses were offered about its original location and purpose. By virtue of heaving the picks and shovels that expose new earth and by occupying a landscape in which objects like these emerge constantly—brought to the surface by rain, wind, and foot traffic—locally hired laborers hone special talents and expertise about the artifacts that constitute archaeological assemblages. Men and women employed to dig at sites in the Middle East often grow up retrieving, identifying, and washing archaeological finds; over decades of close engagement with potsherds and coins, they develop privileged knowledge about the nature and meaning of these objects.

In this chapter, I paint out the nature of that expertise. Using the memories shared by site workers from Hammond's excavation at the Temple of the Winged Lions and Ian Hodder's excavation at Çatalhöyük during 167 ethnographic interviews conducted between 2011 and 2015, I show how their understanding of archaeological finds and methods adds to the existing archaeological record. I demonstrate with network analysis how their expertise compares measurably to the written record from these sites. This analysis illustrates that the locally hired laborers at both sites have developed recognizable archaeological and scientific expertise about artifacts and excavation methodology. However, it also reveals that the opposite approaches to labor management implemented at the two sites have led site workers to develop opposite forms of archaeological expertise. This apparent difference provides evidence for a correlation between labor and knowledge production in archaeology.

EXPANDING KNOWLEDGE ABOUT FINDS FROM THE TEMPLE OF THE WINGED LIONS

When Nawaf described the bronze eagle found in 1983, I was struck by the specificity of his recollection. Later, rereading the fourteen-word documentation of the find, I realized as well the importance of his memory for adding information to the minimal record of this object. Nawaf offers several vivid and significant details that are simply not available from what was written about the object when it was found.

Perhaps the most obvious and concrete detail is the size of the statue. Andrew Jones's notes do not include any measurements or dimensions, but by referencing the photograph of his friend, Nawaf provided an approximation of the statue's size. I had spent weekends watching game-hunting men feed and train the kind of falcons Nawaf showed me in the iPhone photo. Such hunting companions are usually either saker or peregrine falcons, which grow to be 19–22 inches and 13–23 inches, respectively (Porter and Aspinall 2010). So when Nawaf told me that the eagle found in the excavation was a "big one, like this one," he was offering a reasonable measure of just how big the eagle was, particularly since he also recalled that the statue was complete. Both of these details are omitted from the written record.

Nawaf also suggested a possible original location for the statue when he theorized that it came from the roof. There is nothing in the site notebook to suggest this; SU 3—the context from which it was recovered—is not identified as a roof collapse. The only interpretation offered about this unit is that it was deposited during the AD 363 earthquake that destroyed many of the buildings in Petra. But as Nawaf watched the sand fall away from the metal, observing the archaeologists change their interpretation of the object from a pot to a statue, he thought of his experiences working on prior excavations throughout Petra. He linked his hypothesis to other archaeological deposits that had been identified as the remains of Nabataean roofs. And he came to the conclusion that this was a decoration from the roof based on his direct experience with this particular find, its provenance, and analogous finds from the same city.

Andrew Jones's terse description of the bronze eagle is indicative of how finds were most often recorded in the site notebooks from the Temple of the Winged Lions excavation. Even iconic artifacts are treated surprisingly minimally in the project archive—like the stone block depicting the Nabataean goddess *al-'uzza*, referred to by Hammond (1996: 102) as the "Eye-Idol" and by local community members as "Dushara"[3] (figure 2.2), which could be deemed the most famous artifact from the project. It has been reproduced as paperweights, bracelet charms, earrings, magnets, and postcards for sale throughout Jordan. This object was the most common immediate answer to a question I asked former site workers: "What did Hammond's project find during the excavations at the temple?" They described what the tablet looked like—its almond eyes, long nose, and pouty lips—and reached under their collars to pull out al-'uzza pendants dangling from a black cord or zoomed in on mobile phone photographs of al-'uzza souvenirs. A park ranger who stopped at the temple for a tea break while I was working there one day revealed that he remembered the moment when the tablet was found, then skipped off through the rooms of the structure to show me exactly where it was first discovered. Standing on a loose stone in a central room of the building, smoking a hand-rolled cigarette, he called back to me, "This is where it was found, next to these column drums and near the altar."

The evocative stone face drummed up emotion and argument whenever I mentioned it. Although everyone was familiar with the idea of it, having seen

FIGURE 2.2. *Stone block depicting the Nabataean deity al-ʻuzza, originally found during Hammond's excavations at the Temple of the Winged Lions, on display in the Jordan Museum, Amman.*

its miniature clay and plastic clones circulating through the tourist shops, very few people in the community saw the original object before it was transported to Amman. Instead, they were excited about it as a recognizable symbol of Petra, and they wanted to tell—and hear—its story.

One day, I was sitting with a group of Bedouin men and women near the Royal Tombs in Petra, and an older man named Musa joined our group. He sat down, poured a steaming glass of sugary tea, and mentioned offhand that he had been working on the project in 1975 when the al-ʻuzza tablet was found.

Other people sitting in the tent with us immediately started asking him questions about the block. "What level was it on in the excavation?" one man asked. Everyone was silent as Musa answered.

"Oh, I would calculate that it was about 2 meters down. I mean, it was inside a part of the building that I didn't work in. But it was only 2 meters down," he said, and everyone paused to consider this information. I circled and underlined this information in my notebook, excited because absolute depths are almost never recorded in the site notebooks from the Temple of the Winged Lions excavation. About this particular object, the record states only that it was found "E of SU 151/with one side to the pilaster ~ SU 151 and the face to the northern wall was a statue, lying top-down, face to the wall. Only the rectangular lower face of the statue was visible by the excavation. Some other pieces belonging to the stone were found in its neighbourhood. The statue was resting on SU 109. Measurements 1,31 × ,20. Inscribed in Nabataean."

Musa's recollection therefore provides data to complement the details documented by the excavators. To be able to recover this level of specificity and quantitative detail simply by talking to former site workers illustrates how much important scientific information is preserved in the memories of the individuals who spent summer after summer watching monuments and assemblages emerge from the ground, seeing how the archaeologists interacted with these objects. For those relics that go on to be famous, commodified, and symbolic, this knowledge is kept alive and shared with others. The interaction between Musa and the group of engaged listeners sitting around us embodied this process in action.

The ethnographic cases of the bronze eagle and the al-ʿuzza tablet show how scientific details such as measurements and provenance are preserved in oral history and recovered through intimate, in-depth conversations. Most of the interviews I conducted with former site workers, for instance, lasted 45 minutes to 1 hour and were held in their homes and workplaces. We shared food, I played games with their children, I helped with English translation projects. I often went home from these interviews with gifts of dates and apricots spilling out of my arms. The conditions of these interviews led me to recover intimate details about the excavations at both Petra and Çatalhöyük that would have continued to go undocumented otherwise.

But to focus only on individual examples of the specific artifacts and archaeological details site workers remember loses sight of the scale of this hidden expertise and how it compares, broadly, to what *is* documented in the archival record from these excavations. This archival record is extensive; the archives from Hammond's project at the temple consist of 175 site notebooks,[4] several informal reports (Hammond 1976, 1992), and a final published volume (Hammond 1996). Taking a structural view of how the information contained in this expansive archival record compared to that shared in the interviews I conducted offers a sense of how divergent these two sources of information are. More important, taking such a structural view suggests just how much information could be lost from Hammond's excavations in Petra because of the site workers' lack of involvement in recording and documentation.

Network analysis provides this structural view by mapping out how related the interviews and the archival record are or are not. Network analysis also allows for a quantitative and statistical comparison of the knowledge archaeologists have recorded versus the knowledge contained in former site workers' memories. Archaeology itself relies on operating on multiple scales of analysis and marshaling both qualitative and quantitative evidence to make claims about the past. By using network analysis in combination with ethnography, I am appealing to the strengths of archaeology itself in the interest of ultimately challenging institutional traditions in how laborers are recruited, hired, treated, and fired in archaeology.

Figure 2.3 is a graphic representation of the network of recorded and recollected knowledge about the Temple of the Winged Lions excavation in Petra. In this diagram, each "node," or circle, represents an excavation participant—a locally hired site worker, a foreign excavation supervisor, or a foreign student. The foreign archaeological team members are represented by the dark gray nodes, and the Jordanian laborers are represented by the white nodes. The lines between each node, known as links or "edges," connect individuals who mentioned the same artifact in an interview (for a site worker) or in a site notebook (for a foreign team member).

In a network visualization like this one, nodes that are located spatially close to one another are drawn together by having more edges pulling them nearer to one another. In figure 2.3 specifically, two nodes close to one another represent two excavation participants who noted information about many of the same artifacts.

In figure 2.3, the red nodes, representing Hammond's team members, cluster distinctly toward the center of the graph while the blue nodes, signifying locally hired site workers, envelop the cluster of red. This means that the foreign excavators created records of artifacts that were quite similar to one another—but quite distinct from the recollections of locally hired site workers. Indeed, there were categories of artifacts like statues, decorative capitals, and bronze objects that were nearly exclusively (more than 80% of the time) mentioned by site workers and almost never in the recorded notebooks. In

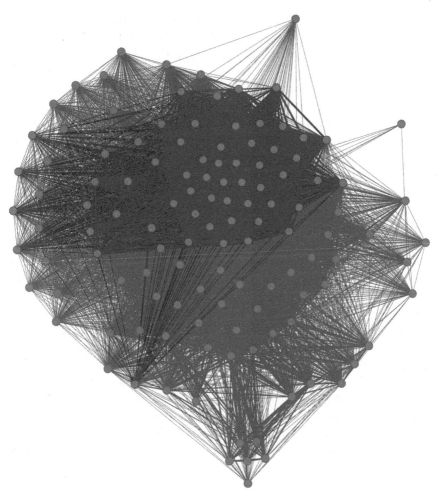

FIGURE 2.3. *A network of seventy-four site workers who have been employed at the Temple of the Winged Lions (blue) and fifty TWL archaeologists (red), linked on the basis of mentioning the same category of archaeological find in an oral history interview or site documentation, respectively.*

contrast, other categories of objects—rings, copper objects, glass, tesserae, and bone—were referenced more than 80 percent of the time in the excavation documentation and almost never in my conversations with site workers.

I argue that this divergence in the structure of site workers' knowledge about archaeological finds at the Temple of the Winged Lions versus the foreign excavators' records is related to labor management at the temple. By "labor management," I mean the strategies for recruiting, hiring, and firing workers as well as how they were motivated, disciplined, and treated overall on the archaeological site.

The difference in artifact-related content between the archaeologists' archives and the site workers' memories is largely due to the disparities in turnover between the foreign and local team members. The same students and excavators returned to Hammond's project from season to season. The site workers, in contrast, changed between the summers. One reason for this was that many of the men who worked at the Temple of the Winged Lions did so when they were very young—eight or nine years old. They were children looking to make a small amount of money over the summer, not adults working to build a career and support a family.

But the team of site workers had a high rate of turnover not only between seasons but even during the seasons or over the span of a single week. The people I met expressed feelings of anger and resentment regarding the employment practices at the Temple. They told me they could be fired for nearly any reason—for being 10 minutes late, for not working fast enough, for asking for a higher wage. They called Hammond and the excavation supervisors "severe," "intense," and "anxious." One of the former workers I interviewed claimed that site workers were "treated like goats" and would be dismissed from the site if they went to drink water at a time that wasn't set aside as "break time" in the daily schedule. Several people equated this treatment with slavery. For example: "He [Hammond] saw the people as slaves, you know? If he saw you working or carrying things you were good, and one moment you go to drink water and he didn't like this. 'Work! Get out! Work! You're fired!' In a snobbish way, I mean. 'Get out! Get out!' He didn't care for any human beings . . . You know, if he visited this place now, you know we will fight."

Remarkably, the excavation supervisors' notebooks support, rather than contradict, recollections like this one. Some of the site notebooks consist almost entirely of daily lists of the workers and the precise minute at which they arrived at the site in the morning. The notebooks from 1978 best depict the strained relations between the excavation team and the locally hired laborers, as they describe the events surrounding a strike by site workers. The comments by the excavators are at first tolerant—although they expose the work conditions on the site: "The little boys were getting sick from heatstroke so it was probably better that this [shorter workday] happened."[5] After a few days, however, the precarity of local labor on the project becomes apparent. In one supervisor's language: "The kiddie brigade decided that they needed more pay and so the director simply fired the whole lot of them."

Not only were site workers constantly fired and replaced, even those working on the site were frequently excluded from the retrieval and analysis of artifacts recovered during the excavation. According to former site workers in informal interviews, "When they [Hammond's team] find something very important they made the people go away." Even though they were working on the site, these men said they could not learn about what was found because they were sent out of the trench anytime anything significant was exposed.

Instead, most of their knowledge comes from talking with one another, sharing stories and memories with family and friends. The conversation I witnessed in front of the Royal Tombs, where Musa shared his memories of the al-'uzza tablet with a rapt audience, was only one instance of this continual process. Of course, stories tend to circulate around the most phenomenal and interesting artifacts, not the broken faunal and glass material repeatedly documented in the site notebooks. And so, former site workers generally possess information about unique finds—idols and bronze eagles, for instance—rather than the more common material categories recorded in nearly every stratigraphic unit. Accordingly, the structure and content of their knowledge is different than that of the site archives, and the network visualization captures this. The site workers' memories of artifacts represent a body of information complementary to that preserved by the archaeological team. The same is true when a similar network is generated on the basis of shared mentions of excavation methodologies by site workers and archaeologists (figure 2.4).

LOCAL AND LEARNED METHODS

In the network shown in figure 2.4, again, foreign team members from the Temple of the Winged Lions excavation are represented by the blue nodes and site workers by the red nodes. Linkages are drawn between individuals who mentioned applying the same excavation method, whether in a site notebook or in an interview.

In this network, again, the site workers are pushed to the outskirts of the network. Centrality measures represent a statistical method frequently used in social network analysis to identify the most "important" nodes in a network (Borgatti 2005). Calculating the eigenvector centralities for the foreign team members versus the site workers reveals that site workers' ostensibly peripheral position with regard to the network structure is deeper than

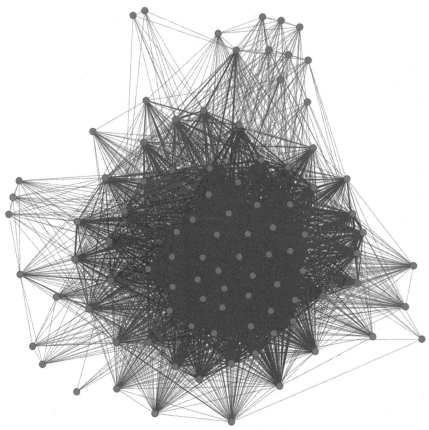

FIGURE 2.4. *A network of forty-eight site workers from the Temple of the Winged Lions excavation (blue) and fifty-six archaeologists (red), linked on the basis of mentioning the same aspect of excavation practice in an oral history interview or site documentation, respectively*

appearance alone. In this network, the average eigenvector centrality of a site worker is 0.504 compared with 0.893 for an archaeologist—a difference of 39 percent.

But the use of the word *centrality* should not be taken as a synonym for importance. Site workers' lack of centrality in this network of archaeological knowledge does not represent a lack of methodological expertise. As with archaeological finds, their knowledge focuses especially on aspects of the excavation strategy not widely recorded by excavation supervisors, and this is what the network is capturing.

The documentation regarding the methods used at the temple does not reference the unique skills locally hired laborers had to possess to carry out their assigned tasks. The site notebooks almost never mention how stratigraphic layers were differentiated and removed. They refer frequently to a "pick-man," implying that a pick was used, although not on which types of deposits or how it was used. This lack of discussion implies that excavation strategies are self-evident and easy decisions to make.

In fact, the opposite is true. The intuition for when to switch tools and techniques is forged through a combination of instruction, awareness of the excavation goals, and direct experience. To master the range of equipment employed by the excavation, one must understand the nature of both stratigraphy and the archaeological assemblage, as Musa Mutlaq told me when I asked him if and how site workers know what tool to use.

"You use the pick when there are many stones," he began. "But when the sand changes you have to switch to the hand pick and the brush if you want to find the floor, coins, small antiquities, and figurines."

When I asked Hamdan Salem, another former Temple of the Winged Lions site worker, how he benefited from working on this project, he answered: "We got real expertise there, the ones who worked there. We learned how to make discoveries without breaking them. Use the trowel, use the small pick, use the big pick . . . Use the pick until it gives way to some pottery. Something would come up . . . [imitates the act of digging slowly in swaths around an object] And at last you can dig it out."

Sixteen separate men I interviewed stated emphatically that using picks, trowels, and even *goofahs*[6] as carefully, quickly, and effectively as possible was something they had to gradually learn through archaeological work experience, in particular how to use the digging tools without breaking the delicate artifacts underneath. The extent of this bodily knowledge of the equipment and of how to dig with it belies language. It is a form of knowledge more accurately evinced by calloused hands, hardened biceps and deltoids, a deftness with even shoddy, heavy, or dull tools. It is embodied knowledge, most apparent in the posture and movement of the members of the renewed, active excavations at the Temple of the Winged Lions and other contemporary excavations in Petra.

Even washing pottery, a duty normally allocated to students and other untrained newcomers, has its own complexity. There is decision-making involved; there is skill in differentiating the materials comprising the archaeological assemblage. Raya Jmeidi was one of a few women hired to wash the pottery from the Temple of the Winged Lions project. She described the process to me: "So we would be in the Nazal,[7] and they would bring us the pottery and we would wash it. And after that, we'd look at the color and say, well, this is pottery, but this is a rock. And so we'd keep the pottery but not if we saw it was a rock . . . So I can say what is a rock and that you can throw them away." After the initial field assessment of the pottery recorded in the notebooks, which provides basic counts and proportions of the ceramics from each stratigraphic unit, the pottery-washing women have both the knowledge and the authority to remove some sherds from that count. They perform an editing role, removing some "pottery" from the archaeological record and modifying the initial interpretations set down by excavation participants. This position requires both a level of familiarity with the materials found through excavation in Petra and some amount of permission to undo the decisions made by excavation supervisors about what should be kept and analyzed.

Despite the fact that project leaders entrusted pottery washers with refining the pottery assemblage from the temple, these contributions by the washing women are not directly recognized in the site records. There are photographs of clean assortments of pottery, presumably missing any stones Raya and her workmates tossed aside as sand and grit mistaken for temper that had slipped away from the edges of the chipped flat shale. But these photographs do not give any hint as to the identities of the people who shaped the assemblages into their final form. Even if the women's discerning eyes were appreciated at the time by project members, the ability of these women to produce more accurate, coherent categories of material finds from the excavation through their practical knowledge of the washing process is not acknowledged in the archive of the research.

I think it is uncontroversial to propose that one of the primary reasons pottery washing and its role in forming the published, curated archaeological record is rarely, if ever, directly addressed in archaeological documentation is because it appears mundane and straightforward. My conversations with pottery-washing women like Raya show this presumption to be mistaken, and anyone who has participated in an excavation has surely encountered others who are undeniably *bad* at pottery washing, suggesting that some level of proficiency must be developed. This is especially true with the emergence of analytical techniques such as residue analysis—techniques that require that artifacts not be washed—and those conscripted to wash pottery and other artifacts must often be able to recognize artifacts that should not be rinsed or brushed. In general, however, this is a task usually assigned to the least experienced members of the research team, and the expertise required to complete it goes unnoticed and unrecorded.

The pottery washing and specific digging methods used at the site are best understood through oral history. These are activities that, despite their integrality to the project's ability to draw conclusions about the past, are constructed by the body of site records as automatic. They are indirectly referenced, never treated in depth. The digging and washing seem to happen without direction or discussion, and the site workers, as participants in these stages of the research process, are similarly simplified. They speak, however, about the amount of active learning entailed in these deceptively uncomplicated methods and approaches.

The site workers from Petra also had ideas and expertise about how archaeological methods adjust to articulate more effectively with local environmental and climatic conditions. Many of them critiqued the methodologies of archaeological projects in Petra on the basis of both their archaeological expertise and their familiarity as locals with the region's environment and cultural resources. One young Bedul man, Ahmed, was candid about his negative view of the Temple of the Winged Lions excavation because of decisions about where to dump the soil they had removed:

AHMED: There was chaos in this work. There was chaos . . . Because to them, there was no problem where the dirt went. You know what I mean? When they took sand out.

ME: Mm. Mm.

AHMED: You know? They didn't care where it went. I think. They didn't care much where it went. They take thirty capitals of, uh, columns. Put it here. You take sand. Put it here. Later . . . later they were forgetting all of this. They just went to put the dirt in another place. This is a problem!

ME: Mm.

AHMED: There was no strategy to the work.

Archaeological workers were upset by dumps like these for several reasons: they cover other sites and monuments that could add to knowledge about and visitorship to Petra; they apply added weight and pressure to potentially fragile remains underneath, and they create eyesores on the landscape. Exacerbating these issues is the fact that many of these men felt they had better ideas for where sifted backfill should be deposited. Their archaeological training had taught them that the sand and stones removed during excavation should be "left close to the site. What if someone comes later with new technology, or what if they want to do restoration with it?" as Darwish Salam Mowasa, who worked at the Temple of the Winged Lions, expressed. "Besides," he went on, "if you take all of this dirt out, no plants will be able to grow in Petra."

Dachlallah Sabah Samahin, a man who contributed to moving several hundred liters of soil from the Great Temple in the 1990s, had a different idea. If the excavation is stratigraphic and careful, he suggested that the soil should be dumped into a *wadi*—one of the valleys in the area carved by water and wind. This way, when the winter rains come, the dirt will be washed down and away, at the very least flattened so as not to transform the topography and viewsheds of the park. Others were in agreement that the wadis are good places to put excavated soil, particularly since there are rarely visible ruins at the surface of the base of these wadis that might be obscured or damaged by piling sand and cobbles on top. From spending their childhoods and adolescences scaling the mountains and traversing these valley basins, they have a familiarity with the distribution of archaeological remains in the area. Integrating this with local knowledge of weather and how it impacts the landscape enables them to make suggestions that are specific and relevant to improving the practice of archaeology in the region.

These types of place-based knowledge are in addition to the information about archaeological practices the archaeologists recorded at the Temple of the Winged Lions. The site notebooks narrate the archaeological team's approaches to dating and analyzing pottery, photographing deposits and finds, and taking measurements. These are all activities site workers did not participate in, did not learn about. The site notebooks, meanwhile, record virtually nothing about the tools used in the digging process or how the location for the soil dump was selected. These are aspects of the excavation procedure that site workers both know and care about because of their identities as local community members and as individuals looking back today on decades of archaeological work experience.

The site workers from the Temple of the Winged Lions excavation therefore possess insight into diverse aspects of the assemblage and the excavation procedure that complements the archaeological research team's core areas of interest for documentation. The American excavators' records follow a template and therefore ensure that the same categories of information are recorded about each stratigraphic unit. At the same time, they sacrifice in their systematism the breadth and idiosyncrasies preserved in local site workers' memories of the excavation work. The site workers form a community of experts that supplement the documentary record on the archaeological finds and strategies from the Temple of the Winged Lions project, and the degree to which their complementary form of expertise has been shaped by the labor conditions of the excavation at the temple becomes clear when viewed along-side the hiring practices and site workers' knowledge at Çatalhöyük.

LABOR MANAGEMENT AT ÇATALHÖYÜK

During a rare quiet moment in which the ladies hired to work in the kitchen were not scrubbing the 40-gallon pot used to cook lentil soup for lunch or peeling the 60 pounds of potatoes to be boiled for dinner, I was sitting on a mat behind the dig house kitchen. Cansu Kurt, who had volunteered to be my interpreter,[8] was sitting next to me; across from us sat the three women from Küçükköy who cooked our daily meals at Çatalhöyük. Cansu and I had begun by asking the standard opening interview questions: how long they had been working at Çatalhöyük, what their responsibilities were. (Actually, we had begun with a promise not to take up too much of their break time.) Fifteen minutes later, we were giggling over stories of mishaps and habits they had observed over their years of working for the project.

Some memories had very direct relevance to the archaeological enterprise. They told me that by watching where people sat during mealtimes and meetings, they could identify whom the other team members would listen to, who the "real bosses" were. They also recognized differences in the behavior of students versus the professors and professionals working on the project. The hidden hierarchies within the team that are so integral to work getting done in an excavation were visible to these Turkish women in the dining room, at mealtimes.

A few of their observations were very funny and charming. When I asked them to describe the most surprising things they had noticed about the team, they told me with incredulity that they had seen a number of people salting their watermelon. "What a strange habit," they told me. "We had never seen anyone do that before, salting their watermelon."

At one point, the ladies took my pen from me and dramatically tossed it behind them as they whispered tales of secret romantic relationships between archaeologists and legends about the raucous, themed dance parties each Thursday night. Some of these stories they had been told, some they had inferred from observing the archaeological team during times when they weren't working. This was information they were uniquely privy to from growing close to team members and participating in the most intimate aspects of the excavation for so many years.

The friendship and familiarity expressed by these women is indicative of how both site workers and the archaeological team have generally experienced their interactions over the course of the Çatalhöyük excavation. Locally hired community members described satisfying conversations with researchers who could speak Turkish. They mentioned mentors from whom they had learned about the prehistoric work and about excavation strategies. "Burcu[9] . . . was like my teacher and a really good excavator," one man told me. "She taught me about counting the volume, using the [flotation] machine, putting the filter in, putting the soil in carefully." Another worker remembered his experience working on an area of the site run by a team of excavators affiliated with the University of California, Berkeley. He recalled, "When I was working for Mira and Ruth,[10] they gave me the soil for sieving and I wrote the labels for the finds. Ruth and Mira taught me . . . I was happy to be trusted with these things and felt I wanted to do good work."

The documentary records from Çatalhöyük express similar positive experiences, appreciation, and closeness with site workers on the whole. Excavators write in particular in their excavation diaries about their admiration for site workers' abilities and insights.[11] In a 2006 diary, for example, German excavator ER (2006a) writes about commissioning longtime laborer Ismail Buluç to repair the site tools, knowing they would be as good as, if not better than, brand new after he fixed them; in the meantime, she marveled at the local workers' ability to use even broken or shoddy tools efficiently because of their impressive strength and experience (2006b). For Kathryn Elizabeth Hall (2007), a British team member, working alongside local community members and watching that rapport develop was one of the most exciting and rewarding aspects of working at Çatalhöyük. American team member CLC's (2013) diary vividly narrates an account that illustrates not only the warmth felt toward site workers but also the ethos of sharing responsibilities (rather than stringent hierarchy and division) that characterized the excavation at Çatalhöyük:

> I was touched that our worker Orhan went beyond his required duties to help me today; it was difficult to clean both profiles as they had dried out so much, and the tools I was using were a small pick and a small trowel. He saw me having difficulty, and came over with a flat shovel and helped clean much of the top of F. 3333. Later, when I was having difficulty again at the base of the wall, I asked him to come in and help, which he did, and JMR happened to be in the trench at the time, and sort of sat back and appreciated the nice job he was doing. I called him "Usta," which means master/master workman/skilled, which he laughed at. Then he went to GWN to see if he wanted profile help as well. Also, after breakfast break, he brought me back an ideal tool for the job: a small hoe with a wide and flat edge. I asked where it came from, if it was his, and he

said no, he found it. He clearly went to the tool shed on his break without me asking him to in order to bring me a better tool. I told him how much better this was, and "You know everything!" which he also humbly laughed at. GWN later used his shovel technique to clean a profile. It is nice to see Orhan enjoying contributing to the work, and also others in the trench appreciating his contribution and skill.

These accounts, from both the site workers and the foreign excavators, paint a picture of a different model of work from Hammond's earlier excavations at the Temple of the Winged Lions. Site workers at Çatalhöyük were much more involved in all dimensions of the excavation process, more readily recognized as stakeholders and as skilled participants. This more inclusive, more egalitarian labor model had definite impacts on site workers' development of specialized archaeological knowledge and abilities, which can be both viewed and measured through network analysis techniques.

NETWORKS OF KNOWLEDGE AT ÇATALHÖYÜK

Figure 2.5 represents a network of all the excavation participants at Çatalhöyük—both archaeologists and workers from the local community—connected to anyone who mentioned the same category of artifact either in an interview context or in the multimedia site archive from Çatalhöyük. At Çatalhöyük, the archival record from the ongoing renewed excavations consists of a vast variety of media created by the contemporary excavation—pro forma, photography, video, maps, 3D models, free-form narrative diaries, drawings, sketches, Harris matrices, end-of-season archive reports, thematic monographs, and peer-reviewed journal articles.[12] All of these records were used to build this network of data, with a particular focus on the pre-printed context sheets, diaries, and archive reports.

The predominance and density of red nodes representing archaeologists is evident in comparison to the Petra networks because the archaeological team at Çatalhöyük numbered in the hundreds, year after year, while the team working at the Temple of the Winged Lions was never more than forty students and supervisors in any given season. But many network statistics, like eigenvector centrality, depend on the overall network structure and are not much affected by the size of the network, allowing for a comparison between networks of very different sizes. In the finds-based network from Çatalhöyük (figure 2.5), the average eigenvector centrality of a site worker is 0.738 and for an archaeologist, 0.741—a 0.3 percent difference. In the

FIGURE 2.5. *A network of 29 site workers who have been employed at Çatalhöyük (blue) and 444 Çatalhöyük archaeologists (red), linked on the basis of mentioning the same category of archaeological find in an oral history interview or site documentation, respectively*

parallel network from Petra (figure 2.3), the average eigenvector centrality for a site worker in this network is 0.819 but 0.938 for an archaeologist (a 12% difference).

This means that at Çatalhöyük, unlike at the Temple of the Winged Lions, site workers and archaeologists occupied similar positions within the overall structure of archaeological knowledge about artifacts. These two groups recalled and recorded similar categories and varieties of finds. Their stories of having shared in the same work do not merely reveal a pleasant work environment; they reflect how different approaches to managing labor have real impacts on site workers' access to developing expertise akin to the scientific training and knowledge the researchers possess. Rather than being sent out of the excavation when artifacts were encountered, workers at Çatalhöyük were included in the recovery and treatment of the objects from the site. Accordingly, their knowledge of the assemblage is structurally similar to that of the research team members.

Site workers' and archaeologists' knowledge of archaeological methods at Çatalhöyük also maps well onto each other. Figure 2.6 links site workers and archaeologists from Çatalhöyük on the basis of mentioning the same excavation approach.

The degree to which site workers and archaeologists occupy similar positions in this structure of knowledge about excavation methods at Çatalhöyük is most observable using a calculation of modularity. Modularity measures how easily a network can be divided into modules, or sub-communities.[13] Optimal modularity in the network from figure 2.6 is achieved when the network is divided into seven sub-communities (figure 2.7).[14] Table 2.1 presents the site workers and the modularity classes into which they are mathematically sorted.

The site workers at Çatalhöyük do not represent one discrete class of research participants with shared methodological expertise. Instead, when the map of team members describing the same techniques and approaches is segmented into natural subgroups, at least one site worker falls within nearly every subgroup (the exception is the group of eight people shown at the very top of figure 2.7 in pink, who carried out and reported on the project's highly specialized ground-penetrating radar activities).

The site workers' dispersion across modularity classes suggests that much like the research community at Çatalhöyük as a whole, the site workers form a group with internal specialties that complement each other so the research process progresses smoothly. Just as the laboratories at Çatalhöyük divide up the archaeological assemblage, using specific and appropriate techniques to examine the particular aspect on which they are experts, the site workers have developed expertise in different categories of methods. There are site workers who are especially interested in and knowledgeable about excavating burials (modularity class 3) and those who remember extremely unusual, specific, or

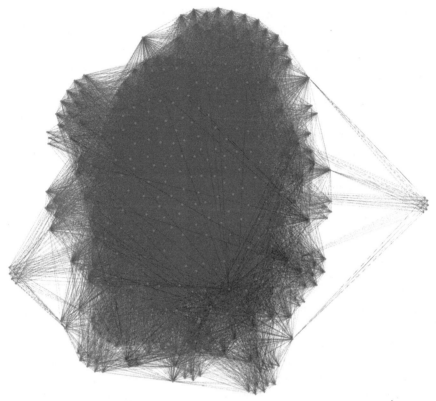

FIGURE 2.6. *A network of 22 site workers who have been employed at Çatalhöyük (blue) and 295 Çatalhöyük archaeologists (red), linked on the basis of mentioning the same aspect of excavation practice in an oral history interview or site documentation, respectively*

rarely applied techniques (modularity class 2). One site worker is the focused expert on stratigraphic excavation, while another group knows particularly about what happens between the initial digging of a soil layer and the examination of artifacts and materials in laboratories (modularity class 0). Just as the archaeological team members are experts in different categories of approaches and techniques, so, too, are the site workers at Çatalhöyük.

These networks reveal a disparate structure of knowledge about archaeological finds and methods versus the structure of the Temple of the Winged Lions team. At the temple, site workers possess expertise complementary to that recorded by the archaeological team and one in which site workers' knowledge overlaps with the contents of the excavation documentation. When site

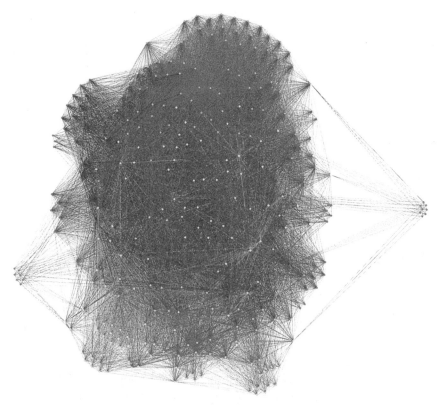

FIGURE 2.7. *Network of Çatalhöyük excavation research participants connected on the basis of describing the same methodologies in oral histories and site records, divided into seven subgroups, or modularity classes, using Blondel and colleagues' (2008) algorithm. Each color designates a different modularity class.*

workers possess unique, special knowledge about the archaeological assemblage and excavation process, it is easy to see what is lost when their perspectives are not recorded. But the understandings of archaeological finds and methods site workers at Çatalhöyük share with the archaeological researchers are important to preserve as well.

OPPORTUNITIES OF THE OVERLAP

Ferdi Söylemez's first season working at Çatalhöyük was in 2014. He had been coming to the excavation, though, since he was three or four years old,

TABLE 2.1. The modularity class of each Çatalhöyük site worker included in the network shown in figures 2.6 and 2.7, which has been partitioned into seven modularity classes total.

Name of Site Worker	Modularity Class	Name of Site Worker	Modularity Class
Abdullah Yaşlı	0	Ali K.	5
Anonymous	0	Hasan Tokyağsun	5
Hüseyin Yaşlı	0	Hüseyin Veli Yaşlı	5
Mustafa Sivas	0	Ismail	5
Ferdi Söylemez	2	Hatice Tokyağsun	5
Hassan Yaşlı	2	Ibrahim Eken	5
Hatice Çelik	2	Mevlut Sivas	5
Ali Akçar	2	Elmas Motuk	5
Mevlut Ferahkaya	3	Hülüsi Yaşlı	5
Osman Yaşlı	3	Saliha Sivas	5
Haşım Ferahkaya	4	Lokman Yaşlı	6

accompanying his mother who had worked in the kitchen since the project's earliest seasons. Two of his uncles had also worked on the site for years. He grew up overhearing conversations about the kitchen, the guardhouse, annoying visitors, and archaeological finds. When he was little, he didn't care about the stories; like any child, he ignored them as adult shoptalk, not something that concerned him. But now that he was participating in the excavation himself, finding bones and obsidian in the sieve, he had developed a new appreciation for these ancient objects: "I'm interested now in the clay balls. And in the skeletons under the floor . . . I always want to pick them up and look at them. I'm also interested in the teeth, the animal teeth. I'm interested because they're so ancient. Sometimes they even find animal bones in the walls. That's so interesting." I asked him if there were any finds in particular this year that his family was talking about at home. "There is one," he said. "A figurine. It was found in Gülbin's square. It was a bull figurine, from the North area. People are talking about that one a lot."

The figurine Ferdi mentioned is identified in the online Çatalhöyük excavation database as 22130.X1.[15] The database records provide technical details about the provenance of the figurine (it came from a friable, orange-ish dark gray arbitrary layer at the base of Building 113). The figurine database contains a great deal of specialist data associated with the figurine (e.g., height, width, length, weight, pose, primary fabric), including the researchers' skepticism about its identification as a bull: "unusually flat, maybe goat-like?"

The information Ferdi adds to the previously recorded data is less obvious than what Nawaf, Musa, and Mahmoud's knowledge contributed to the record of the finds from the Temple of the Winged Lions. Ferdi offers a name of one of the excavators involved in its collection and identification. He also singles out the figurine as a particularly noteworthy find, while none of the site records convey the excitement about the artifact that Ferdi does. A family of seasoned archaeological workers was going home and talking about it, yet it was not singled out for a photograph and specific mention in the archive report for that year (Nakamura et al. 2014). Although it is aggregated into the counts presented, neither the excavators nor the figurine specialists anywhere record the kind of enthusiasm about this figurine that Ferdi's family apparently felt.

But rather than mining Ferdi's knowledge of this find for *new* data, perhaps it is useful to consider how redundant it is with the existing Çatalhöyük archive and what the potential benefits are of this redundancy. Rather than unnecessary, the repeated details can be seen as mutually reinforcing. The archaeological documentation verifies the information given by Ferdi, validating the accuracy of his knowledge. At the same time, Ferdi's account corroborates the archaeological records. This is important not just at Çatalhöyük, where multivocality is emphasized as a crucial component of responsible scientific research, but for archaeology in general. One of the most frequently repeated axioms about archaeological excavation is that it is not a repeatable experiment. Unlike laboratory science, the conditions of an excavation can never be re-created to run independent trials. There is no control in archaeology. But maybe having oral history as a secondary source reporting the same details is a valuable substitute, particularly in cases where there is no substantial amount of documentation about a given unit or object.

Site workers' specialized methodological interests afford a similar mutual reinforcement of what the excavation records say about the research approaches used onsite. Mustafa Sivas, for instance, shared relatively few of his own memories with me, but one of those memories was of mastering the digging and sifting processes at the site. "I really enjoyed scraping slowly with the trowel and sieving," he told me. "Roddy and Shahina [British members of the archaeological research team] taught me how to do everything, all the materials to watch for while I was digging and sieving. It wasn't hard, it was all organized, and they taught me how to do everything."

Mustafa was not the only locally hired worker to emphasize strategies for maximum artifact retrieval. In fact, all the members of modularity class 0 from table 2.1 spent a great deal of time explaining such procedures to me. There are likewise a number of archaeological team members whose written records emphasize careful digging and approaches to sieving. Sieving in particular appears in documents produced by nearly all the laboratories at Çatalhöyük. Faunal specialists Louise Martin and Nerissa Russell (1997) discuss in a Çatalhöyük end-of-season report: "It became clear during the fieldseason, however, that the large quantities of faunal remains produced by excavation, enhanced by excellent retrieval (all deposits are sieved through a 0.4mm mesh; a selection of deposits undergo wet-sieving through a 1mm mesh), would require either a quicker method of recording or a form of sub-sampling."

The archaeobotany team also describes the technicalities of the wet-sieving processes organic materials undergo before identification, sorting, weighing, and counting (Asouti et al. 1999). Pottery specialists, lithics analysts, and figurine researchers all evaluate the impact of sieving on their work in the diaries and reports they have produced. Foreign researchers' and locally hired laborers' shared interest in sieving and maximizing artifacts is an essential component of the knowledge production process at Çatalhöyük.

I have not sufficiently highlighted how surprising it is that with the large and diverse team at Çatalhöyük, there is greater similarity of ideas across the archaeologists and site workers on the project. Within the smaller, more compact team at the Temple of the Winged Lions, meanwhile, more varied different forms of expertise about finds and methodology emerged. These counterintuitive structures of knowledge make sense only when interpreted in the context of the labor management systems employed at the two sites.

ARCHAEOLOGICAL LABOR MANAGEMENT
AND THE NATURE OF EXPERTISE

Even though the site workers on both projects possess specialized archaeological knowledge, two opposing models for organizing labor on an archaeological excavation map onto two equally opposed structures that dictate how site workers relate to and know the archaeological finds from the excavation.

The fragility of employment at the Temple of the Winged Lions and the hostility between site workers and foreign excavators led to these groups developing dichotomous bodies of expertise specifically about archaeological finds and methods. As the site workers described above, working at the Temple of the Winged Lions meant potentially being fired at any time, for unpredictable reasons. Few site workers returned to the project from one year to the next. When site workers *were* working on the site, they were sent away from the trenches during the recovery of artifacts and were on the whole tasked to complete jobs quite separate from those the foreign excavators undertook. And many of the site workers were children—some as young as nine years old—when they were working on the site, marginalizing them further within the excavation hierarchy.

These practices on the site were furthermore embedded within an overall situation of precarity that characterized the archaeological industry in Petra, particularly in the early years of the project. During those years, there were not many opportunities for employment outside of archaeology. Petra became a major tourist destination in the 1980s, with visitation escalating dramatically after its inscription on the United Nations Educational, Scientific, and Cultural Organization's (UNESCO) World Heritage List in 1985. Hammond's excavations at the Temple of the Winged Lions began prior to this event, and those who worked on his project before tourism became a viable alternative sector for employment emphasized that they did so because they had no other choice. Even after tourism expanded at Petra, archaeology remained for some a more desirable work opportunity. Excavation and maintenance projects in Petra took place virtually year-round, whereas tourism continues to be extremely seasonal, unpredictable, and subject to uncontrollable factors like the international perception of safety in the region (Alhasanat 2010). In Petra, these have long been the two major industries for local community members: tourism, where the pay can be high one day and zero the next, and archaeology, where the pay is low but predictable (1 JD per day in the 1970s and 10 JD per day today). For women in Petra, the choices have traditionally been even more limited than those for men; they have been able to work in both archaeology and tourism, but within those sectors the jobs available have been more restricted.

Under these circumstances, the treatment site workers in Petra endured becomes even starker, and its impact becomes clearer. I do not want to suggest that site workers at Petra had no choice in taking the jobs they took. But that choice was structured by historically limited economic opportunities in the region that made working on an archaeological project—even one with such strict and divisive relations between laborers and supervisors—the most appealing or only real option.

Of course, I would characterize the treatment of Bedouin workers, as they describe it, as objectionable in its own right. Archaeologists, though, also lose out under these circumstances. These labor management practices, the relationships between archaeologists and site workers, and the context in which they occurred gave rise to a separation of knowledge regarding archaeological finds and practice, which can be correlated directly to the systems of labor that structured the project's operation. Locally hired laborers frequently learned about some objects found during Hammond's excavation from stories told by their relatives or friends. Their stories of archaeological finds therefore revolve around exciting, exceptional discoveries rather than the broken sherds and ubiquitous materials that feature commonly in the excavators' site notebooks. Moreover, since the site workers on the project were hired to perform supporting roles, tangential to but sustaining the core research activities, they developed expert skills and knowledge different from those the archaeological team possessed.

By contrast, the site workers at Çatalhöyük were retained from year to year, assigned to multiple locations across the site, and allowed or even encouraged to observe and learn about what the excavation was finding and how the excavation was proceeding. In addition, these labor management practices were instituted within a broader economic context in which the site workers at Çatalhöyük enjoyed significantly less precarity than those in Petra. The Çatalhöyük region is by no means a wealthy area, but it is supported by a robust agricultural industry. Many of the site workers at Çatalhöyük also had fields that they or their family members were responsible for tending and harvesting. Except for the Çatalhöyük Research Project (ÇRP), there were no other archaeological excavations in the immediate area for which those living in nearby villages could hope to be hired. These factors combined to make archaeology at Çatalhöyük a less stable and predictable industry than other employment opportunities available.

As a result, those who worked at Çatalhöyük each year were choosing to take their jobs at least in part because they enjoyed the work, not because they needed it. (This argument applies less to the women employed on the project, who had few other employment opportunities in this region besides the archaeological site.)[16] Wages at Çatalhöyük varied across the years, increasing over time as workers used their collective bargaining power to negotiate for higher wages than the previous year. They had other options available to them, they argued, and did not have to settle for working for less than they knew they could earn elsewhere. Some of the Çatalhöyük site workers shared with me that they did in fact end up working for slightly lower wages than they would expect to earn through agricultural work, but they chose the excavation jobs because of the relationships they developed with the archaeological team and the variety of the work.

All of these factors effected a situation in which the content of the Çatalhöyük site workers' memories maps much more onto the content of the information documented by the excavation team. Site workers' presence inside the buildings, alongside archaeologists, exposed them to the same range of artifacts and analytical approaches the excavation team observed. The finds they mention are the central, integral, common artifacts found during the excavation—the same ones the archaeologists thoroughly document. And they have developed methodological specialties like those of the broader archaeological team, forming a sub-community of practiced archaeological workers whose expertise in the research procedure reproduces much of the specialized knowledge the team members apply and possess. The details they share about the artifact assemblage through their memories and stories echo the same data that are encoded in the vast multimedia database from the Çatalhöyük excavation. The CRP's efforts to invite the locally hired site workers to engage with the project, along with the site workers' freedom to decide to do so, have been effective in re-creating the distribution of the research team's knowledge among the site workers.

There is, however, a limit to the scope of expertise site workers develop even on a project that prioritizes community engagement. As I will demonstrate in chapter 3, even though there are certain interpretations from the archaeological research at both Petra and Çatalhöyük of which site workers are aware, the involvement of local community members even at Çatalhöyük has not extended to ascribing meaning to the archaeological evidence collected at the site. At both sites, this is an aspect of archaeological knowledge production to which site workers have little access and make a minimal contribution, despite the implementation of more inclusive labor organization structures.

3

Access to Interpretation

Haşım Ferahkaya had driven 45 minutes from the fields
where he worked specifically to answer my questions. For
more than an hour, we sat on his front porch together,
sipping orange soda, as Haşım vividly narrated the
process of discovering a stamp seal, of learning how
to differentiate soil colors and textures, of getting to
know the Turkish archaeologists on the research team at
Çatalhöyük. I discreetly checked the time on my scratched
and dusty iPhone, conscious that he still needed to eat
lunch before driving back to the farm. I flipped to my list
of interview questions at the beginning of my notebook,
scanning to make sure I hadn't missed anything.

"Thank you so much for all your time," I said as my
interpreter, Tunç, translated. "I really appreciate you
coming home to talk to me. All of this information is so
helpful." Haşım's dimples creased as he grinned modestly
from one corner of his mouth, shaking his head. "I only
have one more question. Is there anything that you're
interested in learning more about?"

He thought for a second before answering. "Yes." I
rested my pen in the crease of my notebook. "I'm very
interested in the burials inside the houses. Why did they
do that?"

I had asked other site workers what they were
interested in learning about, but a colleague had recently
suggested that before responding, I should invite them to
share their own ideas. "I'm happy to tell you the theories
we have, but to be honest we don't know for sure. What
do you think?"

DOI: 10.5876/9781646421152.c003

Haşım looked pleasantly surprised to have the question posed back to him.

"Well . . . first of all, I wonder if everywhere around them was too wet, if maybe there weren't other good places to bury them because of the rivers and marshes and wet soil."

"That's a really interesting idea," I remarked, writing it down. I thought of the researchers at Çatalhöyük working to reconstruct the Neolithic environment in the region, how their ideas have changed over time, and what they might think about Haşım's hypothesis.

He continued: "Second of all, I think it might be because they loved their ancestors and didn't want to forget them."

I raised my eyebrows as I jotted this down in my notebook. I wasn't expecting him to offer both material and symbolic answers to the question he had posed himself.

"And finally," he said thoughtfully, "if they buried them outside, maybe a wild animal would get to the graves and open them and eat them [the bodies]. They probably didn't want that."

This exchange with Haşım stands out in my mind for his contemplative delivery, for the pleasantness of sitting on his front porch watching the sunset kiss the rows of rustling crops stretching out to meet the horizon, and for the undeniable archaeological expertise his theories exhibit. This moment was memorable, though it was not the only time a site worker I spoke to offered a novel hypotheses or interpretation of the archaeological evidence. The excavation workers I met posed knowledgeable questions about the sites on which they work and proposed answers to those questions.

In general, however, they asked more questions than they had hypotheses for and expressed an overwhelming feeling of knowing little about the conclusions archaeologists draw about the past, in contrast to other aspects of the excavation such as finds and methodology. Their perception is supported by network analysis comparing the archives from the Temple of the Winged Lions project and the Çatalhöyük project to the oral historical accounts. The network visualizations show minimal overlap, minimal complementarity, and, indeed, few connections between the knowledge presented by the archaeologist and site worker communities regarding archaeological interpretation and analysis. This commonality across such different archaeological research contexts, I argue, is due to barriers and reward systems that have been an entrenched part of archaeological work in the Middle East since the nineteenth century and that continue to structure the research endeavor even on excavations like the Çatalhöyük Research Project that prioritize community outreach. Locally hired laborers have not and do not participate in archaeological interpretation despite their privileged insight into artifacts and methods and their willingness to engage in the creation of scientific narratives about the human past.

NEW NARRATIVES, HYPOTHESES, AND ARCHAEOLOGICAL INTERPRETATIONS

The intimate experience site workers possess about the local area benefit archaeological excavation in myriad ways; these men and women know where to find new sites, understand the soil, and can anticipate weather patterns. Their environmental knowledge also underpins the original hypotheses they develop to interpret the archaeological record. At Çatalhöyük, excavation workers offered explanations of the behaviors and choices of the site's Neolithic inhabitants based on the modern community's relationship to the landscape. In my very first interview, a white-haired man sitting on a bench in the center of the village—who rapidly rattled off his ideas about the site and left before I could even ask his name—recalled playing on the mound during his childhood and seeing what would happen when it started to rain. The channel between the East Mound and the West Mound filled with water and soon became a strong current. He suggested that if this river had flooded or become a rushing rapid when the ancient residents of Çatalhöyük were living there, the dangers and destructive potential could have been a factor in their decision to eventually move away from the site and resettle elsewhere, providing a climatologically grounded hypothesis for the abandonment of the site—a continuing question at Çatalhöyük.

In Küçükköy, different strategies are used by living residents to mitigate this enduring flooding problem—constructing a ledge, for instance, at the base of exterior doorways or building a house on a platform several inches above the ground. Many of the site workers who had dug inside the Neolithic houses at Çatalhöyük, who had seen where the ladder was wedged into the plastered floor of the house, remarked appreciatively on the ingenuity of building entrances to the houses through the roof. They noted that making the entrance to the houses through these ladders would have been an effective—if labor-intensive—solution to the unavoidable problem of rainwater from annual spring deluges pooling and seeping into the houses.

Hüseyin Veli Yaşlı had an alternative but equally environmentally informed explanation. As one of the men recruited to plan and build the experimental house at Çatalhöyük, meant to be an informed approximation of a typical Neolithic house at the site for visitors to explore, Veli arrived at his own realization about a possible reason for the rooftop entrances to the houses. As he placed one brick atop another and the walls gradually grew in height, he realized that each wall was effectively becoming a taller and taller fence. Today, some predators are living in the region, such as foxes and jackals, but "at that time—in Neolithic times—there were a lot of wild animals," Veli reminded me. "So they built their door through the roof to stay safe from them." Like other Çatalhöyük site workers I spoke with, Veli drew on his own experiences of the local environment to form logical conclusions about the enigmatic practices of the Neolithic inhabitants of Çatalhöyük.

The people I met also brought their life experiences to bear in forming interpretations of the symbolic significance of artifacts recovered during the excavation. One man, particularly intrigued by the stamps found at the site, said that they reminded him of stamping implements used by the *muhtar*—the village political leader best compared to a mayor. Acknowledging that the Neolithic people wouldn't have had bureaucratic documents to stamp, the man maintained that "still, the stamp seals were probably for an important person who needed to mark things as part of his role." Another man who had worked in Building 77, a structure with several bucranium installations, suggested that these dramatic skeletal installations were put in place to ward away the "evil eye," comparing the Neolithic features to protective objects in modern Mediterranean and West Asian societies meant to guard against malevolent powers. To understand the most intriguing findings from the project, the locally hired site workers applied their own religious experiences of the figurative meanings ascribed to material things they had observed themselves.

As I began to collect these perspectives on the past, informed by the direct experiences of native inhabitants of the area, I grew increasingly excited about how willingly people ventured their own evidence-based interpretations about the nature of Neolithic people and their material culture, which often did not conform exactly to archaeological understandings. During a meeting with the Çatalhöyük project director, Ian Hodder, I expressed this enthusiasm and shared a few examples of ideas former site workers had conveyed to me and the reasoning behind them. "You should ask about why we have both ovens and hearths in the houses," he suggested. "We haven't been able to get a straight answer on that."

Pleased to have such a specific and direct question to ask, the next time I sat down with the women hired to sort heavy residue at the site, I put it to them. They responded with a debate, rooting each of their theories in personal life experience:

ŞENAY: Maybe one of them was used to cook food and the other one was to bake bread.

HATICE T: They would make the oven part of the wall below the ladder, and they would take the fire from the oven to light the hearth to distribute the heat more evenly. It was a heating system, since it gets cold.

HATICE Ç: No, one was for food and one was for bread. We have two ovens in our houses in the village like this as well. It's good for when we are expecting guests. We put beans in one and bread in the other.

All of these comparisons—to modern cooking, modern responses to the environment, modern politics, modern religion—are at their core ethnographic analogies. They are comparable to the types of relationships archaeologists draw between past human societies and contemporary living communities to better understand archaeological assemblages. Only in this case they are not based on an evaluation of contextual and structural similarities between the two groups of people under comparison but rather on a feeling of affiliation with the Neolithic society by the locally hired laborers. The site workers I interviewed at Çatalhöyük repeatedly and explicitly emphasized the close affiliation between their own lives and those of the Neolithic people, given the traditional lifestyle and aesthetic of rural Küçükköy. They claimed the part of the ethnoarchaeological subject, asserting that they perceive similarities between the ancient material culture and their own and that these parallels can be used to explore possible meanings, functions, and objectives of the things with which the Neolithic inhabitants of Çatalhöyük surrounded themselves.

To be sure, many people in Küçükköy have computers, internet connections, and smartphones; the connections they are asserting between their lives and Neolithic life at Çatalhöyük should not be taken to mean that they are in any way "anti-modern" (or that anthropological expletive, "primitive"). But highlighting these parallels between current and ancient life at Çatalhöyük has proven advantageous and even monetarily beneficial for those who work at the site. Archaeologists have solicited and utilized these types of memories and perspectives offered by village residents in project publications. *Çatalhöyük Perspectives: Reports from the 1995–99 Seasons* (Hodder 2005) features several chapters in which information about traditional life, collected during community meetings with site workers and their families and friends, is printed in bold and put directly into context with the data, analysis, and hypotheses put forward by the archaeological researchers. Sadrettin Dural, the longtime site guard at Çatalhöyük, has enjoyed an unusual amount of direct benefit from his knowledge of traditional practices relevant to understanding the archaeological record at Çatalhöyük. His book *Protecting Çatalhöyük: Memoir of an Archaeological Site Guard* is an autobiographical account primarily of his time spent living at the site, engaging with tourists, and guarding the entrance in which a great deal of the text links his knowledge of traditional behaviors with the Neolithic settlement. "Our life was also similar to the Neolithic life," he states. "The lifestyle of the Neolithic people was also experienced by the people who have lived around here for many years. Maybe that is the reason I am in love with Çatalhöyük" (Dural 2007: 58, 61). He goes on to describe constructing houses out of mud brick, whitewashing the walls, hunting wild animals, and his father sending logs down the river to transport them—all tasks he states the archaeologists told him were performed by the ancient inhabitants of Çatalhöyük. Dural's book is still in print by a major press—and he recently wrote and released a second book, which is a fictive imagining of Neolithic life at Çatalhöyük (Dural 2015). Dural represents a unique case; most of the site workers at Çatalhöyük have not enjoyed the same levels of recognition and compensation for their insight into the similarities between their lives and those revealed through the archaeological record. The archaeological team at Çatalhöyük *has* encouraged and financially rewarded site workers in general, though, for sharing the aspects of their lives that are relevant to interpreting the archaeological assemblage and deposits—creating a market that pays for this type of ethnoarchaeological insight.

For Bedouin site workers in Petra, a comparable market does not exist. The Bedouin community has rapidly moved away from agriculture, pastoralism, and other traditional lifeways in recent decades, particularly following the construction of and relocation to government-allocated settlements (Bille 2009; Comer 2012; Kooring and Simms 1996; Shoup 1985; Wooten 1996). Instead, archaeology in Petra is a total industry in which many men and women have made lifetime careers, working on project after project, every year through the spring, summer, and autumn. The site workers I interviewed from the Temple of the Winged Lions project accordingly offered historical interpretations that closely resembled the types of conclusions drawn by the archaeologists themselves. The Bedouin site workers' analyses of the archaeological assemblage are not based on comparisons to their own lives, cultural practices, or contemporary interactions with the environment but instead are shaped and substantiated by their lifetime professional excavation experience.

For instance, the following is an excerpt from Hammond's (1996: 29) discussion of the construction of the temple:

Transporting prepared, or semi-prepared, blocks from the quarry areas to the work-site could well have been done solely by donkey-back, since those animals, and their modern burden-bearing descendants, are well-adapted for use in the rugged terrain of the Petra Basin. The carrying ability of such animals would probably only have permitted each animal to transport a single ashlar block at a time, however . . . The use of camels may also have been employed and might have facilitated load-carrying over long distances . . . Dray horses, oxen, or other draught animals could likewise have been used (cf. Landels 1978: 173–177) on the more level terrain . . . Sledges, or carts, including those drawn by man-power, would also have been possible on the more level terrain.

The parallels are apparent with this portion of a conversation I had with Dachlallah Qublan al-Faqir, one of the foremen for the Temple of the Winged Lions excavation:

DACHLALLAH: The rocks were from Wadi Siyagh. You know Wadi Siyagh? The Wadi, the valley, down in the Siyagh. Cut stones from there.

ME: Mm-hmm.

DACHLALLAH: They cut all of them, all the stones from there, so big. So big! Huge!

ME: And how did they bring the stones from there?

DACHLALLAH: With a wagon.

ME: Ah.

DACHLALLAH: A wagon with camels, with cattle. A cart, I mean. And how did they cross? They put the stones on the livestock. They made a path, you know, a path. And the cart went across.

Consider, too, Hammond's (1996: 2) explanation of how the temple was identified as such: "The recovery of the unique, feline-decorated, capitals and capital fragments, in the vicinity of the Altar Platform, led to the identification of the Temple as one dedicated to a female deity and to the popular designation of 'The Temple of the Winged Lions.' The recovery, in 1975 of the 'Eye Idol' (AEP '75, RI #217), inscribed 'the goddess of . . .' finally confirmed the dedicatee." This explanation echoes both the content and structure of Atullah al-Faqir's explanation of the same question:

ME: What makes you sure that the Temple of the Winged Lions is a temple and not some other kind of building?

ATULLAH: Because, uh, from my experience, you know, the temple has many columns. And inside, when you dig, you find a lot of art. Or statues. And the Dushara, the god block.

ME: Yeah. Of course.

ATULLAH: The, uh . . . Houses, they're just houses. You can find rocks or something.

What is remarkable in both of these examples is not only the repeated language ("camels"; "cart") but also the similarity in the ordering, layering, and buildup of information across the two accounts. In the first comparison, both Hammond and Dachlallah trace the movement of the stones from quarry location to the construction site. They both conclude by addressing the problem of the mountainous and rocky desert terrain across which animals and carts would have had to traverse, as if, in mentally following the path of the stones from start to finish, they each hit the same sort of rut or boulder the Nabataean workers would have encountered, forcing them to resolve the problem in their description by relegating the carts to "level terrain" or the creation of a "path." In the second example, both Hammond and Atullah first describe columns and capitals—elaborately decorated ones—as an important key to the designation of this monument as a temple. They both mention the idol secondarily, re-creating an excavation process in which this statue served to corroborate a hypothesis about the function of the building that had already taken shape on the basis of other evidence by that time. It is not merely the information that is shared between the analyses and theories presented by Hammond and the site workers I spoke to but also the way they build their scientific narratives.

In some cases, the people I spoke to held stances diametrically opposed to the archaeological consensus. Multiple individuals did not agree with the base understanding that the Temple of the Winged Lions was a temple. "It was a big home for someone high up in the government," Ismail Mowasa told me. Another night, while sharing a pan of *gallayat bendura*,[1] the man working as the site guard for the Temple of the Winged Lions told me he was certain that the "temple" was actually a complex of houses. "You can tell," he pressed, "because it had that second floor. And the rooms look just like the houses here in Umm Sayhoun. People would have been sitting there, just like we are now, with their families. What is there to make you think it is a temple?"

I assured him that I was really looking to hear his opinions but that others had mentioned the al-'uzza idol as a key find indicating that the building was a religious space. He clicked his tongue and shook his head. "That's a decoration, like '*Bismillah*,'" he said, referring to the phrase recited before each phrase of the Qur'an and one of the most common texts displayed in calligraphic form in homes throughout the Muslim world. Religious objects, he maintained, would not be out of place in a domestic context.

I then asked about the workshops, named by Hammond the "painters' workshop," the "marble workshop," and the "metal workshop." Hammond (1996: 111) suggests that these complexes were associated with manufacturing "altars, probable votive objects, metal-working, and local, if not commercial, production of oil" to support the religious activities in the temple as well as the long-term residence of cultic leaders. I asked our site guard what these areas were for if not supporting the religious activities of a temple. "They're kitchens and craft workshops for the families living there," he replied.

I want to set aside for the moment the question of whether the alternative hypothesis about the function of this structure is better than the currently accepted interpretation—or even whether it is a good one; I address further on the issue of theories and ideas that contradict archaeological evidence. What is more important initially is recognizing that this "House of the Winged Lions" theory does make use of the material evidence recovered during the excavation. It relies on observations of domestic space, subsistence, and economics to assess the meaning and purpose of the building. Our debate was in the same register; I presented evidence usually interpreted as supporting the designation of the temple as such, and Ismail explained how this evidence fit into his alternative view. The conversation felt little different from a discussion with an archaeologist about his or her take on a curious site or artifact.

Initially, it appears that the impact of particular labor management strategies on site workers' access and relationship to developing archaeological interpretations is nearly opposite the way these strategies have affected site workers' expertise about finds and methodology. The Çatalhöyük site workers bring a perspective that is unique to them—the viewpoint of the self-identified ethnoarchaeological subject, drawing comparisons between archaeological evidence and their own memories and experiences. The site workers from the Temple of the Winged Lions, meanwhile, present hypotheses and analyses that closely resemble those of the published archaeological literature, often in content and certainly in language and structure. This is very different from the situation described in chapter 2, in which the more inclusive organization of labor at Çatalhöyük engendered two very similar bodies of information about the site between the written archive and the site workers' oral history, while the hierarchical system used on the Temple of the Winged Lions project resulted in distinct, complementary sets of knowledge between site workers and the archaeological team. Why does the situation for interpretation look so different?

The answer is not that the site workers at the Temple of the Winged Lions were somehow, suddenly invited or inserted themselves into conversations aiming to put together and read the evidence as a whole, to construct holistic explanations for why the archaeological record appears the way it does. Instead, the similarity between the way they describe and contextualize the archaeological evidence at the Temple of the Winged Lions comes from the many decades of archaeological work they have participated in since then, at other monuments at Petra. The people I met in Petra were engaged in debates parallel to ones taking place in academic archaeological literature. A group of men and women selling souvenirs on the stairs to the Royal Tombs engaged in a debate about how disruptive the Roman annexation was for the cultural practices and lifeways of the community living in Petra in the beginning of the second century CE—an ongoing conversation in the archaeological community as well (Fiema 2003; Kouki 2009, 2012). Another man wanted to have a dialogue about how integral agriculture was to the stability and growth of the Nabatean kingdom (see Beckers and Schütt 2013; Erickson-Gini 2012; Kouki 2009, 2012; Nasarat et al. 2012).

By far my favorite conversation about life in Nabataean Petra was with Bassam Alfakeer, a core member of the renewed investigations and conservation efforts at the Temple of the Winged Lions. We were sitting in the shade during a midmorning tea break. As the fat and heavy *pum! pum!* of a stoically beating drum punctuated the morning desert silence, we rolled our eyes at each other. Over the hillside, men hired to dress up as Nabataean soldiers were performing a simple marching formation to the beat of a drum, bringing history to life for tourists walking down the colonnaded street of the city center. This happened every day, several times a day, and like listening to a Top 40 station for an entire workday, it was feeling noticeably repetitive.

This time, though, Bassam started to laugh. "You know what's funny?" he asked. "They're supposed to be like Nabataeans. But the Nabataeans wouldn't have had time for that. They would have been in the buildings, on the mountains. Working. If they spent all this time doing this every day, there would have been no Petra."

I almost spat out my tea. I pictured a Nabataean army wearing full uniforms and armor, simply waiting for their hourly cue to walk around rhythmically in a circle. Bassam's assessment was so succinct and so funny; plus, it made complete sense from an archaeological standpoint. The archaeological record may not provide much insight into whether Nabataean soldiers ever stomped around for the purpose of sheer performance, but the image of Nabataean society that scholars have constructed on the basis of archaeological and historical evidence is one of a vibrant community engaged in long-distance trade, extensive building projects, dedicated religious and funerary practices, and intensive agriculture. Bassam's remark highlighted the gap between the vision of the past built from material remains and historical records versus that created to engage tourists. His identification of that gap rests on knowledge gained from extensive employment on excavations all around Petra, concerning cross-cutting aspects and subgroups of Nabataean society and therefore allowing him to make an informed assertion about how its inhabitants most likely spent their time and divided the workforce.

The multi-sited, comprehensive archaeological experience the Temple of the Winged Lions site workers have developed is also apparent in the number and nature of hypotheses about undiscovered sites in the Petra area. A Petra Archaeological Park ranger from the Bedul community who was visiting the current Temple of the Winged Lions excavations stood with me at the peak of the prominence on which the temple was constructed and pointed out all the visible areas where he had noticed an especially dense concentration of pottery and coins on the surface. He had worked with archaeologists before who had used this evidence, recorded through pedestrian surveys, to determine where to excavate and easily applied this knowledge of site identification practices to propose new potential sites for investigation. I asked if he could offer a conjecture as to what the sites might be. There was one in particular, on the crest to the south of the Temple of the Winged Lions where we were sitting, that he supposed might be a bank. I asked why, and his answer thoughtfully took into account previous archaeological findings in Petra. "It's a big building," he said, "and it's central. And the city would have needed one. This was a big, important city, and no bank has been found yet."

Again and again, the most experienced site workers among the Bedouin community in Petra posited new theories and analyses of what may lie beneath the surface of the archaeological park. Dachlallah Qublan al-Faqir, who has worked on archaeological projects almost continuously since the 1950s, proposed his theory:

> And maybe, maybe after a little while, there will be a school . . . There must
> have been a school. There must have been a school. Where, I mean, could they
> have had a city without a school . . . Where would they have studied? Where
> would they have learned? They would have studied. They wrote. In Nabataean
> civilization . . . In Nabataean civilization there was writing. There was study.
> There was studying and education, I mean.

Not everyone who was present during this conversation agreed with his assertion, however. Talal Ammarin, a Petra Archaeological Park employee from the Ammarin Bedouin tribe, suggested an alternative idea:

> It's possible there wasn't one. Yes, they would have studied, but it could have been within the religion . . . People could have studied in places like the church. There were many religious places where they could have studied . . . Not very many people would have been learning, and the church would have been where they were learning. Of course, there were scientists and engineers and an army, but the path to education was not like this. There might not have been a building for a school. They could have studied in other places.

Importantly, Talal's response—with all its "possibles" and "could haves"—comes out of both practical experience participating in archaeological excavations and academic study of archaeology. When we had this conversation, Talal was preparing to leave for Germany to complete graduate work in cultural heritage studies. His expertise is a marriage of university scholarship and his native knowledge of the site. But Dachlallah's expertise, too, marries the archaeological and local perspectives, combining decades of applied onsite learning with a lifetime spent among the caves and carved facades of Petra. This is why Talal and Dachlallah share so much in common rhetorically, why both of their ideas are carefully conceived, based on solid reasoning and comprehensive understanding of the local archaeology.

I listened as Dachlallah offered thoughtful ideas about the nature of the Nabataean education system and Talal assessed how well those ideas fit with established scholarly views. With the exception of Dachlallah's certainty against Talal's discussions of possibility and probability, reflected in their statements above, the way they expressed their points of view shared the same grounding in what has previously been found in the Petra region and logical expectations of a functioning city of this complexity and scale. But over the course of my interviews with site workers in Jordan and Turkey, I also encountered plenty of theories and hypotheses that contradicted material evidence in more obvious and potentially un-resolvable ways. These contradictions raise the question of what the ethical scholarly response should be to claims that read archaeological evidence in ways entirely opposed to academic interpretations. Should the archaeological team aim to correct, to educate, to engage, to consider, or to document these alternative views, which do not seem to be firmly based on the personal memories and experiences of local community members, as at Çatalhöyük, or on their extensive cross-site work history, as at Petra? What role can fringe theories like these—coming from individuals with demonstrable archaeological skills and understanding—play in the process of knowledge production?

INTERPRETIVE DIALOGUE AS EXPERTISE

Most questions I asked in interviews were designed to elicit examples of the specific expertise site workers had developed from working on excavations. This was my overt goal, and I was excited every time someone offered a recollection about the measurements of a figurine or the conversations between excavators about when to change digging strategies. I was happy to write down these memories. They fulfilled the objective of my research project; each memory was a direct piece of evidence illustrating the knowledge and capabilities locally hired laborers possess. But once in a while I felt caught in uncertainty about how I should react to a particular theory or interpretation.

One afternoon, after an hour of speaking with the women responsible for sorting the heavy residue at Çatalhöyük, I asked what they most wanted to know about the site.

"Well," one woman began, "we're curious about how the Neolithic people died." I nodded and noted this down as my interpreter, Cansu, translated her words into English.

Cansu then paused and turned toward me, uncertainly. "She thinks it was either a tornado or an earthquake because this place is so much higher than its surroundings."

I understood Cansu's hesitation. She knew that my goal was to document examples of impressive expertise on the part of site workers, and this hypothesis did not accord with the archaeological record from Çatalhöyük. There is no evidence of the kind of destruction associated with a natural disaster such as a tornado in the latest levels of the mound. This hypothesis, therefore, would be difficult to motivate as "expertise" when writing to an anticipated audience of archaeologists.

But both Cansu and I were committed to multivocality, to considering and engaging with all thoughts and viewpoints, a principle guiding the overall Çatalhöyük project and my research in particular. It would be wrong for either Cansu or me, both researchers on the excavation team, to simply tell this woman her idea was misguided.[2] At the same time, it would be disingenuous to simply ignore a problematic idea, one that did not fit easily into the image of professional, knowledgeable communities of current and former site workers. This moment was like finding a piece of tin foil in a secure prehistoric context; it did not fit with our expectations or hopes for talking to longtime site workers at Çatalhöyük, but it needed to be documented and explored nonetheless.

As I started to think of an appreciative way to ask for more information about why the woman had developed that hypothesis, another woman in the group jumped in. "The people living here would have died of old age or disease," she explained. "If it was a tornado, then the whole site would be destroyed. You see how the surrounding area is so flat and this area is so high? A tornado would have destroyed this place, made it more flat like everything else around."

I watched as the group of women collectively considered this point, one of them nodding as she realized how it fit with what she had seen and heard while working on the project. The value of inviting the proposal of a radical idea like the tornado was immediately apparent; in this group conversation, it opened up a possibility that would never otherwise be considered and immediately invited the comparison to data, observations, and perceptions. By proposing her natural disaster theory, the first woman opened a dialogue that laid out the logic and information that was either consistent or conflicted with her ideas. This is the same process that happens within the excavation team on a daily basis, about the interpretation of a given soil layer or a mysterious architectural feature. By discussing the merits and flaws of emerging hypotheses among themselves, archaeologists come up with new ideas, transform paradigms, and, over time, improve the robustness of their conclusions about the past. The conversation I witnessed illustrated how this happens in parallel among the community of site workers at archaeological sites—an example of how this community *becomes* a group of professionals and experts by sharing and comparing ideas and information among themselves.

In some instances, I watched as a single individual, thinking out loud, would propose a new idea and start weighing it aloud against evidence they had heard about or seen. One of the site workers in Petra initially hypothesized that the temple had served as a domestic structure, then began listing the evidence: "the complete lamps, jars, and coins that were being kept there as storage for the people living in the house." He started to realize that these finds did not clearly demonstrate that the building had served as a house and began to show some uncertainty: "It would have been a really *big* home, maybe . . ."

I wanted to see how strong he felt about his assertion. "It wasn't a temple?" I asked.

"I don't know," he responded carefully, after a pause. In that "I don't know" is possibility, openness, the potential for confirmation and contradiction. That "I don't know" expresses liminality in interpretation, a space and time in which the temple's identification is rocked out of rigidity for at least a moment, where the "process" part of the "research process" becomes visible. It is scientific not-knowing, the kind of uncertainty from which questions are developed, research agendas are designed, and evidence is collected to evaluate hypotheses—a process this man began instinctively.

Ferdi Söylemez, a site worker at Çatalhöyük, also went through these visible stages of inspiration and self-imposed critique when he brought up the ongoing debate at the site regarding whether burned houses were set aflame intentionally or accidentally and why:

> Fire wasn't that common in that period. It would have been hard to burn their houses in those days, so maybe the burning happened because of fights between neighbors. Or, or maybe they wanted to make a new house, so they burned theirs and built a new one. So then, if there is a new one on top, it must have been intentional. [pause] But . . . why would they have done this on purpose? Why would they have needed to burn it? Why wouldn't they just build the new one on top of the old one? [pause] That's not right.

These instances of critical reflection on alternative theories—whether introspectively or interpersonally driven—demonstrate that the same sorts of processes that lead to the modification, improvement, and slow solidification of theories within the archaeological scholarly community happen among locally hired laborers as well. The same sorts of dialogues or internal deliberation in which evidence is considered in terms of how effectively it either supports or contradicts an interpretation occur equally among site workers as among excavators and other archaeological researchers. The fact that they do not always come to the same conclusions demonstrates even further that locally hired laborers are fellow producers of knowledge.

All of this is not to imply that all outlier theories are constantly reshaped to accord comfortably with standard archaeological interpretations—or that they should be. What these conversations and stream-of-consciousness monologues evince, however, is that even the interpretations that contradict standard archaeological readings of the material evidence have been thoroughly, thoughtfully reviewed within a community of experts. They are the outcome of processes that resemble the practices of knowledge construction used by research team members but that are, importantly, separate and their own. These dialogues and internal thought processes, as well as the hypotheses they produce, represent an archaeological hermeneutic that brings together the specific local knowledge and scientific expertise site workers develop under highly particular labor conditions. The degree to which their interpretation of archaeological evidence is distinct from analyses suggested by archaeological team members can be both visualized and measured with network analysis.

MAPPING OUT EXCLUSION FROM INTERPRETATION

When excavation team members and site workers who address the same research topics in archives and in oral history are linked to one another, the resulting networks reveal the relative positions of these individuals in terms of their interest and knowledge. Figure 3.1 shows a visualization of a network in which all Çatalhöyük excavation participants are linked to other participants who mention the same research questions, with archaeologists appearing as dark gray nodes and site workers as white nodes. Unlike the networks shown in figures 2.5 and 2.6, the Çatalhöyük excavation laborers are situated at the edges of this network.

Calculating and comparing the centrality of the team members versus the site workers supports this visual assessment. In a range from 0 to 1, the average eigenvector centrality of a site worker in this network is 0.59, whereas the average eigenvector centrality of a team member is 0.67. This 0.08 difference reflects a role site workers played relative to the process of reading and interpreting archaeological evidence that is distinct from their relationship to the material finds and methodologies. At Çatalhöyük, the arrangement of labor, designed to encourage reflexive dialogue and minimize hierarchy, has provided access for site workers to the material evidence recovered during the excavation and to the tools and techniques of archaeological research, allowing them similar views and perspectives to those the team members have acquired and documented in the standard recording systems. But even though interpretation is certainly happening throughout the stages of excavation, beginning "at the trowel's edge" (Berggren et al. 2015; Hodder 1999), the moments in which it is happening appear to be relatively off-limits to site workers.

Albeit in different ways, the analogous network for the Temple of the Winged Lions case is equally different from the previous networks under consideration (figure 3.2). The site workers are not in this case identifiably peripheral to the network, as they were in figures 2.3 and 2.4. This is opposite from the Çatalhöyük networks, where the site workers *only* appear on the fringes of the network when linkages are made on the basis of common topics of analysis. On the Temple of the Winged Lions project, analysis and interpretation appear instead to be a sort of equalizer. The centrality statistics bear out this assertion. For the network shown in figure 3.2, the average eigenvector

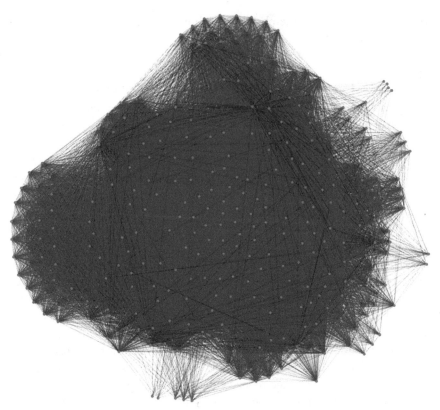

FIGURE 3.1. *Visualization of the network linking Çatalhöyük research team members (red) and locally hired site workers (blue) to each other, based on the topics of analysis they discuss in site archives and oral histories, respectively.*

centrality for the site workers is 0.44, while the average eigenvector centrality for a team member is 0.39. In this case, the site workers are actually very slightly *more* central than the team members. How is it possible that they could have enjoyed comparatively more access to the moments and points in the excavation where analysis and interpretation were occurring compared to the recovery of objects or the implementation of specific methodologies? In the following section, I explore in depth the reasons for the network structures presented here in terms of the organization of labor leading to these maps of expertise and consider the ramifications of these relationships for the overall production of archaeological knowledge.

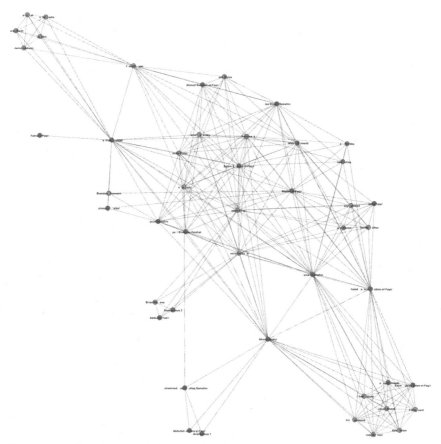

FIGURE 3.2. *Visualization of the network linking Temple of the Winged Lions research team members (orange) and locally hired site workers (blue) to each other, based on the topics of analysis they discuss in site archives and oral histories, respectively.*

CAUSES AND CONSEQUENCES OF EXCLUSION FROM INTERPRETATION

The initial appearance of equal involvement in drawing conclusions from the archaeological evidence at the Temple of the Winged Lions by site workers and excavation team members is misleading. Instead, the overlap of information between the two sets of data more likely comes from differences in the nature of the site notebooks versus the oral historical record. The notebooks, as mentioned, are rigidly structured documents with detailed instructions for how to complete them, and there simply is no place in which the site notebook creators were directed to inscribe their emerging thoughts and theories. The excavators, accordingly, recorded very few analytical topics (only 1.52 per person on average).

Accordingly, none of the people I spoke to recalled having theoretically oriented discussions with the excavators of the Temple of the Winged Lions, but they did have these sorts of conversations on other projects. The nature of oral history, as a living and continuously evolving record, allows this accumulative knowledge to fold into site workers' memories of the Temple of the Winged Lions. As these men and women acquired greater experience in understanding and proposing meanings of the archaeological record by working on project after project, they could think back and reexamine what they saw and heard about on earlier excavations so that when I asked them in 2015 about the significance of what was uncovered at the Temple of the Winged Lions twenty, thirty, or even forty years before, they offered an analysis based on those twenty, thirty, or forty years of working on archaeological research endeavors. The broader industry of archaeology in Petra—the near-constant excavation of sites in the region and the according reliability of archaeological employment—provides site workers with the opportunity to develop their interpretive abilities.

Archaeology is not as expansive a sector of employment at Çatalhöyük as it is in Petra; as explained in chapter 2, none of site workers I met at Çatalhöyük had worked on any other archaeological site. Therefore, any privileged insight the Çatalhöyük site workers possess into how archaeological interpretation proceeds must have been cultivated while working on the excavations at this specific site, with this team (or, in the case of two individuals still living in Küçükköy, with James Mellaart). The opportunity to develop a comparative framework simply does not exist.

Site workers who have been employed at Çatalhöyük on the whole tend to have little awareness of or involvement in the theories of the past drawn from the material evidence recovered at the site. This assertion is supported not only by the network analysis presented above but also by site workers' own descriptions of their interactions with archaeologists. On the very first day I went to conduct interviews in Küçükköy, I spoke with two men who had worked on the contemporary excavations and one who had worked with Mellaart in the 1960s. The man who had worked on the Mellaart excavations reported that he dug without knowing what the goal of the excavation was or what Mellaart learned.

"No one explained anything about Çatalhöyük then," he said matter-of-factly. This was no shock to hear; disciplinary trends toward greater public engagement accelerated in earnest more than twenty years after the initial excavations at Çatalhöyük. What was more surprising was how directly this account resonated with the recollections of the other two men I met that day, who had worked with the current project. One of them said he never learned what happened in the laboratories while he was digging there, what the archaeologists were learning in those rooms, but he stated that he wanted to know. The other said he had participated in a taphonomic experiment, burying sheep bones to see what happened to them while underground, but he never learned the findings of that experiment. Again, he expressed a desire to learn them, asking if I knew what they had determined.

As my interviews continued, I confronted this issue again and again—the Çatalhöyük site workers wanted to know more about the findings of the project but for various reasons felt blocked from accessing this information:

No one asks us 'What aren't you understanding?' because of the language problem. The result is that we don't get information about what's happening at Çatalhöyük . . . It makes me angry when these foreign people don't explain the finds and the artifacts to workers! . . . There should be more information sharing.

I've seen some interesting things being found. But I can't understand when they talk about them in English. If they spoke in Turkish I would ask, but the language barrier makes me feel like I can't.

We have no idea what they're doing and finding in the labs. We've never been to the labs. Of course, we would like to see what happens after [the work we do], but we are not involved in doing it.

I don't know what happens to the finds at all after they leave the mound. I know you put them in a bag and study things in labs, but I don't know what happens there. I'm not allowed in the labs. And I can't ask; that would be too rude.

Three or four years ago, the news about what archaeologists were finding would come back to the kitchen, but now it doesn't. So we have no idea what you are finding.

These statements illuminate a series of stopping points, both tangible and intangible, blocking the exchange of ideas and interpretations about archaeological contexts and materials. An incredible artifact is lifted by trowel, the sandy loam is brushed out of its crevices, and the archaeologists begin excitedly trading ideas about what it could mean—but the site worker, standing nearby, can't understand or participate because they are speaking in English and he only speaks Turkish. He might consider asking, but the difficulty for both parties of trying to explain and understand is too much of a deterrent.

Once the artifacts are taken down from the mound, sorted into their appropriate laboratories, and examined by specialists, a host of new barriers prevent site workers from participating in interpreting the material. There are the physical locks and closed doors to the laboratories, with the attendant rules on who can enter these rooms and when. There is the continuing problem of language, along with related questions of cultural expectations and etiquette, raising the problem of when it might feel inappropriate or disrespectful to a member of this local community to ask directly about what the archaeological researchers are doing and learning. There is the presence or absence of friendship, which the women I interviewed in particular named as the best way to engage with ongoing conversations about the significance of recent discoveries. All of these barriers block the transmission of ideas in both directions; although the quotes above frame these blockades in terms of an inability to learn from the archaeologists, they also close the openings for questions to be asked both by and of archaeologists, for hypotheses to be offered both by and to the site workers.

Many different programs implemented at Çatalhöyük and at other community-oriented archaeological projects aim at breaking down these barriers, working to expand site workers' access to all aspects of the excavation and to open up avenues for two-way communication with the archaeological team. Ayfer Bartu Candan, a Turkish anthropologist, worked closely with local community members in Küçükköy beginning in the 1990s to involve them in the archaeological process—especially the interpretation and presentation of the site. She collaborated with local women to design an exhibit in the onsite museum about local plant use today and 9,000 years ago (Bartu 2000). Ian Hodder frequently brings site workers—especially the site guards and those who work in the dig house—around the mound during the excavation season, telling them in Turkish about what we have found most recently and what we are learning from these findings. These efforts necessarily entail sharing archaeological interpretations as well as encouraging and utilizing local knowledge.

By far the most comprehensive and intensive community engagement project has been the Community-Based Participatory Research (CBPR) program led by Sonya Atalay, which started in 2006 (see chapter 1). Atalay (2010: 422) notes that "initially, discussions involved the familiar framework of questioning local residents about their daily lives and practices (e.g., annual barley storage, meat drying and processing)—something they were experts in and felt comfortable discussing." The initial stages of her CBPR project addressed "the overwhelming concern that local residents had about their limited knowledge about the site" (Atalay 2010: 422) and included an annual festival where residents of three nearby villages could learn about the laboratory analysis happening on the project as well as take a site tour in Turkish to learn about recent progress and discoveries, archaeological lab-guide training for young residents, a regular comic and newsletter series distributed in the local community, a paid internship program, and an archaeological community theater program. All of these elements of the CBPR project worked to increase local archaeological knowledge so community members would feel better equipped to act as equal partners in decision-making and planning for the site.

All of the network analysis, oral historical, and ethnographic data examined so far suggests that the community engagement strategies implemented at Çatalhöyük have been very effective in encouraging the sharing of knowledge and information access in some dimensions. The way labor has been arranged and managed at Çatalhöyük, predicated on this same commitment to engaging and involving local stakeholders, has had an apparent impact on the role site workers play in archaeological knowledge production on this project. Site workers have acquired expertise that closely resembles the content of what is documented in the excavation records about the archaeological finds unearthed and have developed methodological specialisms that remake the division of specialisms within the research community at the site.

But the interpretative and analytical dimensions of the work operate in places and ways very separate from those in which the site workers are involved. This is one area in which community engagement has not affected the organization of labor enough to break down the divisions between foreign archaeologists and locally hired laborers that have always characterized excavations in the Middle East. Despite the well-intentioned, thoughtfully designed, carefully planned, and in many ways successful initiatives to include locally hired site workers in the entire archaeological process, labor relations at the site remain in other ways too exclusionary for local site workers to act as knowledgeable, confident participants in the analysis of the archaeological materials from the site. The community engagement strategies employed at the site have been led by individuals rather than being project-level structural initiatives that resonate through every dimension of the project. The limitations of these fairly small-scale and short-term commitments to social engagement (in comparison to the overall time span and reach of the project) are apparent when attention is intently focused on site workers' knowledge of what interpretations are drawn from the archaeological assemblage at Çatalhöyük. The dimension of archaeological analysis that has been most financially rewarding and consistently accessible to local residents is to act as the subject of ethno-archaeological research performed by the archaeological team; to understand and know or even to ask about other conclusions archaeologists are drawing about the archaeological assemblage at the site does not afford a comparable level of capital, hindering the success of the numerous outreach efforts implemented by the project.

The Temple of the Winged Lions and the Çatalhöyük excavations represent two contrasting but consistent case studies in how the arrangement of archaeological labor impacts site workers' engagement in the production and preservation of knowledge. At both sites, site workers have acquired expertise in some areas while experiencing obstacles to either gaining or expressing their expertise in other areas; the similarity or difference of their knowledge and memories to those contained in the excavation archives from the two sites clearly reflects the ways locally hired laborers have been invited to participate or disallowed from participating in particular events, practices, and conversations. A parallel exists, however, across the two contexts, which I have not yet addressed. In both areas, as I listened to people express all the intimate and professional archaeological knowledge outlined here, I would tell them how grateful I was that they were willing to share their perspectives, how clear it was that they had attained considerable archaeological expertise from working in excavations.

"Oh no," person after person told me. "I don't have any expertise in archaeology."

In chapter 4, I describe this phenomenon in detail—when, where, and with whom it kept happening—and offer an explanation as to why local community members who possess significant expertise in archaeology would choose to disavow this expertise rather than proudly assert their status as professional, skilled, and knowledgeable participants in the process of archaeological excavation and knowledge production.

4

Lucrative Non-Knowledge

The person who told me "I know how the Roman pottery is different from the Byzantine pottery and how they are different from the Nabataean pottery. They can be broken down into three groups. The first group is the Nabataean, the second group is a bit bigger and more black, and that's Roman. When it's more white, here, it's Byzantine" later said in the same conversation, "The people here, I mean the people from the Bedul, don't remember anything about the ruins. They don't know anything about the science of archaeology."

The man who told me how to recognize cooking areas and bathrooms in ancient structures by looking at the assemblage of tiles and pipe fragments, who recalled a comprehensive list of artifacts recovered from the Temple of the Winged Lions ("pottery including green glazed pottery and cooking pots, tear jars, oil lamps, necklaces, stone beads, gold flakes"), also said he "didn't have expertise" and "just worked as a worker" on the excavation.

When I asked one of the site workers from Çatalhöyük if there were any additional jobs or tasks he would like to perform, such as drawing or photographing, he said: "I wouldn't like to do those jobs. I'm always watching and it looks really boring, always the same, measuring and dig-ging. I like my own job."

Moments later, this same man took out his cell phone to show me the pictures he had taken of burials and finds from the area of the excavation where he had been work-ing. I tried to point out the irony, but he just shrugged and reiterated that he wasn't interested in taking pictures.

DOI: 10.5876/9781646421152.c004

These conversations became predictable: after an hour of hearing a person's intimate knowledge of the archaeological process and their nuanced ideas about how to interpret archaeological assemblages, they would deny having experience and knowledge of these same things. At first, I assumed that this repudiation was based on a real lack of information and abilities, that for various reasons site workers across these projects had either forgotten or never acquired insight into most of what goes on during the course of an excavation. Some of what people said confirmed just this: that their jobs on the site were too detached from the rest of the excavation procedure, that the archaeological team was never interested in sharing and explaining, that they were too young or too disinterested to remember the answers to questions I was asking now, decades later. There are reasons for a real absence of expertise in both of these contexts, which can help us understand how labor management structures can exclude workers from participating wholly in the production of knowledge on archaeological projects.

A look at the economics of archaeological labor in both of these contexts, however, makes clear as well how powerfully these structures work to alternately reward and devalue certain kinds of expertise and performance. An examination of the testimonies of locally hired laborers at Çatalhöyük shows that when site workers self-identify as ethnoarchaeological subjects, they receive compensation in the form of both money and prestige. Site workers in Petra report something similar but even more dramatic, sharing stories that portray an archaeological industry that rewards those who claim not to have archaeological expertise and present themselves as less knowledgeable than they are. Local community members are more likely to be hired and to avoid being fired if they appear less expert to archaeological project directors.

This effect, in which locally hired archaeological laborers receive financial benefit from disavowing their expertise and knowledge, is a phenomenon I call "lucrative non-knowledge," to link the ways money making is maximized by professing one's ignorance. Lucrative non-knowledge is characteristic not only of these two sites but of archaeology more broadly and of closely connected industries like tourism and cultural heritage management. Tracking how excavation and heritage workers are systematically rewarded with money and employment for performing ignorance provides insight into the economics that structure the creation and dissemination of narratives about the past. Understanding how pervasive this process is helps us see it in its total historical, political, and socioeconomic context; seeing how it operates specifically in the context of Middle Eastern archaeology may point to solutions for more inclusive, multivocal archaeological knowledge production.

THE CASE FOR MEMORIES NEVER MADE

Some of the reasons site workers give for why they have not been included in the full and total knowledge production processes at the site were discussed in chapter 3. Locally hired laborers at Çatalhöyük have felt prevented from being completely involved in and able to learn about all dimensions of the excavation because of the language barrier, because of the closed doors on the laboratories, because, as one interviewee said when I asked why he didn't feel like he knew very much about many aspects of the excavation, "*you didn't show us.*"

Many of the individuals I met readily expressed how little they knew about the site or about archaeology before working at Çatalhöyük. "If I saw obsidian before I worked at Çatalhöyük," one man told me, "I would have thought it was just natural stone." Another man said he always thought the glimmering black shards he saw on the ground were broken fragments of glass. Several individuals did not know the mound was manmade before excavations began there. And some of the older people who had worked at the site recalled moments from their childhood when farmers would find pieces of pottery or figurines and simply throw them aside without considering that they might have some significance for learning about the past. In a context in which local residents arrive at the project with very little archaeological experience and are prevented from accessing a range of the steps of the archaeological research process, one can often interpret later statements by these workers about their lack of knowledge at face value. In many cases, they are offering truthful descriptions of their lack of access and opportunity to build substantial archaeological knowledge.

There is, as well, the equally real issue I was interviewing many people about, often many years after the fact: short periods of employment. In several conversations, the former site workers I was speaking to apologized for failing to recall all of the specific details I was asking about, telling me they had worked there decades ago and their memories had faded. I interviewed dozens of men and women who had worked on the Temple of the Winged Lions project in the 1970s and 1980s. Not only were they reaching forty years back into the annals of their memories, but these memories were created when many of them were very young—some teenagers and many as young as nine or ten years old. Talat Tweissi, who worked at the temple when he was ten years old, described how he felt about working on an excavation at such a young age:

> For me, it . . . it was, like, good to learn language. Plus, for me, the two-and-a-
> half dinars [per day] were great in this time. [Laughing] I was dreaming of, like,

one dinar a day . . . So to get a job for two-and-a-half dinars a day was great . . . I was a little child working things. Trying this, trying that . . . The experience comes when you are older. It's different. But as a child, you work once or twice. You don't really get experience.

One man, who was a great admirer of Philip C. Hammond, commended this practice of hiring children for the excavation. "I think he was very smart," this man told me, "because children, when they are a young age, they really like to work. They don't know how to play games, like old people [do]."

This was not, however, the overwhelming point of view from the community members I interviewed. Most who had worked at the site in their adolescence—who now had children of their own—condemned the practice of hiring children as a means of setting up a workforce that would have little choice or agency over its pay or working conditions. As young boys and girls, they lacked the organizing power or financial security to negotiate for better treatment and compensation.

Oral historical accounts from former Temple of the Winged Lions site workers illustrate this lack of empowerment and stability. "If we couldn't work with trowel or brush and only could use the pick, we would be fired," said one man who had been sent away from the excavation for precisely this reason. Another former site worker had watched several of his friends lose their jobs for taking too many breaks. "We got three breaks," he explained. "One for tea, one for breakfast, and another one for tea. If you stopped at any other time, you were fired." Site workers were fired for being late, for working too slowly, for taking too many breaks, for having difficulty recognizing differences in the stratigraphy, and once because a rodent was making holes at night, which the archaeological team suspected were made by site workers coming after dark to loot the site. With such a high turnover rate for laborers, the majority of people I interviewed only worked at the site for a single six-week season at most. A number of them only worked on the excavation for a week before being fired for one or a combination of these many reasons.

As I spoke to more and more of the people who had been hired to dig with Hammond's team at the Temple of the Winged Lions, the list of reasons why they were unable to gain insight into all aspects of the archaeological research process expanded. They tended to work on highly specific and isolated tasks, like washing pottery or carrying buckets of soil, and had minimal to no knowledge of anything that happened to the artifacts outside the procedural events in which they were acting. This sort of highly specialized division of labor is precisely the management structure that creates the conditions for

Marxian alienation (Marx 2012 [1844]). In addition to generally exploitative labor conditions, like low wages and long hours, Marx describes how the transformation of the worker into an instrument leads to his dissociation from the eventual outcome of a complex production process in which he is only a small part. This is arguably the case for workers at the Temple of the Winged Lions. What could be a clearer indication of the identification of a person with an instrument than roles titled "pick-man" or "goofah boy"? It follows that they would experience *entfremdung*—disconnection from and a lack of awareness of the eventual findings of the total archaeological research process.

The degree to which site workers were prevented from accessing a comprehensive view of the excavation process is laid bare by the memories of what happened during the discovery of particularly important artifacts. In many of my early interviews, former temple site workers gave accounts such as "they [archaeologists] would move me whenever I came upon something good, and they'd put in people who wouldn't understand [the significance of] the thing" or "when we found something important, they would send the Bedouin away and come back in the evening when the workers had gone to excavate these good things."

I initially interpreted these stories as somewhat hyperbolic—certainly rooted in truth but shaped and retold in such a way as to highlight particular feelings of mutual distrust. While I could see the archaeological team taking over the excavation of a delicate or particularly significant object, the idea that they would sneak back to the site under cover of night to excavate seemed outlandish—an angry metaphorical expression of a local perception that both foreign and Jordanian archaeologists play a role in Petra's antiquities being taken, stolen, or sold to museums and antiquities dealers far beyond the site. Even though the account was repeated by numerous individuals, I understood it as more legend than fact.

Then I met one man who worked with the project, a Jordanian who had grown up in the immediate area of Petra. He shared his contribution to the excavation methodology employed at the Temple of the Winged Lions:

> [Hammond] also wanted to work with someone who would keep an eye on his project because you know how the Bedouins are. If they see something, they come and take it. So that's why usually all your staff must know when they're trying to see if something is appearing, to hide it and not to dig it in front of the public. Always to be careful is better . . . And then we can come and do this as archaeologists without [the Bedouins] there. But if they [the Bedouins] see

that [the archaeologists] find a bit of gold or bit of silver or a special thing, they might immediately come and dig it up . . . And [Hammond] replied, he said well, usually we do everything when we can. I said no. They can put some ash on top and dig somewhere else, and then we come with our quietness . . . That was my idea . . . This is the technical work we have to do. And we should not do it in front of them and to show them, you know, how we find things and encourage them to come and break what we find. And he accepted the idea. And that was good for me.

They were true, then, the stories of archaeologists hiding remarkable artifacts from the locally hired site workers and returning in the nighttime to remove them from the site. Not only this, but the originator of the practice, the man whose original idea it was for the excavators to return after dusk to retrieve artifacts uncovered during the day, still regarded it as an effective means of protecting the artifacts from site-workers-turned-looters. From the perspective of those who were presumed to be the potential looters, however, it was alienating—a sign of suspicion by excavators who hastened to pile loose dirt on top of an emerging pot base or figural statue fragment, glancing over their shoulders to see if the site workers were noticing (which, of course, they were). The insult felt particularly acute once the site workers had already been unfairly accused and fired for looting when a rodent was the true culprit.

The practice of nighttime excavation was instituted to combat looting—an undeniable threat to archaeological remains and one archaeologists continue to struggle to document and prevent. I do not want to suggest that it is not a problem or that it does not continue to take place; many studies have shown that it absolutely is and does, including in Petra. (Parcak et al. 2016; Stone and Bajjaly 2008; Vella et al. 2015). But the solution chosen in this case—to stealth-excavate complete or potentially valuable objects—has done more harm than good, and not only to local community members. Indeed, the mutual suspicion underlying and fortified by this practice limited the opportunities for both foreign and local groups to exchange expertise. Given how much archaeology has to gain from the original ideas and insights site workers possess, this was arguably even more detrimental to the production of knowledge about the Temple of the Winged Lions than to the daily lives of young Bedouin men working a summer job.

Furthermore, digging up Petra's artifacts away from the view of local residents goes against more recent publications proposing solutions to looting in the Middle East and elsewhere. These scholarly projects have advocated more nuanced approaches, challenging archaeologists' exclusive right to determine who should benefit economically from tangible cultural heritage and how and ultimately pointing to legal and market-level strategies for decreasing looting (Brodie et al. 2006; Kersel 2007, 2011; Matsuda 1998; Pollock 2003; Smith 2005; Wylie 2005). The problem is not, in other words, excavating in the presence of community members but rather the totality of laws, interest in purchasing antiquities, ethics of the consumer base, and lack of enforcement that make up the antiquities trade.

In light of this (noting as well that some of this research was published while the Hammond excavation was still ongoing), the decision to excavate at night is particularly unfortunate. It fostered the environment of division and tension between laborers and supervisors, preventing supervisors from hearing the observations and ideas the site workers had to offer. For the site workers, in terms of access and participation in the production of knowledge at the site, the effects are apparent. Without being able to see or ask about all the artifacts from the excavation—particularly those in which the excavators were most interested—or how they were recovered, site workers were prevented from gaining the same knowledge recorded by the archaeological team members who did witness these objects and practices. This is clear from the analysis presented in the foregoing chapters. With regard to the finds and excavation methods, former site workers from the Temple of the Winged Lions (TWL) do not as a whole recall the same information contained in the formal archive.

But the same analysis presents a problem for fully accepting all of these compelling reasons why site workers may lack knowledge of archaeological assemblages, methods, and interpretations. The preceding chapters clearly demonstrate that the site workers from both Çatalhöyük and Petra *do* possess evident, measurable expertise about these subjects. The structure of their expertise and how closely it resembles the body of documentation created by the archaeological team differ between the two contexts, with former site workers from Çatalhöyük recalling objects and research approaches that match those recorded in the archaeological archives and former TWL workers recalling very different ones. Still, despite the real obstacles suggested as reasons why the site workers could not acquire wide-ranging knowledge about all aspects of the excavations in these two contexts, many actually did gain such knowledge. This is not to discount those obstacles or the way labor organization on the two sites has materially limited the abilities of some groups to be completely integrated in knowledge production processes. When community engagement is not a priority and sometimes even when it is, locally hired site workers' views of and voices in many dimensions of archaeological research are restricted. But in the areas to which they do have access, it is equally clear that local laborers, regardless of labor management practices, develop important in-depth knowledge and expertise.

The descriptions, then, of the many ways they were prevented from participating, or at least not invited to participate, in certain aspects of both projects are only a partial explanation for why so many people I spoke to claimed they were "just workers" and had no particular special knowledge or information about the archaeological work or even about what they did there. There must be a more persuasive explanation for why this assertion was so pervasive. There must have been some incentive for site workers who claimed a lack of archaeological expertise rather than an abundance of it.

THE POWER OF NOT SPEAKING

Somewhere between asserting a professional identity and avowing ignorance or inexperience is the decision to simply *not* share one's knowledge or insights. Answering a question with "I don't know" is claiming absence of knowledge, whether real or professed. There is also the option not to answer at all, which is not to deny having had access to a privileged perspective on archaeological work but is also not to share it. I experienced this twice while conducting interviews at Çatalhöyük, in two noticeably similar encounters.

In the first twenty-one of the twenty-two months of oral historical research I conducted, not a single person in either Çatalhöyük or Petra refused to be interviewed, unless it turned out that they had not actually worked on an archaeological excavation and had been identified mistakenly. Toward the end of my final month of interviews, my interpreter, Tunç, and I were driving down the main road of Küçükköy, hoping to find someone who could point us to the houses of the last few people I was looking to interview. As we saw a man walking down the side of the road, Tunç slowed the car to a stop, rolled down the window, and tried to get his attention. "Excuse me," Tunç called out. "My friend here is trying to find some people in the village to interview. We have a list of names here; could you tell me where to find them?"

The man readily gestured for us to hand him the list, and Tunç got out of the car, holding out the frenetically flapping white pages with the columns of names printed on them. They started examining the list together, and I watched from the passenger window as the man gave more directions for a person on the list. Suddenly, he stopped to scrutinize one of the names more closely. He looked at Tunç, pointing at the name. Tunç raised his eyebrows and smiled. "Allison," he called back to me. "He worked at Çatalhöyük!"

I gathered my notebook and pen and hopped out of the car, ready to ask him questions on the spot or take down his information so we could contact him later. But by the time I reached the two men, the conversation had turned. The man's tone had become adamant and combative and Tunç's had turned imploring and apologetic. They were speaking rapidly, and as the man walked away, Tunç explained that as soon as he mentioned Çatalhöyük, the man became agitated and started repeating over and over that he didn't want to talk about his experiences on the project. From a few houses away, we heard him calling back to us, inviting us to dinner. A second, female voice joined the man's, repeating the offer to join them for dinner. As we reached their gate, we could see both of them as they peered over the fence and together repeated the same statements like a chorus: "We won't tell you anything about Çatalhöyük. But we'll talk about anything else you want to know about. Please, have dinner with us tonight." And again, "We won't tell you anything about Çatalhöyük. But we'll talk about anything else you want to know about. Please, have dinner with us tonight."

Only five days later, over a different fence, we found ourselves having the same conversation. Standing in the road, Tunç and I were talking to another man we had identified as a site worker, who was responding from his yard on the other side of a closed gate. He was steadfastly refusing to be interviewed about his experiences at Çatalhöyük while also happily offering information about any other topic I could imagine and inviting us to share a meal with his family. He repeated the same three messages: you are welcome in this home, I am willing to speak with you for your research, but I will not talk about that time, place, job, or group of people.

The effect of this response is to at once suggest the speaker's potential contributions to the research project—that is, these men did not deny that they possessed knowledge or information about the Çatalhöyük excavation—while also closing off access to it. At the same time, certain kinds of access were opened in the form of invitations to dinner in their homes with their families. Their refusal to talk about Çatalhöyük should not be taken as an indication of unfriendliness or an unwillingness to help. Some limits were being lifted in these series of statements; others were set in stone. These men and this woman dictated exactly what aspects of their lives and experiences I could even ask about, let alone what they would share. Before I asked a single question, they firmly asserted control over what topics I would be permitted to address as they rather poetically stood on the opposite side of a tall, constructed physical barrier.

To list any possible specific reasons why these men did not want to share their experiences about Çatalhöyük would only be speculation and would disrespect their desire not to answer questions on the topic. Even without pursuing this avenue of inquiry, however, these encounters illustrate an important aspect of the politics and economics of site workers' role in archaeological knowledge production, namely: whether these individuals were deciding not to reveal their expertise or skills, not to share a specific critique of the project, or not to open themselves up to the vulnerability of participating in an ethnographic interview, they were taking advantage of an opportunity to take control and assert power. By simultaneously establishing themselves as sources of privileged knowledge but also unavailable ones, they asserted control over the normal relations between archaeologists and site workers, redirecting the flow of information by determining when, where, and especially about what they would speak in a conversation with an archaeologist.

These exchanges illustrate how the decision not to reveal the extent or content of one's archaeological experience can be a way of establishing power and influence. It is a means of interrupting archaeologists' access (including my own) to the particular expertise of locally hired laborers but still presenting oneself as a valuable source of potentially useful or important information. It is still, however, very different from presenting oneself as someone *without* potentially useful or important information, a claim made by many locally hired laborers in Jordan and Turkey.

THE ECONOMICS OF SIMPLICITY

While site workers at both Çatalhöyük and Petra denied having advanced archaeological knowledge, this repudiation was expressed in slightly different language. The people I spoke to at Çatalhöyük, after denying high-level insight into the operations, goals, or findings of the excavation, most often went on to characterize themselves as traditional villagers with old-fashioned lifestyles in opposition to progressive-minded scientists. They positioned themselves as kindred spirits to the Neolithic inhabitants of the mound, closer to these people in livelihood and culture than to the international team coming to conduct research for several months each summer. "I am the daughter of this soil," one of the women who had worked on the project for several consecutive years summarized her feelings elegantly. "We are the same as the Neolithic people."

This is not the same as claiming genetic descent from the Neolithic community. Those who expressed these feelings of kinship articulated the sentiment on a more observational basis, pointing to specific artifacts or behaviors the excavation had uncovered. In chapter 3, I described how the sorting women explained the presence of separate hearths and ovens in Neolithic houses on the basis of having two separate cooking installations in their own homes, one for baking and one for meats and vegetables, which proved especially essential when they were expecting company. Other people I spoke to drew similar direct comparisons to other artifacts recovered during the excavation, such as the mini clay balls: "We were children. We made these small clay balls as toys and threw them to each other. We played games like marbles with them." The figurines: "When I was a child, we made miniature animal and human models and models of the houses. They were like small toy versions of the village." And bins: "They are for saving grain, wheat, and salt. This is what my grandparents used."

Often, these points of personal connection to and memory of the Çatalhöyük archaeological assemblage led to a steady flow of descriptions of traditional ways of life that interviewees saw as analogous to those employed by Neolithic people. In a single interview, one woman, who started by telling me that she already knew how to recognize the different seeds and botanical remains found at the site before she started working there, then went on to talk about her childhood memories of making cheese in animal skin, storing yogurt and meat in pottery, using charcoal as eyeliner, washing clothes and cookware using clay and ash, and having to collect wood for this very purpose.

Another man led me through his house, giving a tour of the parallels he perceived between his own life and that of Neolithic Çatalhöyük society. First he brought me into the paddock where he kept his sheep, which shared a wall with his home. He pointed out how close he lived to the herd, described how he could hear them shuffle and bleat as he fell asleep, and suggested that this close relationship with animals was something people in the past would also have experienced. He framed this sensory experience as something that made him feel a close affiliation with those who built Çatalhöyük. We walked to the storage building that held the feed for the animals, which was decorated on the side with paint and, notably, handprints—one of the recurring motifs found inside the houses at the site. He touched one of them and looked at me, smiling and making sure I noticed. We went inside the storage building, and I saw a ladder leading to a loft area. The ladder was identical to the one on display in the experimental house. "Just like the Neolithic people," he exclaimed, patting the sturdy post.

Initially, I found these claims to traditional or old-fashioned identities difficult to rationalize in the context of the archaeological project. Wouldn't it be beneficial to play up being scientifically minded, modern, quick learners in order to secure jobs or better positions on the archaeological project? Especially since they all knew me as an excavator, why would these men and women want to highlight their ancestral ways of life or "simplicity" and to say things like "I didn't learn anything from the excavation" or "I wouldn't want to do any jobs besides the ones I already do?" It was striking to hear so many people profess a lack of both knowledge and motivation to learn or advance in the archaeological excavation, especially when the rest of our conversations illustrated how much expert archaeological knowledge they possessed. Their stories, however, intimated some of the reasons why such a large proportion of the people I spoke to emphasized the affinity they felt with the Neolithic inhabitants of Çatalhöyük.

For example, one man, describing how his wife knew about the archaeobotanical materials before she worked on the excavation, said, "One time, when some archaeologists found some seeds, they asked my wife what they were for. They were medicine we use for dry skin and hair. She got this knowledge from her grandfather and grandmother." In this exchange, his wife provided valuable insight to the researchers. This same dynamic was described by a woman working to sort the heavy residue recovered from the flotation process: "Things like grinding grain . . . I know about these things from my childhood. I've lived them. I'm not learning anything by working here. People in the village, we can teach archaeologists about ovens and how to heat the houses at Çatalhöyük. We live the same way as the Neolithic people." Her description of the relationship between the local community and the archaeologists is one in which members of the local community are potentially very valuable to the research team *because* of their traditional knowledge. In other words, it is not their advanced archaeological skills or excavation experience that makes locally hired excavation workers essential contributors to the production of archaeological knowledge. It is instead their familiarity with the traditional building, subsistence, and production practices that can be examined as an ethnographic analogy to better understand the Neolithic assemblage that renders local community members integral to the archaeological research team.

This impression, expressed by nearly half the people I interviewed, is supported by the number of experimental programs and ethnoarchaeological research projects in which local community members and site workers in particular have participated. These initiatives have been described at various points throughout the discussion presented here. There is the ethnographic work conducted by David Shankland (1999a, 1999b), analyzing the folklore and spiritual meanings ascribed to the mound by local community members. Wendy Matthews and her colleagues (2000) list eighteen separate ethnoarchaeological projects in which they consulted with the local community, covering specific topics as diverse as architecture, settlement organization, soil chemistry, ethnobotany, dental wear, posture and bodily movement, faunal remains, ground stone, uses of clay, and social anthropology. Mirjana Stevanović (1999) outlines an experiment with sourcing raw materials and construction bricks using the same techniques as those employed by the Neolithic community—an experiment that relied on locally hired site workers for both their labor and knowledge, as residents of Küçükköy continue to build houses using mud brick. I spoke to one of the men involved in designing and constructing the experimental house, who had been a professional construction worker employing traditional mud brick building strategies for thirty years. He was the one who mixed the mud, built the molds, and put the mud in the molds. He knew what would happen if there was too much or too little moisture or grass in the mud used for the bricks and how long they needed to dry. I asked him directly why local people like him were hired for this job, and he said that those directing the project "asked my little brother if someone from the village would be able to do all of these activities. My brother sent them to me because I knew what to do. I know the mud bricks, and they were specifically looking for a craftsman of mud bricks. It's an old technology. Not everyone knows it."

His memory of and experience with traditional technologies were what made him an ideal candidate for this job. Because he had seen and utilized the same sorts of environmental resources in the same ways as the Neolithic community members and had not studied them from a scientific or scholarly perspective, he was better suited to carry out this experiment than the scientists on the research team.

The archaeologists themselves, then, by the opportunities they have created for site workers and other local community members, have constructed a site-level economic system that rewards the overt performance of traditionalism. For members of the local community, establishing themselves as ideal ethnoarchaeological subjects has consistently proven an effective means of securing employment and involvement in the project. Outside of the excavation at Çatalhöyük, there are few similar sorts of employment opportunities. Most of the people from Küçükköy who do not work on the excavation either farm or raise livestock, both of which require large areas of land and specialized equipment and are heavily affected by the weather. Agriculture, moreover, does not provide regular reliable wages. Participating in the excavations offers a weekly salary, even if it is only seasonal.[1] In addition, many site workers told me they joined the project at Çatalhöyük simply for the fun of excavation and being part of the team. For all these reasons, for many residents of Küçükköy, working on the project at Çatalhöyük is desirable, and emphasizing their traditional identity is a crucial way to gain access to more paid opportunities with the project.

Importantly, though, it is not only archaeologists who have financed this performance of traditional identity. One of the women who offered some of the most vivid childhood memories of old cooking styles and cleaning methods told me about a documentary in which she was paid to appear. Four people from the village, including she and her husband, were recruited to pose as Neolithic people at Çatalhöyük. They were instructed to comport their bodies as the Neolithic inhabitants would have done, to move around in the same way, to grind grain using a stone mortar and pestle. "The directors told us some things to do, like where to look and where to go. But the grinding of the grain . . . My grandmother, even my mother ground grain like this. So I knew from them what to do," she said. She added, "I've never even seen the documentary. We were told when it was on [on] European television, but we don't have access to that channel," drawing out even further the gap between herself and the technologically modern world. This was not a one-time opportunity, either; when I later asked Ian Hodder which documentary the woman was talking about in hopes of sharing it with her, he said that a number of film crews had hired people to re-create Neolithic scenes, so he couldn't be sure which production she was describing. This was a recurring opportunity on which local community members could capitalize by focusing attention on the ways their lifestyles are similar to those of the inhabitants of the 9,000-year-old settlement at this site.

The son of the man who led the construction of the experimental house at Çatalhöyük was working on the excavation in 2015. For him, "It is a good opportunity for me to work here because it's just like my home." That connection, that identification of likeness between themselves and the ancient settlement, presents the possibility for more jobs, more involvement in the investigation and presentation of Çatalhöyük. The archaeological researchers working there and the associated media producers involved local site workers and their families in a number of activities that rewarded the outward performance of those affiliations and concomitantly the downplaying of the workers' advanced archaeological knowledge. The intimate and personal knowledge of Neolithic objects and behaviors has brought more recognition and monetary reward than a scholarly knowledge of the same would have done. The structure of archaeological labor at Çatalhöyük is such that a certain kind of non-knowledge—that is, the denial of knowledge of the science of the excavation—becomes more lucrative than claiming and performing one's rightful role as an archaeological expert.

This same sort of reward for local community members who embrace and highlight aspects of their lives and identities that affiliate them with the past also exists at Petra—although in this case, it is the Nabataean past that is of interest. But a dominant framework of labor on archaeological excavations in the region encourages these local inhabitants to assertively deny their archaeological experience. Once again, archaeological non-knowledge is lucrative, and instead the knowledge of how to be a good worker is reliably rewarded.

A GOOD WORKER IS NOT AN EXPERT

"I am Nabataean," Noora Qublan told me after giving me a tour of the cave where she and her family live. She had shown me how her family diverted the water for their waste facilities to minimize erosion of the stone, how they carefully chose where to start fires so the smoke wouldn't damage the interior of the cave. When I asked how she had selected which cave to live in initially, she said it had been important for the Nabataeans, who had carved elaborate features in the mountainside around it, and it therefore held significance for her: "I will never leave this place, ever. It was important to the Nabataeans, and I follow the Nabataeans."

Nabataean or Neolithic—the time period in focus is different, but the past-facing representation of self is the same. Other scholars have documented and closely examined the performance of the past by the Bedouin community at Petra. Both Kenneth W. Russell (1993) and John Austin Shoup (1985) have demonstrated that many members of the Bedul tribe claim to be genetic descendants of the Nabataeans because of the proven traction of this argument in influencing negotiations with government and heritage management agencies. In fact, when my research assistant Eman Abdessalam and I met a man who confidently asserted that he knew what the Temple of the Winged Lions looked like originally, Eman asked how he had determined all these details. His response was, "Because my genetic DNA is Nabataean." Often, however, the affiliation with the past takes a much less specific form, as Mikkel Bille and Cynthia A. Wooten have illustrated. Bille's (2012, 2013) work on the material culture and cultural practices of the Bedouin tribes at Petra analyzes how different, overlapping, and sometimes contradictory heritage management policies effectively legitimize certain aesthetics and behaviors over others, often reinvigorating rapidly disappearing or nearly extinct practices. The effect is an amalgamation of many interlocking images of different kinds of "pastness" that is marketable within the heritage industry. Wooten (1996) makes a similar argument, suggesting that the tourist experience of Petra is an exaggerated vision of "hyper-nostalgia" that overemphasizes the camel herding and cave dwelling Bedouins have engaged in, not only now but throughout their history. Particular rhetoric, material culture, clothing, and practices prove profitable in a place with such an active tourist economy while they have little relevance to a specific, identifiable, or historically accurate moment in the past.

The performance of traditionalism represents a distinct point of crossover between the Petra and Çatalhöyük case studies and serves to illustrate that this is not an isolated phenomenon. Indeed, communities in many different areas and circumstances, for cross-cutting economic, political, and historical reasons, make the most effective use of the tourism industry by performing against modernity, by emphasizing traditionalism and difference from foreign tourists. It is apparent that the Bedouins at Petra have capitalized on the opportunities to benefit from this kind of performance, and archaeologists excavating there have helped create this opportunity. Still, there are political and economic structures specific to archaeology that point to focused and satisfying explanations for the common repudiation of uniquely archaeological expertise I recorded.

One of the most archaeologically professional Bedouin men in Petra is Suleman Samahin. When we were introduced, he was assisting another archaeologist with an ongoing research project in the area and planning ahead for an upcoming excavation on which he would be the foreman. Suleman's first experience as a site worker was in 1988; since then, he has worked almost continuously with archaeologists from around the globe: Jordanian, Polish, American, German, and French archaeologists. Over the years, Suleman has developed enough familiarity with the region's soil stratigraphy to be able to predict how deep one would have to dig in a given location to find the Roman occupation layers or the Nabataean layers at a given site. He has received physical recognition of his proficiency; two of the projects he worked with gave him formal certificates attesting to his excavation skills and historical knowledge.

When he told me this, I was excited. These certificates were an ideal form of evidence for local archaeological expertise—official, signed, laminated verification provided by archaeologists who had witnessed and benefited from this man's remarkable abilities. I asked Suleman if I could photograph them for my project. He sighed and rubbed his head.

"I'd have to go looking for them. I don't know where they are. Maybe my wife knows . . . I can ask her."

"Really? You don't have them mounted, framed, on display?" I asked, half joking.

He waved his hand dismissively. "No. I've never shown them to anyone. I never would."

This surprised me. I wasn't expecting that he would have made the certificates the focal point of his *diwan*,[2] but to hear that he would not show them to anyone was startling. "What about when you're trying to get a new job?" I probed.

"No," he replied firmly. "I wouldn't want to seem arrogant."

Suleman is decidedly polite, so this statement was hardly out of character. Viewed in the context of other accounts provided by former excavation site workers, however, it takes on additional meaning. Take, for example, one Bedouin man's perspective, offered during a conversation on why he had vowed to never again work on an archaeological excavation:

AHMED: Sometimes, you find some stuff and one of them [the archaeologists] say[s] this stuff is, uh, from 200 years before Christ.

ME: Mm-hmm.

AHMED: And then on another excavation we find the same stuff. The same. And they look at it, they say this is 400 years before Christ.

ME: Yeah.

AHMED: And you don't know what's right, which is wrong. Everyone, every archaeologist, they tell a different story.

ME: So what do you do when that happens?

AHMED: Huh?

ME: What do you do?

AHMED: We don't do anything! What could we do?

ME: You could say something, right? You could say, "Well, I worked on this other excavation . . ."

AHMED: If you say that, they will say, "No. We are right. We are the experts." . . . And if you are a worker and if you come all the time to ask them, they might, uh . . . They will become angry, you know? And they will say "stop!" Uh . . . "We only brought you here to work. You're not here to ask."

Memories of the Temple of the Winged Lions excavation, provided by another man who worked there, resonate powerfully with Ahmed's account of the normal exchange of information—or lack thereof—between foreign archaeologists and locally hired site workers: "There are so many things to discover in Petra. I tried to bring them up to Halia [one of the American team's excavation supervisors] and she respected me, but she couldn't do anything about it. The other people just thought I'm stupid . . . When they found something, they wouldn't believe my ideas because they thought I was just a Bedouin."

From what this man and Ahmed say, informed suggestions or questions brought forward by experienced excavation workers are typically dismissed or even viewed as annoyances. It is easy to imagine in a setting like this that someone like Suleman would not find it advantageous to advertise his experience or professionalism. Over the course of my time in Petra, I met two other men who had received similar certifications from archaeologists recognizing their digging and artifact-handling abilities—both of whom also matter-of-factly stated that they had never, would never, show the accreditations to an archaeologist beginning a project in the region.

Furthermore, on a project with the high levels of employment insecurity for site workers that the Temple of the Winged Lions seems to have had, the "arrogance" Suleman was so wary of conveying could have meant the difference between a reliable salary and none at all. Especially in the 1970s, when this project was just beginning, there was very little tourism to the area. "People would fight to work there," pressed one man who lived at that time in a cave with a view of the Temple of the Winged Lions. "There was very little chance for people to make money outside of this." But while the salary might have been stable, the position of a site worker on this excavation was far from it. As I have shown, locally hired excavation laborers were frequently fired for a range of reasons ranging from tardiness to drinking water at undesignated times to being accused of digging holes actually created by vermin. A worker viewed as presumptuous or difficult for raising questions, new ideas, or concerns could have suffered severe consequences. Suggesting an alternative methodology or interpretation could cost someone the job they had fought to obtain.

This collective understanding that one should pretend to be less adept, less knowledgeable than he or she really is in order to secure employment is once again not relegated to the realm of archaeological labor alone. In the Petra context, I observed this same belief put into practice when I spent time with men involved in the tourist industry in the park. One man, Ahmed, after introducing me to several of his family members who had worked on Hammond's excavations, sat with me on a bench while we took a break and I wrote field notes on the interview while my memory was still fresh. Ahmed had his camels with him, one white and one brown, wearing colorful saddles that normally attracted tourists interested in paying for the experience of a lilting ride. After watching a few groups of visitors walk past, he nudged me and said, smiling, "watch this."

As a couple approached, he listened closely and identified the language they were speaking as French. They neared our bench and he called to them, "*Voulez-vous monter un chameau? Je peux vous offrir un bon prix . . .*" The couple shook their heads. After a short time, a group of students chatting animatedly in Spanish passed by. "*¡Amigos!*" Ahmed cried, grinning. "*¡Ven aquí! ¿Ha montado un camello?*" They continued their conversation without seeming to notice him. A British husband and wife walked in front of us next, and Ahmed offered them a camel ride in a proper English accent. Australian, German, American . . . he had mastered all these languages, grammars, dialects, and accents.

Then Ahmed sat back and chuckled to himself. Another group soon approached, but instead of politely offering to negotiate fairly with them or singing the merits of his camel, he called out in broken Arabic-accented English: "Camel ride! Camel ride! Very cheap for you! I give special price!" The people laughed together and came over immediately to admire the haughty animals. After a few more minutes of joking with them in stilted sentence fragments and animated gestures, Ahmed had two of them on the saddles and was waving to me as he tugged on the ropes and the camels dispassionately lumbered after him.

Ahmed knew exactly what would happen when he began this demonstration. He knew the tourists would not respond to his fluent offers of camel rides in their native tongues but that speaking in a-grammatical, choppy English full of trilled r's and misplaced diphthongs would pique their interest. He made a marketing decision—to downplay his familiarity with other cultures, other places, and instead advertise himself as a type of camel herder more akin to what a visitor might expect a "Bedouin" to be. So it is not only in archaeology and not only in Petra that workers are rewarded for downplaying their capabilities or education.

The alienation from sense of self is, after all, the third and final stage in Marx's (2012 [1844]) theory of alienation. Site workers in both Petra and Çatalhöyük derive minimal recognition or direct benefit from their intellectual contributions to the scientific enterprise of archaeology. They experience and express a lack of connection not only to the outcomes of that intellectual work—published data sets and analyses—and to the particular activities categorized as scholarly—laboratory work and technical recording—but also to their own identities as contributors to the production of archaeological knowledge. They lay claim instead to only partial aspects of who they are and what they bring to the archaeological research process. They represent themselves as emblems of the past or as passive laborers, not as vital and experienced excavators with privileged insight into artifact assemblages and archaeological methodologies. The labor conditions underpinning the production of archaeological knowledge in the field prevent such a full, holistic articulation of their identities—at least in their interactions with archaeologists.

Marx offers the theoretical link between the divisive management of supposedly unskilled labor and the experience of alienation from one's self-identity. Adding to this view, Michael Herzfeld's (2004: 4) concept of the "global hierarchy of value" suggests why the particular international encounters involved in the archaeological industry lead to the self-abjection expressed by tourism workers and excavation laborers:

> The global hierarchy of value has emerged from processes of world domination that colonialism began and that international commerce and the international arrangement of power bid fair to complete. One aspect of these processes is the way in which certain places, ideas, and cultural groups appear as marginal to the grand design. These are the places and cultures that do not fit the design to perfection; the more they protest its domination, they more they seem to confirm their own marginality.

The way the former Temple of the Winged Lions site workers disparage their archaeological skills and the way Çatalhöyük site workers identify themselves not simply as the descendants of the Neolithic community but as Neolithic themselves share in common this relation of self as somehow marginal to the archaeologists. Their language is strategic. It correlates with the realities of economic opportunities and vulnerabilities at the two sites.

What Herzfeld's framework suggests is that the site workers' laying claim to marginality cannot be explained by viewing this as an exclusive problem of labor management. Rather, the ongoing legacies of colonialism and Orientalism, which underpin foreign archaeological work in the Middle East, have strengthened the view of Middle Eastern communities as backward, unskilled, uneducated, and anti-modern. Even archaeological research projects actively working to counteract these legacies must deal with the political and economic realities structured by these long-term processes.

Archaeological labor management—the way local community members are hired, fired, paid, and placed on the archaeological site—is one dimension of these colonial effects. In reinforcing either their lack of expertise or their simple, traditional lifestyle, the site workers in both settings make clear that they are aware of how archaeological labor relations are structured, as well as how they can best take advantage of those relations. The most desirable site workers, they have found, are not the ones who declare their profound scientific knowledge or notable skills. It is, in fact, quite the opposite. In disavowing their expertise, locally hired laborers exploit this structure to serve their own interests, even if it means they play into the global hierarchies of value that continue to structure labor management practices in archaeology. The effect is cyclical. Therefore, the structure itself must be changed at a foundational level if both archaeologists and local community members are to benefit from locally hired laborers' particular archaeological expertise. Expressing their privileged perspectives rather than denying them must become the more lucrative option.

ACCESS TO INTERPRETATION FROM BOTH SIDES

To be sure, there are a number of ways locally hired site workers at Middle Eastern archaeological sites such as Çatalhöyük and Petra have not acquired or been granted insight into the full range of processes involved in the archaeological process. For this reason, when former excavation laborers respond to specific questions about an assemblage or research approaches by saying they don't know much, this reply may not necessarily signify anything more than what is directly stated—that these people actually never saw or learned about the topic in question. This is especially true for highly hierarchical or unstable labor contexts where workers might have little access to certain areas and aspects of the excavation or might spend only a few days or weeks working on a given project.

Most of the time when I received this response, however, it was after an in-depth conversation covering the very topics about which interviewees were asserting they had little knowledge. The experience was much like the structure of this text; only once had I already glimpsed the high levels of particular expertise by virtue of how people answered questions about the history of archaeological research to which they contributed when they then said directly that they were not experts and instead maintained their "simplicity," whether in lifestyle or in lack of archaeological expertise. The differences between the forms this simplicity took across the two research settings, Petra and Çatalhöyük, map onto the disparities in labor organization and economic opportunities in the two archaeological contexts under study. At Petra, where archaeology is an industry unto itself—albeit a competitive one in which the labor supply far outstrips the demand—local community members have developed a clear comprehension of how they can best present themselves to project directors beginning excavations in the area. From experience, they have determined that highlighting their scientific aptitude and special knowledge actually costs them wages and employment, whether because they are seen as counterproductive to a fluid excavation process or because they simply won't be hired in the first place.

At Çatalhöyük, in contrast, the current excavation program and external affiliates have made it economically exigent for local community members to act as ethnoarchaeological subjects, using their knowledge of traditional subsistence practices and the local environment to provide insight into how the Neolithic community would have lived in this area. This is the economic niche local community members at Çatalhöyük uniquely fill, and so despite possessing a great deal of both practical and scholarly knowledge particularly of the archaeological finds and excavation strategies employed on the project, it is their traditional lifeways and their felt affinity with the Neolithic inhabitants of Çatalhöyük that they foreground in speaking to me—a member of the same archaeological project that has hired them.

Perhaps the most compelling argument for the notion that this devaluation of one's own expertise is strategic is to view it from the other side, from the perspective of archaeologists who are assembling these workforces and making labor management decisions. The first time I introduced this argument to another archaeologist, who also works in Jordan, I expected a critical reaction. I imagined that the idea that archaeologists have created a situation that penalizes people who proudly assert their earned expertise might elicit some indignation. I anticipated needing to very carefully explain how this contemporary reality is the result of a long and fraught history of interactions between foreign archaeologists and Middle Eastern communities, of archaeology being intertwined with imperialist and colonialist programs, of centuries of research establishing distance between modern Middle Eastern societies and the ancient archaeological remains. This wasn't what happened, however. When I explained the argument to a fellow archaeologist, it was met instead with collegial laughter: "I can understand that. I think if someone came to me with a card, saying they had so much experience, I *would* maybe think they were looking for extra money. I might be hesitant to hire them. We only have so much money, you know, budgets are so tight in archaeology." The more archaeologists to whom I described the concept of lucrative non-knowledge, the more indication I had that the site workers I interviewed were not mistaken in their perceptions of how archaeologists make decisions on who to hire and who to keep on an excavation team. Some even offered stories of their own, describing local site workers who could predict the archaeological remains to come with almost miraculous accuracy.

Many archaeologists told me about local community members who minimized the full extent of knowledge they possessed until a level of trust had been firmly established. One woman who had excavated on several projects in Petra asked if I knew a particular Bedul Bedouin man who for the first several weeks of her project had pretended not to speak any English. Nearly a month after the excavations started, during a tea break one day, he suddenly entered a conversation with complete English fluency.

I confirmed this story with its protagonist. When I related the narrative back to him, he chuckled at the memory, confirmed that "of course" it was true, and disclosed that he made a habit of not showing the full range of his capabilities to each new research team he worked with. "Once we're friends and I can trust them, okay," he stated and shrugged. "But at first? I don't like them to know how much I know."

The politics and economics of labor in archaeology in the Middle East have served over the centuries to make non-knowledge, the disavowal of expertise and special abilities, economically beneficial for local community members hoping to secure employment in excavation. These processes are still ongoing; in archaeological contexts as different as Petra and Çatalhöyük, on projects as disparate in their labor organization approaches and the attention paid to community engagement as these, former and current site workers continue to claim simplicity, traditionalism, lack of scientific experience: overall, non-knowledge. They perform certain kinds of identities and are paid for doing so through economic structures that have been in place in Middle Eastern archaeology since the nineteenth century. But the concept of lucrative non-knowledge, the idea that it is financially beneficial for archaeological workers to deny their scientific experience and instead perform an inexpert identity, has relevance to archaeological excavation contexts around the world. In chapter 5, I locate forms of lucrative non-knowledge on archaeological projects in South America, Mexico, sub-Saharan Africa, India, and Australia—seeing what is specific to the history of archaeology in the Middle East, attempting to understand what makes this a global phenomenon, and asking what can be done about it.

5

Lucrative Identities in Global Archaeological Labor

In Petra, I entered home after home, sat in courtyard after courtyard hearing stories upon stories describing the ways archaeologists have rewarded site workers for pretending to lack specialized archaeological expertise. Stories like these flowed from the doorways of houses in the Bedouin village until these similar experiences began to reach out toward each another, resonating with one another, transforming from isolated memories into a cross-cutting web of shared experiences with complexity and coherence.

Five hundred and twenty-four miles away, in Küçükköy, a similar web of shared experience began to form with each Çatalhöyük site worker I interviewed. One person's memories echoed another's and connections formed between the houses, between the people who had enjoyed the rewards of emphasizing their traditional lifeways while downplaying their scientific knowledge. The similarities and linkages of their memories recast individual experiences as collective ones, as a shared narrative of the way archaeology works, the way it has impacted people in this particular context.

These villages each emerge as a rich, thickly woven case study that illustrates how labor management on archaeological excavation shapes the knowledge produced through archaeology. I have here drawn a line between them, linking them to each other, drawing out the similarities between them, and arguing for what they demonstrate about the archaeological

DOI: 10.5876/9781646421152.c005

endeavor when considered alongside one another. While instructive as individual case studies, like nodes in a network, their meaning becomes much clearer when tied together.

In this chapter, I draw out that network, dropping points all around the world and investigating their connections. By examining other contexts where local labor has been used in archaeological excavation and tying them to the concept of lucrative non-knowledge that has emerged from the Petra and Çatalhöyük cases, connections appear across countries, across continents. A multifaceted global image develops of the systematic rewards archaeology offers local community members—not only for working in excavation but for the performance of a certain kind of identity as they dig, sift, sort, and wash.

THE MIDDLE EAST AND NORTH AFRICA

I outlined in chapter 2 the nature of interactions between archaeologists and local communities in the Middle East and North Africa (MENA) from the earliest expeditions in the eighteenth century to the present day. The narrative of this history is fraught, characterized by the colonial encounter and continued conflict. There is more continuity than rupture across these centuries, allowing threads to be traced over 200 years—producing a vision of the contemporary legacy of Mariette's decision to close the school of Egyptology, Petrie's selection of laborers according to a checklist of physical traits, excavation labor across the region being supplied by the soldiers enforcing colonial rule.

In Syria, for instance, Laurence Gillot (2010: 12) states that excavation "organisation is inherited from the 'Colonial' model introduced at the beginning of the twentieth century by British, French, and German excavators." He describes how labor is still recruited via the social and kinship networks of the foreman, how foremen are still chosen through inheritance as the job passes from father to son, how excavations in Syria still employ teams of workers who are separated and associated with one of three key instruments of excavation (pick, shovel, basket). As in the early days of archaeology in Syria, archaeology represents seasonal, temporary employment rather than long-term, secure, and reliable employment. Most important, even though local community members "can help archaeologists with the interpretation of remains with their own knowledge and local memory . . . local populations are far from being involved in the interpretation process and are still regarded as 'passive'" (2010: 13).

Gillot describes the general behavior of local populations toward foreign archaeologists as "friendly," characterizing the interaction between foreign archaeologists and local Syrian communities as one that emphasizes personality, not expertise. Enabling those friendly interactions are the same sorts of complex skills and perspectives that local site workers contribute to the archaeological process at Petra and Çatalhöyük; underneath this amiability are the essential processes and interpretations site workers contribute in unseen ways. Syria represents another context in which the economic dynamics of archaeological excavation (1) separate site workers' physical labor from the epistemological process of the archaeological endeavor, (2) instrumentalize site workers in an alienating way, and (3) structure interactions between local communities and archaeologists that are simply affable instead of intellectual and challenging in the way of scientific collaboration.

Egypt, too, represents another link that ties together the archaeological labor dynamics of the MENA region. With Egyptian independence in 1922 came the end of conscripted, or corvée, labor for archaeological excavation but not the end of the hierarchies and tensions this system entailed (Doyon 2014; Reid 2002; Wynn 2008). Today, lower-class individuals are still primarily recruited for archaeological work and paid minimal wages, and as L. L. Wynn (2008: 288) has remarked, their contributions are hardly ever recognized "other than brief expressions of gratitude" in Egyptological field reports and not at all in media accounts of exciting new findings in Egypt.

Wynn's account of the excavation of the pyramid builders' tombs in Giza provides further insight into the attitudes and identities Egyptian laborers are rewarded for presenting. She describes how the Old Kingdom pyramid builders were interpreted and publicized as patriotic participants in constructing the still-standing and iconic monuments of Egypt's glorious past. Wynn argues that such a reading of the builders was used to engender parallel feelings and expressions on the part of modern-day Egyptians regarding their own labor as they worked under similarly restrictive conditions. The narrative pulled from the objects and structures the excavation laborers were uncovering functioned to justify the use of difficult, under-compensated labor by recasting that labor as a nationalistic duty. Here is again a particular sort of working identity that laborers are expected to portray through their bodies and their actions—this time, a patriotic persona, one of a laborer eager to sweat and shovel for the state. It is not their scientific expertise Egyptian excavation workers are encouraged to bear but instead a willingness to labor for the good of the nation.

In highlighting these separate case studies, located across the borders of different countries in the Middle Eastern region, the connections between them become apparent. Where the labor management principles are the same as those inherited from the early days of the archaeological discipline, economic dynamics do not reward site workers for directly offering or advocating for their particular archaeological experience. They are instead paid for performing particular identities antithetical to that of a confident scientific expert prepared to advocate for novel or challenging interpretations of archaeological remains. The labor relations and interpersonal dynamics at play in each of these excavation settings are the outcomes of the historical developments of archaeology, which differ in their specific instantiations at the country, province, and site levels. But they are connected by the shared colonial origins of the discipline that gave rise to the global practice of archaeology. Those origins continue to inform the principles of labor management practices in locations as distant and different as Turkey and Egypt. Those origins also link the archaeology of the Middle East to archaeology around the globe, based on the perpetuation of labor relations dating from the discipline's early days.

INDIA

As in the Middle East, early archaeology research in India was closely tied to colonialism—specifically, the British administration (Chadha 2002; Chakrabarti 1997; Lahiri 2000; Paddayya 2002). The relationships between early archaeological scholars and local Indian communities also evolved along the same lines as the Middle Eastern context, evoking similar themes. In India, too, colonial agents shared a persistent belief that contemporary Indian communities represented a degradation from the glorious civilizations of the ancient past. This is best exemplified in the work of Indologist James Fergusson (1848: 11), who argues that by comparing two artifacts in terms of which is "more perfect," a researcher would be able to tell which is older and by how much. He goes on to state, "It only requires sufficient familiarity with the rate of downward progress to be enabled to use it as a graduated scale by which to measure the time that must have elapsed before the more perfect could have sunk into the more debased specimen. And I fear the characteristic is not less applicable to all the institutions, both moral and political, of the people than to their arts" (1848: 11). This vision of contemporary India as somehow devolved from the ancient past affected historical interpretations as well as the practices that led to those interpretations for more than 100 years.

Early Indologists actively distanced themselves from living Indian communities in their research practices. Sir William Jones, who came to India in 1783 as a magistrate for the East India Company, employed almost exclusively philological methods, delving into historical texts rather than working among material remains and contemporary communities (Johnson-Roehr 2008). Meanwhile, Jones's contemporaries Francis Buchanan and Colin Mackenzie—both employees of the East India Company—began to take local folklore seriously, including what they learned from stories and myths in their survey reports (Guha-Thakurta 2004). These reports, however, were intended to serve as informative documents for the British military (which patronized the archaeological survey expeditions) to aid in controlling the populations of newly acquired territories in India (Dirks 1994).

As in the Middle East, early interactions between foreign archaeological researchers and Indian communities were distanced and fraught, character-ized by power dynamics that reified the broader imperialist policies occur-ring at the same time. Also as in the Middle East, the colonial underpin-nings of the archaeological endeavor persisted through the nineteenth century and continued to structure the relations between foreign researchers and Indian communities. This legacy is evident in the conditions of local labor on Mortimer Wheeler's excavations in India during the mid-twentieth century, when he was serving as director general of the Archaeological Survey of India. Wheeler (1954) famously saw archaeological excavation as a fundamentally military endeavor; bringing the discipline of the military to the research proj-ect led not only to efficiency and scientific precision but also to a very tightly controlled workforce. Photography formed a crucial component of an accu-rate and closely surveilled excavation procedure, according to Wheeler (1954), who used photography extensively in his documentation and publication. A scientific photograph needed a scale, and Wheeler often used people as props in his photographs to illustrate the scale of architectural features.

"It is not coincidental," says Ashish Chadha (2002: 389–390), "that Wheeler never appears as the human epistemic marker in any of the images that were produced during his excavations in India. Invariably it is the nondescript workman/woman, the subaltern, who plays the dual role of the human epis-temic marker and the ethnic marker—an anthropological motif crucial to the visual representation of colonial archaeological projects . . . Wheeler's visual vocabulary borrowed these tropes from the depiction of native workers in the service of the Raj, where they performed the role not of a primitive sym-bol but rather of a tame and adaptive labor force." Once again, the laborers are required to perform inexperience, to perform an identity that makes the archaeological endeavor easier and more efficient. The locally hired laborers in Wheeler's workforce are made to represent not the producers of knowledge but the mute instruments of the research project, akin to any one of the tools archaeologists must manipulate to uncover the past. Their contribution to the archaeological project is physical—bodily and entirely silent. They are included in the production of archaeological knowledge only when they act as an easily positioned and carefully controlled metrical object. This is literal instrumentalization of the laborer (Marx 2012 [1844]), photographed and archived.

The network of places linked together by archaeology's role in constructing a performance of non-knowledge as lucrative extends beyond the Middle Eastern and North African region into South Asia, into twentieth-century India. These are not parallel phenomena; they are not incidental comparisons. The colonial expansion that allowed archaeological expeditions to first begin was global in nature and in intention. The visions of empires with such expansive political reach may have ultimately fallen apart, but archaeology—used to scientifically and materially justifying this vision—persisted, with its labor systems virtually unchanging over these centuries. Laborers in the Middle East and India—hired during the eighteenth century for manual jobs, paid minimal wages, and alienated from the knowledge produced by their labor—continued to work under the same conditions of the global archaeological discipline for centuries. These conditions have systematically rewarded them for performing roles that deny their positions as co-producers of knowledge about the past.

SOUTHERN AFRICA

"The secret history of archaeology in Africa," says Nick Shepherd, "is the history of 'native' labour." He continues (2002: 335):

> In many cases, they were and are skilled practitioners: not Archaeologists, or even "archaeologists" (for such is the politics of naming in the sciences), but something else, field-hands, or assistants, or more usually just "boys" . . . Yet, in the ironised contexts of the construction of archaeological knowledge in the colonies and former colonies (and the essential tenor of this enterprise is that of irony), they are almost never referred to, or are referred to in passing or with contempt.

This makes it extremely difficult to locate the particular contributions African excavation workers have made or the conditions under which they have labored. As Shepherd says, these topics normally go un-discussed. For his part, Shepherd looks for the traces of these local laborers in the photographic archive of John Goodwin, a South African archaeologist who undertook numerous excavations throughout southern Africa in the 1920s and 1930s. He is able to identify a number of consistent assistants and workers across the photographs but cannot determine their names, as the written archive is almost entirely bereft of even anonymous references to the laborers on the site. Shepherd (2002: 340) muses that "when the hand that holds the trowel is black, it is as though holes dig themselves and artefacts are removed, labelled and transported without human agency."

There are a few references to workers from various locations in Africa in letters Goodwin sent to his wife from excavations in Nigeria. He referenced, for instance, Justus Akeredolu, whom Goodwin (1955, quoted in Shepherd 2002: 341) said "has little power to think things out" despite being "an expert woodcarver." Goodwin did not note the dissonance between these remarks in any way. He also described two of "his" laborers as "both very nice men, not very hard workers"—then, when discussing the character of a third worker, Enobi, whom Goodwin found to be quite hardworking, Goodwin (1955, quoted in Shepherd 2002: 342) said he "can only suppose he [Enobi] has escaped justice by coming here." Goodwin's only explanation for a worker who is dedicated to the excavation activity is that he must be a fugitive trying to evade detection.

Shepherd links these contradictions in Goodwin's descriptions of the workers to the underlying fantasy of the colonial (and, later, the apartheid) state in South Africa—one of a landscape void of black Africans but one in which manual labor is still performed, seamlessly and invisibly. This vision is little different from Wheeler's ideal tame and adaptive labor force in India or the friendly local laborers in Syria or the workers in Petra who await direction and interpretations from students and supervisors even when they are experienced enough to determine the best next steps themselves. In all these places, there is a masking, a hiding, an ideal of quiet and unproblematic service to the excavation.

The labor of African site workers continues to go relatively unexamined, even in recent literature rightly celebrating the proliferation of community archaeological initiatives across the African continent (e.g., Muringaniza 1998; Ndoro 2001; Parkington 2006; Taruvinga 2007). Many, however, have been wary of overstating the successes of these projects (e.g., Chirikure and Pwiti 2008; Katsamudanga 2015; Segobye 2005), pointing out that even community archaeologists often continue to view local communities as passive, only consulting community members at times and in ways that suit the archaeological process. Paul Lane (2011), for example, argues that the continued colonial legacy plays out in archaeological practice across sub-Saharan Africa in that recent calls for community engagement set up an unfounded opposition between "scientific" and "indigenous" or "local" knowledges. The impetus to include local perspectives on archaeology essentializes "local knowledge," falsely creating a dichotomy between scientific and indigenous expertise—one that is meant to be informed and clinical, the latter traditional and romanticized.

Lane's words call to mind a woman in Küçükköy, the "daughter of the soil" of Çatalhöyük, a woman saying she is "the same as the Neolithic people." And another woman talking about how she learned to grind grain from her grandparents. And a man describing the sensory experience of living among his sheep, again, "just like the Neolithic people." These are all people with years of experience in the scientific practice of archaeology, highlighting instead their traditional knowledge, evincing that dichotomy Lane is describing, connecting the history of archaeological labor in southern Africa to that of Turkey, of the Middle East more broadly, of the other contexts examined here.

But in southern Africa as elsewhere, the extent and duration of archaeological fieldwork completed has trained local excavation participants to become archaeological experts—that is, they possess scientific skills and insights that could be integral to archaeological knowledge production if recognized and rewarded. Instead, local knowledge is framed as opposite to empirical scientific reasoning in these different locations because the same structural disciplinary developments have occurred across continents contemporaneously. The key scientific contributions of local laborers to the excavation process have been kept "secret," as Shepherd describes it, not simply because of foreign archaeologists' oversight or because archaeologists once behaved in accordance with now outdated disciplinary standards.

Instead, the "secret history of archaeology in Africa" has been kept secret by intentional, rational decision-making on the part of locally hired laborers looking to locate and preserve economic opportunities within the colonial vision of a landscape devoid of their very presence. In this context, deference and dutifulness pay; initiative and independence are costly. Goodwin may have been right about one thing at least: Enobi was likely trying to keep a low profile, just not from his hypothetical jailers. Conspicuousness, after all, is the enemy of lucrative non-knowledge.

Today, black African excavation workers may not have to be silent to be seen as diligent or as contributing to the research process, but stepping into the role of the traditional villager is far from a dramatic restructuring of local community members' contribution to the production of knowledge. If local communities' expertise can no longer be constructed as wholly antiscientific, it is often instead exoticized, essentialized, rendered primitive and Other. It is still not quite seen to be intellectual or analytical. The pervasiveness of this phenomenon across regional contexts points to shared, underlying disciplinary structures, as well as a shared failure to reconfigure the kind(s) of work (in an economic and epistemological sense) entailed in archaeological knowledge production.

LATIN AMERICA

Lucrative non-knowledge is by no means an exclusive Old World or Eastern Hemisphere phenomenon. The colonial origins of archaeology, after all, are not; nor is the conceptual and financial separation of manual and intellectual labor in archaeological fieldwork. Another instance, a vivid image of performing invisibility in the archaeological endeavor, links Mexico's Yucatan Peninsula into the network of workers enacting lucrative non-knowledge. At Chichén Itzá, local Maya residents have been involved in excavating, conserving, reconstructing, and protecting the site since the nineteenth century. Mentions of Mayan workers' personalities and contributions and occasionally their breadth of archaeological knowledge appear in excavation memoirs from the late nineteenth and early twentieth centuries. The Austrian archaeological explorer Teobert Maler (1932) remarked on his impressions of the villagers at nearby Piste, calling the village "sad" and saying that the local residents were lazy, only working when they were entirely out of money. Other contemporaneous descriptions cast workers in the image of the noble savage, remarking on their physical features ("small in build but with strong bodies" [Brunhouse 1971: 209]) and their willingness to work without question or complaint ("They were as efficient, as dependable, and agreeable as any group one could hope to find in any land" [Morris 1931: 9]). Lisa C. Breglia (2006: 104), who has conducted extensive ethnographic research among the contemporary site workers at Chichén Itzá, critiques these characterizations of the local community, through which she says "credit to Maya workers is erased from the projects in which they have reconstructed their cultural patrimony."

This history bears immediate resemblance to the development of archaeology and its relationship with local labor around the world. The comparisons continue into the present, as the archaeological site custodians at Chichén Itzá have handed down their positions from father to son over three generations. Breglia (2005: 386) calls the work of protecting and maintaining Chichén Itzá a "family business" or a "dynastic enterprise"—as is the case in the Middle East and elsewhere. As at other sites around the world, Chichén Itzá "does benefit from such skill and dedication passed from generation to generation" (Breglia 2005: 388).

One rather different aspect of archaeological labor at Chichén Itzá that sets it apart from many of the other global case studies considered is that site workers are aware of the value they add and in fact use it, rather than their local or descendant identity, to motivate their claim to the site. For site custodians at Chichén Itzá, the skill and expertise they contribute to the long-term protection and upkeep of the archaeological site earns them the right to benefit economically from the site—from their perspective, their knowledge rather than their non-knowledge should be lucrative (Breglia 2005, 2006). In fact, arguing this position enabled local site custodians in the 1980s to successfully broker an agreement with the Instituto Nacional de Antropología e Historia (INAH) allowing them to form two tourism cooperatives that control and run souvenir shops and cafés at Chichén Itzá.

The agreement, however, was a compensation the site custodians demanded in return for the bulldozing of their houses when the INAH determined that, in Breglia's (2006: 126) words, "a contemporary Maya scene of rambunctious children, laundry hanging out to dry, and roaming dogs and chickens alongside the monuments was incongruent with the modern representation of [a] tourist destination." Despite the distance between them and their differences, the tie between Chichén Itzá and Petra is tight and strong. In 1985, the United Nations Educational, Scientific, and Cultural Organization (UNESCO) arranged a similar deal for the Bedul Bedouin in return for leaving their homes in the caves and tombs of the archaeological park. UNESCO's aim was the same as INAH's in Chichén Itzá—achieving an aesthetic sort of historical authenticity.

It is unsurprising, then, that at Chichén Itzá as at Petra, the archaeological workers "blend into the infrastructure of the ancient ceremonial centre and international tourism destination" (Breglia 2005: 386). The site workers at Chichén Itzá wear bright uniforms and whistles; ostensibly, they should be highly visible. But instead their job is in many ways to disappear, to fade into the material remains of the past, to act as "docile descendants," to use Breglia's (2006) term. Even with their advocacy for their own expertise, the ideal site workers in this context are invisible and are rewarded for being so.

Mary Leighton's ethnographic work with archaeological laborers in Tiwanaku, Bolivia, complicates the notion of what constitutes invisible labor. As she points out, in reality, the texts and interpretations archaeologists produce are intangible, in contrast to the highly visible mounds of earth and piles of pottery sherds workers' physical efforts produce. "Workers are only invisible," Leighton (2016: 751) argues, "if one already assumes the purpose of the excavation is to generate texts." While this point is significant, it seems that the apparent visibility of the manual labor site workers perform still serves to distract from and obscure the invisible, intellectual, or tacit labor they contribute to the archaeological enterprise. Indeed, Leighton describes an incident in which a leader from the local community asked to replace one of the local workers at the site with another individual. The worker had been placed in charge of supervising the artifact laboratory and processing archaeo-botanical materials—a highly specialized position requiring training and experience—and the proposed replacement had no archaeological experience. The archaeological team would not accept this change because they needed someone for this position who had adequate scientific expertise.

Leighton demonstrates how this incident shows a contradiction of views regarding the purpose of archaeological employment. Archaeologists hire site workers on the basis of their ability to perform visible, physical work and to make intangible intellectual contributions invisibly; local commu-nity members seek employment primarily for economic reasons—to sup-port themselves and their families. Leighton (2016: 744) is right that it is essential to be skeptical of claims that "all indigenous people would prefer to be involved in the interpretive work of archaeology rather than the manual work of excavating a site." I argue, though, that local workers in archaeology are already involved in the interpretive processes of archaeology by virtue of the skills and expertise they bring to all stages of excavation—digging, sifting, flotation, artifact and sample processing, and everything else in the knowledge production process. The challenge is to make these contributions visible and vocal in an effort to create more nuanced and complex under-standings of the past. One key way to do this is to acknowledge the financial appeal of excavation for locally hired laborers and to make their immaterial contributions to the archaeological process as financially viable as their tan-gible contributions.

Otherwise, local community members will continue to protest that even after years of working on archaeological excavations, their work is not part of scientific research, saying they know "nothing about that" (Maldonado 2011: 9). This quote comes from yet another location in Latin America where archaeo-logical labor has been studied and where locally hired workers are rewarded for performing particular non-expert identities: the archaeological site of Currusté in Honduras. Doris Julissa Maldonado interviewed experienced site workers living in the area, who claimed that they did not know anything about archaeology or were not interested in it, regardless of their experience level in terms of years. With a note of frustration, Maldonado (2011: 13–14) says that in her experience working in this region, archaeologists "rarely stop and look up from our clipboards and holes in the ground and think of the people doing the brute labor as more than employees there to perform a job. We train them to do straightforward things . . . and once we are satisfied with their competence, less babysitting is involved."

In response to these observations, Maldonado pioneered the Pilot Program in Participatory Archaeology at Currusté, which created an apprenticeship model for working and learning about the site, easing the division between the identity categories of local laborers and archaeologists. Four local community members who had much more experience served as "master archaeologists" from whom the apprentices would learn on a rotating basis. Maldonado provides ample evidence of the recipients' positive reception to this program and of the novel narratives and ideas participants felt empowered to offer. Maldonado links the success of the program to the collaborative relationships it created—relationships founded on an expectation of mutual benefit. Read through the global network of lucrative identities that locally hired laborers are traditionally paid to perform, her work suggests as well that the reconfiguration of the labor model to an apprenticeship system rather than the stringent militarism that has dominated most of archaeology's history was also critical to the program's ability to engender a more multivocal archaeological record. This is a dramatically different labor paradigm than the one traditionally employed; in the Currusté case, it is the learning and the development of expertise that is being rewarded rather than the movement of soil. Maldonado's Pilot Program made knowledge lucrative.

The same is true of the community mapping initiatives of the Maya Area Cultural Heritage Initiative (MACHI) (McAnany 2016). Patricia A. McAnany (2016: 206) states that archaeologists working in the Maya region "could not become renowned without the productive labor of Indigenous and local guides, excavators, field cooks, cleaners, and launderers. Yet the people often were undervalued and perceived as pale shadows of the renowned and celebrated archaeological culture." In an effort to counteract what it refers to as the "gestation" of colonial dynamics, MACHI instituted a collaborative project in which five Guatemalan communities created digitized maps of types of sites important to them. All elements of this project—the categories of places chosen for mapping, the actual mapping activities, and the purposes to which the maps would be put—were negotiated with the communities involved. As in Maldonado's project, their knowledge was valued and respected. According to McAnany (2016), these community members expressed feelings of ownership over and responsibilities toward the landscapes they documented. This is again nothing like the alienation of identity documented in so many places in the Middle East. It is empowerment through a transformation of the archaeological encounter and a broadening of archaeological knowledge as a result.

A similar process occurred, if less intentionally, at Santarém, Brazil. Denise Maria Cavalcante Gomes (2006) outlines the ways archaeologists on this project benefited from hiring local workers. At first, she describes the situation as extremely fraught. When the archaeological research project initially began, a local political faction filed a report accusing the archaeological researchers of biopiracy, and the excavation had to be halted until the allegations were sorted out. This initially hostile encounter forced the archaeologists to reconsider how they were approaching local community members, and, as Gomes (2006: 152–153) states, it "marked the start of a relationship built on dialogue and based on constant renegotiation, close cooperation, friendship, and reciprocity during three years of working together." By participating in local social activities, holding informational meetings at the community school, and directly addressing the residents' fears of land seizure, the archaeologists gained the trust of the populations that had initially forcefully rejected their work.

Importantly, Gomes recounts that when the excavators taught some of the workers to register notes and draw profiles, they were impressed with the interpretations of settlement patterns these workers developed, and the traditional local knowledge became entwined with the academic research practices employed by the project. As the site workers took on these documentation and analysis roles, the archaeologists, in turn, learned more about the region, identified individuals willing to disseminate information throughout the local community, and received useful advice concerning security concerns and social dynamics.

The cases from Honduras and Brazil illustrate the possibilities for alternative labor models to change not only interpersonal interactions on the archaeological site but also the epistemological processes that occur during an excavation. When local community members are hired for intellectual work—mapping, recording, drawing, drafting, and analyzing artifacts—the knowledge that is created about the archaeological past is made more complex, nuanced, informed, accurate. This is according to the archaeologists who have made these hires, who have begun to dismantle the instantiations of the old colonial divisions of labor, the old ways of doing the business of archaeology. These examples in Latin America provide a snapshot of how archaeological methodology might be transformed enough to undo the legacy of lucrative non-knowledge.

These two examples might be distinct and relatively isolated case studies. But they are structurally linked to other archaeological projects in Central and South America, Africa, South Asia, and the Middle East because these regions share a disciplinary history. Archaeology in all these contexts was built up through a particular kind of native labor—recruited, paid, and treated so as to reward workers for making their contributions invisible. Archaeology in all these contexts is therefore related, linked together. As in any network, these links enable flows of information, ideas, and interventions. Just as the network of archaeological work spread around the globe, relating these places and re-creating itself, with the same ideas around excavation labor reproducing again and again, a transformation in the nature of archaeological work could travel back through the network of the global archaeological discipline. Enough still connects these disciplinary contexts—not just their shared histories but similarities in continued practice and the global nature of academic archaeological discourse—that it is hardly radical to imagine that the expectations and economics of archaeological work could change all around the world. It is unlikely to happen quickly. It is unlikely to happen without resistance. But models exist within the network of global archaeological work for how laborers might be financially rewarded for something other than a performance of ignorance and traditionalism. These models, too, show how vital these changes are for an improved archaeological science.

LABOR MODELS AND ARCHAEOLOGICAL INTERPRETATION

There are labor models in archaeology that do not employ members of the local community—models that lie at the periphery of or beyond the network I have just drawn out. These labor models may not be equitable in terms of whose voices are heard in the analysis, interpretation, documentation, and publication of an archaeological site. Some of these models share similarities with contexts in which local labor is predominantly used. I argue, however, that locally hired archaeological laborers are subject to particular vulnerabilities and are enmeshed in quite specific (and often locally determined) structural dynamics that give rise to the phenomenon of lucrative non-knowledge. Any path forward for redressing this must be designed with full recognition of the economics as well as the expertise of local archaeological labor.

One example of an archaeological labor model that does not employ local community members is that which relies on volunteer, rather tha paid, labor. Volunteers are often recruited as a means of encouraging public appreciation for historical knowledge and archaeological research, with especially notable examples from the United States (Little and Shackel 2007; Nassaney and Levine 2009), the United Kingdom (Brown et al. 2004; Simpson and Williams 2008), and Israel (Abu El-Haj 2001). Critics of this model have pointed out negative impacts on the scientific rigor of excavation (Clarke 1978) and possible ulterior motives to inculcate particular ideologies among volunteers (Abu El-Haj 2001). Other studies suggest that enrolling members of the public in digging does not itself guarantee that these individuals will gain more complex, comprehensive understandings of the past or of archaeology as a discipline (Simpson 2008). Similar to volunteer-based excavations in terms of labor structure are those that rely on student labor, either by running an archaeological field school or by providing opportunities for graduate students to complete research on the recovered materials.

Student and volunteer-supported excavations have some structural similarities to archaeological projects that rely on local labor. In all these models, there is the same distinct hierarchy and concomitant gaps in authority between the designers, directors, and administrators of the project and the people carrying out the physical work. At the same time, however, on student and volunteer-based archaeological excavations, the students and volunteers do expect to receive compensation for their contributions to the archaeological endeavor. Students are provided with instruction and professionalization opportunities in the field they will pursue, and volunteers normally join the archaeological project with some level of interest in archaeology or history and receive the opportunity for tactile, embodied engagement of those interests. These contexts, like those with local labor, can also be exploitative. Still, there is an expectation of some recompense for the contribution professional, student, and volunteer diggers make to an excavation.

Furthermore, what is most important is that this return is not only for the physical digging these excavation participants perform but also for their participation in the documentation efforts of the project. Students and volunteers working around the world generally take measurements and photographs and complete pro forma records. As a result, their observations, perceptions, and ideas are recorded, directly influencing the knowledge that results from the archaeological research endeavor.

The same cannot be said for locally hired laborers on excavations led by foreign project directors. While local site workers have historically been paid to dig, their wages are often surprisingly low—what Curt W. Ceram (1968: 284) called "delightfully modest" in describing the salary of a worker at Nimrud in the Ottoman Empire, on Austen Henry Layard's excavation in the 1840s. Of course, laws, expectations, practices, and enforcement of fair pay for excavation workers vary from country to country and even from site to site, but in general, locally hired laborers do not experience the same sorts of benefits from their excavation work as do students, volunteers, or other types of hired workers. Locally hired site workers, moreover, do not participate directly in documentation efforts on the archaeological site—and perhaps more to the point, they are not paid to vocalize their interpretations or analysis during the archaeological process. As a result, unlike professional excavators, field school students, or interested volunteers, the ideas and observations of site workers recruited from communities living on or near archaeological sites are absent from the body of recorded knowledge that comes from excavations. The way locally hired laborers in particular have been rewarded for not recording their observations and interpretations has an undeniable immediate effect on archaeological knowledge production.

Although these labor structures and the attendant economic dynamics have represented a core part of archaeological practice for more than two centuries, they do not have to remain in place in the decades to come. In chapter 6, I examine the capabilities of diverse and multimedia recording technologies to alter this economic exchange, to adjust the labor economies of the archaeological site so that locally hired laborers' ideas, not just their sweat, are financially rewarded.

6

Inclusive Recording

"I have some advice for the Çatalhöyük project," Hassan
Yaşlı offered, gesturing for me to take my pick from an
overflowing bowl of candy. "There need to be some rules
onsite—some more clear and consistent locations for
workers. It is important to work in the same place."

"Yes," I replied. "I agree." Many of the site workers
I had spoken with had stated that they appreciated
getting to know an excavation area rather than
being moved interchangeably around a project from
day to day.

"And you need mutual trust," Hassan went on. "When
I felt there was mutual trust, I felt that I wanted to do
good work."

"When did you feel especially trusted?" I asked him,
unwrapping the butterscotch I had selected.

He thought for a moment. "In the beginning of the
project," he determined. "When I wrote the labels for
the finds."

Hassan described a period of several years in which
he was given a Sharpie and entrusted with filling out labels that would be slipped into the bags of
recovered faunal bone, obsidian flakes, and ceramic.
This job is often given to students or other trainees on
excavation teams, but writing the numbers correctly
does require knowing a great deal about the current
stratigraphic progress of an excavation since writing them incorrectly means some artifacts will be lost
from the record entirely. Hassan was right: being
asked to fill out the information on these tags was a

DOI: 10.5876/9781646421152.c006

job that encoded an unspoken trust between the supervisor and the person asked to complete it.

More important, perhaps, when Hassan was asked to complete writing these labels as a site worker, that moment transformed the normal economic interaction between archaeologist and locally hired worker. In this moment, he was paid to understand and participate in the intellectual activities of the excavation. His job description as a site worker expanded from physical labor to mental work as well; his tacit contributions to the smooth progress of the excavation and the development of knowledge were made lucrative.

Changing what a person is paid to do will equally transform what they produce and perform. This is true not just in archaeology but in other labor sectors and has specifically been recommended for transforming scientific practice by Stephen Barley and Beth Bechky (1993). In their study of the ways scientific technicians' roles have been devalued since the Industrial Revolution, they argue that reversing this trend requires both economic interventions (i.e., higher wages for science technicians) and a cultural shift. Instituting these changes, according to Barley and Bechky, will not only improve laboratory morale but will also result in improved scientific knowledge by rewarding technicians for contributing intellectually and explicitly to all stages of the knowledge production process.

Following this logic, in archaeological excavation, locally hired laborers must be paid money for offering their intellectual contributions directly and freely. Their explicit job duties need to include the recording, documentation, and analysis of the archaeological site. As Hassan suggested, this is a way to create mutual trust between locally hired workers and the rest of the archaeological team—to engender the cultural shift Barley and Bechky advocated. Changing what site workers are paid to do also restructures the financial calculus of what identities are lucrative to perform within the excavation context by rewarding expertise rather than non-knowledge.

In this chapter, I consider the potential for a number of recording strategies to redefine the economic dynamics of the site workers' role on an archaeological project. While any one of these strategies offers possibilities in this regard, I show how effective photography was in making tangible the particular forms of knowledge site workers possessed at both Petra and Çatalhöyük. I argue that open-ended methodologies such as photography and video are the most promising options for making site workers' visible participation in the production of archaeological knowledge rewarding and for ultimately leading to a more nuanced, inclusive, and complete archaeological record.

THE DEMOCRACY OF PRO FORMA

Standardized recording sheets have been used to some extent on archaeological excavations since the early 1900s, particularly by British archaeologists such as Augustus Pitt Rivers and Flinders Petrie (Pavel 2010). Their use, however, expanded during the 1950s as archaeology itself developed into a professional employment sector. During this time, increasing numbers of field technicians were hired in the United Kingdom and the United States, requiring recording methods that could be completed equally by individuals with varying levels of experience, with minimal supervision (Berggren and Hodder 2003). Standardized data sheets, with pre-defined fields and boxes, were an ideal solution that ensured comparability between records and thorough data collection.

Catalin Pavel (2010: 8) has called the use of pro forma sheets "a democratization of stratigraphy" and praises their potential to "encourage multivocality and safeguard against any monopoly over interpretation." Indeed, the intuitiveness of a well-designed recording sheet, with easily understood questions and multiple-choice answers, allows a broad range of excavation participants to document their observations and interpretations of the archaeological process. Students, volunteers, and visitors can easily select which categories of artifacts were found in a given deposit, measure the length and width of a stratigraphic unit, and check a box to say whether the deposit was sieved. The context sheets, by design, pose questions in a way that enables all team members to offer their ideas about the excavation process and findings, particularly when they are prompted to provide longer, more interpretive and analytical descriptions of a given deposit.

But the ease of use of these forms simultaneously circumscribes the types and range of information that will be recorded. In fact, the simpler the form is to use—the more questions that are made multiple choice, the more instructions that are given on how to answer a question—the less diverse the responses on the form are likely to be. There is a tradeoff: the more structure built into a form to allow less experienced excavation team members to complete it, the less freedom those team members have in the responses they give. As they are directed how to complete the form through its language and material design, excavation participants are increasingly unable to insert interpretations and ideas outside of the questions that are directly included. In addition, the context form works to convey the impression that it is a complete record. It looks thorough and detailed, and it may be—but it is unavoidably incomplete. There are always pertinent questions that won't be asked on a standardized form. The number of data fields on the recording sheet, the way it is designed to fill the page visually, gives the illusion, however, that there are no other possible questions, which further circumscribes the diversity of data elicited by a recording form.

While pro forma expands the range of people who can contribute to the archaeological record, it does little to invite new content into that record, to make room for unusual observations or interpretations. For this reason, standardized recording sheets have little potential to preserve site workers' unique and local perspectives on archaeology, instead asking them to make their ideas and analyses conform to fit a structure predetermined by the archaeological community. If site workers were invited to participate in the pro forma recording on an archaeological site, the effect would be the same as when pro forma initially proliferated in the 1950s; new groups of excavation participants would be doing the recording, but the information would be strictly controlled and standardized.

An additional structural limitation at many sites would prevent locally hired site workers from participating in completing excavation recording sheets. Many local laborers do not speak the language of the excavation team, and many are not literate at all. Certainly, this lack of literacy is true in Petra, where children frequently leave school in third or fourth grade, if not earlier, to earn money in the tourism industry. The adults hired to work on archaeological projects in Petra, therefore, frequently cannot read or write and would be unable to complete a written standardized recording sheet.

Accordingly, despite the affordances of standardized recording sheets that allow newcomers to archaeological excavation to participate in documentation practices, they are not ideal for engaging the unique archaeological perspectives locally hired laborers possess. Any recording strategy designed to include more diverse voices in the creation of the archaeological record cannot rely on literacy to complete it, or it will exclude the particular expertise of many local site workers whose perspectives have already gone unrecognized throughout the history of archaeology in the Middle East. Further, it cannot be so structured that alternative ideas that do not easily or directly respond to prewritten questions have no place. Archaeological excavation, however, routinely involves a number of recording strategies that complement preprinted context sheets in these ways, and a number of them could be opened to locally hired laborers to invite their unique insight into the creation of the archaeological record.

STYLES OF SEEING AND DRAWING

Drawing has been used as a recording strategy in archaeology since the early excavations in the eighteenth century to document architecture, stratigraphic deposits, and special finds and to propose reconstructions. Producing drawings at all stages of the excavation process is a critical component of archaeological epistemology; as drawings are composed, combined, and refined, the archaeological team arrives at new conclusions about a site (see Wickstead 2013). Jens Andresen and Torsten Madsen (1992: 57) call drawing "the most important of our means of documentation" because through drawing, archaeologists record information about the formation and locations of layers and objects not documented by any other means.

Drawing in archaeology, moreover, is a recording strategy with room for creative adaptation. Each individual brings a particular way of seeing and translating to the artistic style with which they complete a drawing. This has, in the past, brought about debate within the archaeological community; Mortimer Wheeler (1954: 59) famously criticized Gerhard Bersu's drawing techniques, calling them "impressionistic" and "nebulous," saying they create a "lack of precision." Although Wheeler determined in 1968 that Bersu's drawing style was "obsolete," Geoff Carver (2010: 117) points out that today there exists "a wide variety—a spectrum—of drawing styles, not just the binary opposition of Wheeler vs. Bersu." These differing styles convey different ways of seeing, different priorities—a schematic scientific view, in the case of Wheeler, or a more artistic but naturalistic expression, like Bersu. Locally hired laborers and others who have been traditionally excluded from archaeological recording could offer innovative, alternative modes of drawing the excavation process that might capture their particular experience and perspective on archaeology.

At the same time, however, nearly every field and recording guide gives particular rules for the appearance of drawings in the field. In *Field Methods in Archaeology*, Thomas R. Hester and colleagues (2009) give recommendations for the type and size of paper on which to produce section and plan drawings, the scale at which they should be drawn, and the data that should be included with the drawings. In Philip Barker's *Techniques of Archaeological Excavation* (1993: 173), he recommends that "all draughtsmen should coordinate and draw in the same style." In fact, Michael Fotiadis (2013: 305) has argued that the "well-defined codes" of technical drawing in archaeology allow it to be seen as a more scientific and reliable mode of recording than photography. Even if archaeological drawing allows for a range of styles and perspectives, it seems that drawing is most recognized as a scientific recording method within the discipline when this diversity is flattened.

This is a barrier, then, to the potential for drawing to engage new and different views on the archaeological process and on the past. Importantly, though, it has been effective before. In 2001, during Denise Maria Cavalcante Gomes's archaeological survey in Amazonia, she hired several individuals from the local Parauá as workers on her field project to draw profiles of the excavated sections. Gomes (2006: 154–155) states, "At this point they started to feel a bit like archaeologists and to suggest interpretations of intrasite distributions, identifying different areas of concentration of archaeological refuse and patterns of settlement that might be represented by the sites observed during the survey."

Inviting workers to participate in drawing engendered a dramatic change in the identities these individuals chose to perform on the archaeological project. They offered analyses of the archaeological record, giving answers to the very questions Gomes's project was designed to investigate. In this case, they were paid not only for their physical labor but also for the intellectual insights they recorded through drawings. This led them to express their expertise in other ways as well and ultimately produced a more nuanced archaeological record of the region forged through competing hypotheses, dialogue, and debate. Any recording strategy that could be equally successful in creating a more inclusive and multivocal view of archaeology needs to share the same flexibility and intellectual character that drawing offers.

EXCAVATION STORYTELLING

Diaries were once a flexible medium for recording. Archaeological diaries from the earliest periods of the discipline record the personal experiences of excavators, interspersing scientific detail with vivid feelings and descriptions of interpersonal relationships (Hodder 1989; Lucas 2001). They feature many of the tropes of travel writing—the sense of adventure, peril, and plight; the humanity of the narrator. But during the mid-twentieth century, as standardized recording forms became increasingly prevalent in archaeological practice, the autobiographical character of archaeological diaries began to fade. As the discipline increasingly emphasized objectivity in recording and comparability across records, diaries became more structured and less emotive (Pavel 2010). Field projects through the 1940s, 1950s, and 1960s established rules for how diaries would be formatted and what they would—and would not—contain. Diaries from this period often require topographic plans, equipment inventories, and lists of pottery baskets. They are designed to be comparable and standardized like pro forma—very much the opposite of an inclusive, dialogic record of the excavation.

More recently, however, many archaeological research projects have begun adopting more flexible diary recording strategies, designed after the archaeological diaries of the eighteenth and nineteenth centuries, in an attempt to capture the moment-by-moment transformations by which assemblages are collected and knowledge is produced (Bender et al. 1997; Berggren 2009; Pavel 2010). The diaries that have been implemented for this purpose are intentionally open-ended, with no templates or detailed instructions, so excavators are inclined to offer emerging hypotheses and observations otherwise excised as tangential or potentially incorrect. They represent a powerful tool for establishing some control over the story one tells about the excavation process. While the diaries kept on most research projects are written, it is easy to imagine how they might be adapted to other languages and media to include locally hired laborers in the diary record.

Regular interviews could be conducted, for instance, with site workers in their own languages and recorded as audio or video. Interviews have formed a key component of collaborative and multivocal work at sites as diverse as the Greenham Common Women's Peace Camp in England (Marshall et al. 2009), Quseir, Egypt (Moser et al. 2002), the Nevada Test Site in the United States (Stoffle et al. 2001), and Currusté, Honduras, where Doris Julissa Maldonado (2011, 49) makes explicit reference to needing to accommodate workers' non-literacy in engaging with their perspectives and values.

Consistent interviews with site workers can be incorporated into the archaeological research process and can transform the site workers' role into an intellectual and scientific one if interviews are not just aimed at gaining insight into potential ethnographic analogies but encourage a more open-ended sort of storytelling that weaves together the excavation procedure, findings, and developing interpretations. In other words, interviews conducted in a way that approximates the life-writing style of the early archaeological diaries. It seems fitting that to remediate the legacy of labor management practices inherited from this era, laborers could engage in the storytelling-based recording systems that originate from that time—like retracing and reshaping the early history of the discipline. At the same time, a number of contemporary tools and technologies may enable locally hired site workers to tell their own stories in new and dynamic ways.

EMERGENT NETWORKS AND TECHNOLOGIES

"The World Wide Web," George P. Landow (2006: 345) states, "provides a particularly important opportunity for the empire to write back."[1] He argues that the internet represents a democratization of power over representation that "permits those in postcolonial countries to represent themselves . . . rather than having critics from Europe, the United Kingdom, and the United States write for them" (2006: 345–346). Indeed, the internet and social media have been touted within archaeology as tools with an enormous potential impact for both sharing archaeological data with broad non-specialist communities and encouraging them to contribute their own ideas and hypotheses (see Bonacchi 2012; Kansa et al. 2011; Morgan and Eve 2012). Andrew Dufton and Stuart Eve (2012), for instance, have demonstrated how archaeologists might use "guerrilla" tactics to subtly embed archaeological information in commonly used commercial social networking platforms such as Foursquare, using central London as their case study. The MicroPasts project is another crowd-based archaeological initiative that invites online users to participate in tasks such as the preparation of photographs for 3D modeling and the transcription of object cards from the British Museum (Bonacchi et al. 2014). Sarah Parcak's TED-funded GlobalXplorer (2017) project takes on, as the title suggests, a global approach to crowdsourcing data in archaeology, asking anyone with an internet connection[2] to become a "space archaeologist," detecting looting of and encroachment on archaeological sites around the world using satellite imagery.

One can imagine applications of social media in the contexts where archaeologists work that make use of local community members' particular expert identities. Many site workers have accounts on Facebook and Instagram; their photos and statuses could be shared and signal-boosted by the research project's social media accounts. The Temple of the Winged Lions Cultural Resource Management initiative, in fact, began experimenting with this; in the spring of 2015, the project started having local team members administer the TWLCRM Facebook page. This has created a multi-year body of stories, updates, and photographs controlled and presented entirely by experienced local team members—one Facebook users from around the world have routinely interacted with since this campaign began (TWLCRM n.d.). While it is essential to be cautious about potential unintended uses of data shared through corporate social media platforms like Facebook, having an online presence is an essential part of any research project that prioritizes public engagement—one that entails another aspect of intellectual labor from which locally hired team members have traditionally been excluded.

Archaeologists today are also experimenting with new tools and equipment that promise to change the recording procedures in excavation. Paperless, mobile recording (e.g., Banning and Hitchings 2015; Fee et al. 2013) pens like the Bamboo Spark that upload strokes directly to the Cloud and increasingly efficient, easy-to-use 3D modeling applications (e.g., Forte et al. 2012; Howland et al. 2014; Remondino and Campana 2014) all have the ability to change both the workflow and content of archaeological recording. As these dynamic and innovative technologies become increasingly prevalent in archaeological work, the extent to which they can be used to engage a broader range of voices in the creation of the archaeological record will need to be a subject of ongoing examination. Angeliki Chrysanthi has led such an investigation of the Looxcie 2, a wearable camcorder mounted over the ear on which the user can push a button to save the last thirty seconds of recording. Experimenting with this device on multiple archaeological sites, Chrysanthi observed that each of the individuals who wore the video cameras chose to record different aspects of the excavation process. Some created a visual record of the deposits they uncovered, some created audio recordings of conversations with supervisors to refer back to later, and some documented "notes to self" so they would recall why they made the decisions they did. Site workers did not participates in this particular study, but Chrysanthi contends that the wearable camcorder led to "a democratisation of the recording process," suggesting that it could be productively extended to enable local laborers to record their particular perspectives on and experiences of the archaeological process (Chrysanthi et al. 2016: 267). As new recording technologies proliferate and fade from archaeological practice, it is precisely this democratizing potential, as well as the possibility of transforming the nature of site workers' labor, that will need to be constantly and critically studied.

These new technologies are expensive, though, at least when they first appear. They are out of reach as inclusive recording strategies for most archaeological project budgets. There remains, however, another standard recording medium of archaeological work not yet discussed—one locally hired laborers used at the Temple of the Winged Lions and at Çatalhöyük to document their diverse expert perspectives on the archaeological process.

PHOTOGRAPHY AS INCLUSIVE RECORDING

Photography has been a crucial component of archaeological research and publication for more than 100 years. It has also served in many contexts outside of archaeology as an emancipatory technology—giving voice to underrepresented groups around the world because of its ability to be used dynamically and creatively—in programs such as Kids with Cameras, Through the Eyes of Children, the Skid Row Photo Club, and Lensational. The low barrier to entry in terms of both cost and difficulty to learn, the capacity to capture nearly limitless views on any given subject, the easy integration into the archaeological process, and the demonstrated potential for photography to contribute to confronting long-standing power dynamics all influenced my decision to experiment with photography as a means for engaging locally hired laborers in the recording stages of archaeological research.

During a two-month season on the contemporary project at the Temple of the Winged Lions in Petra and for the same amount of time at Çatalhöyük, I gave four locally hired site workers at each site a camera[3] and asked them to document their experiences of the project. By the time I began this photography initiative in 2015, I had spent several years getting to know and interviewing these workers, and they were familiar with my goals—namely, that I was interested in the unique forms of expertise and knowledge local archaeological laborers possess compared to those held by the archaeological team.

When I first suggested the recording experiment to the group of site workers at both sites, the reception was positive and enthusiastic. No one had questions about why I wanted to implement this photography initiative; the few questions I received were much more technical in nature. "What happens if we break the camera?" one of the men at Çatalhöyük asked. When I assured him that they would not be held responsible, the group of site workers looked at each other and one asked, "When will we start?" The first day I brought the camera to the Temple of the Winged Lions (TWL) excavation site, one woman who had never operated a camera immediately asked me to show her how to use it. I demonstrated the basic operations and she took a few test snapshots, then circled back to ask how to zoom, how to review her photos, and what the other buttons on the apparatus did. Perhaps the greatest indicator of the enthusiasm for this experiment was the number of photos taken: in total, the site workers at Çatalhöyük took 253 photos and the TWL team members took 519 photos.

Agelah al-Jmeidi was the woman who immediately asked how to operate the camera the day I brought it to the Temple of the Winged Lions. During the eight weeks in which the photography initiative ran, Agelah was by far the most passionate participant. Nearly every day she had the camera, she created a dozen or more images and the other team members started jokingly calling her "Agelah the photographer." She frequently went over the photos she had taken with me, sharing the reasons why she had captured a particular snapshot. When visitors—usually other Bedouin men and women also working inside the park—came to the excavation location for tea and a cigarette, she would show them her photos and inevitably a conversation about the subject of the image would begin.

Most of the photos Agelah took conveyed a coherent theme: by far the majority were of outward views, in all directions, from the Temple of the Winged Lions (figure 6.1).

FIGURE 6.1. *Photos taken by Agelah al-Jmeidi from the Temple of the Winged Lions excavation area, looking outward in all directions.*

These photos represent an inversion of the usual photographs taken by archaeologists. Normally, photographs taken for research purposes are of a site, of a landscape being surveyed, of specific deposits or objects that have been uncovered. But Agelah's photos are taken *from* that site, from the monument, looking outward at the structures, roads, paths, and mountains all around. Rather than an intensive, close view of all the elements that make up an archaeological site under study, Agelah's photos provide a panoramic 360-degree context of everything surrounding the site, everything in its immediate environs but outside the borders that delimit the area under study.

In the course of applying for permits, setting out research questions, laying down an excavation grid, and selecting the squares or trenches that will be excavated, archaeologists delineate boundaries between what is the object of investigation and what is not. The edges and perimeters of the archaeological site, along with the deposits, features, and objects that comprise it, are created by the activities of archaeological research. Recording methods participate in this boundary making. The photographs archaeologists make are meant to show, at varying levels of detail, all aspects and angles specifically of the archaeological site and its components. They are set up to provide a clear view, for instance, of the site under excavation, a single trench in that excavation, a single burial in that trench, or even a single bead in that burial. Agelah's photographs do not wholly undo this delineation and categorization. They do not break down the boundaries between site and off-site. But they do provide insight—or perhaps simply sight—into what is sorted into that category of "off-site."

This viewpoint draws on her dual identity as a Petra native and a participant in archaeological excavation. Her background gives her detailed knowledge of the landscape as an interconnected whole as well as the divisions and distinctions drawn over the course of the archaeological process. Agelah's photos perfectly evince this dual expertise. They fit into categories established by the archaeological research endeavor; they do not challenge the separation between the site under study and its immediate context, but they do look directly and unapologetically at the material not defined as part of the Temple of the Winged Lions excavation area. Her photos give a comprehensive view of the region and the landscape in which this area is embedded, filling in the blank space of what lies just outside the boundaries of the archaeological site without erasing or challenging that boundary. This is not the standard set of photographs archaeologists might take as part of the scientific investigation and documentation of a site, focused as they are on that which is out of scope. Instead, her photographs marry her perception of the landscape as a local inhabitant of it with her position as an archaeological expert.

The body of photography produced by the TWLCRM foreman, Shakir al-Faqeer, represents a radically different class of images in terms of content and style. Nearly all of the pictures he created over the weeks of having the camera onsite were either candid portraits (figure 6.2) or "selfies"—photos people take of themselves (figure 6.3).

As primarily candid photos, Shakir's portraits evince what Walter Benjamin (1980: 202–203) identifies as the most unique and specific power of photography—the fact that despite the extensive aesthetic and creative decision-making undertaken by the photographer, a photograph provides at least a glimpse of realism that resists the careful, intentional planning or posing by its creator:

> All the artistic preparations of the photographer and all the design in the
> positioning of his model to the contrary, the viewer feels an irresistible compul-
> sion to seek the tiny spark of accident, the here and now . . . While it is possible
> to give an account of how people walk, if only in the most inexact way, all the

FIGURE 6.2. *Portraits of individuals created by TWLCRM team member Shakir al-Faqeer*

same we know nothing definite of the positions involved in the fraction of a second when the step is taken. Photography, however, with its time lapses, enlargements, etc. makes such knowledge possible.

Benjamin argues that the camera's speed and capacity for capturing detail are what makes photography such an evocative medium, one that feels as though it provides a glimpse into real, unplanned, authentic moments. Shakir's candid portraits make use of this precise attraction of photography; they are fleeting

FIGURE 6.3. *Selfies created by TWLCRM team member Shakir al-Faqeer*

and wild, often with an imbalance between light and shadow, closely cropped or containing distracting objects jutting into the foreground. His snapshots are not carefully directed or set up in advance; they are instantaneous, spontaneous, and natural—visions of "the positions involved in the fraction of a second" by members of an archaeological research project.

Benjamin goes on to assert that this particular advantage of photography, to document glimpses of unmitigated reality, is especially powerful when applied to portrait photography. Portraiture, he states, moves "out of the realm of esthetic distinctions into that of social functions" (Benjamin 1980: 211). These affordances of portrait photography have been applied by archaeologists in several contexts, for different but overlapping reasons. Dave Webb's collection of photos titled *Diggers* provides gritty, high-contrast, black-and-white portraits of excavators in the field in the United Kingdom that provide emotional insight into the socioeconomic positions these men and women occupy (Bateman 2005; Swain 1997; Witmore 2007). At the Seventh World Archaeological Congress convened in Jordan in 2013, Jesse W. Stephen and Colleen Morgan (2014) undertook the *Faces of Archaeology* project, an assemblage of bright, clear, close-up headshots of the archaeologists and heritage workers attending the conference intended to highlight the diversity of people at the event and in the discipline more broadly. Yannis Hamilakis and colleagues (2009) carried out portrait photography of site workers as a component of their archaeological ethnography project on the Kalaureia Research Programme in Poros, Greece. There is clearly, within archaeology, a recognition of the potential for portrait photography to add something new, unusual, and important to the disciplinary discourse, even though pictures of people are overall lacking in the photographic corpus produced during archaeological excavations (see Bateman 2005; Shanks 1997; Tringham 2010).

The selfie, moreover, as a highly specific form of portraiture, has its own dimensions and perspectives to contribute. Because of its informality, because it requires only basic equipment (usually only a mobile phone), the selfie is democratic, allowing a much broader class of individuals than ever before to make themselves seen, to take control of the representation of their bodies and subjectivities (Senft and Baym 2015; Warfield 2014). In being simultaneously behind and in front of the camera, the selfie taker manages all aspects of how he or she is framed, positioned, lit, feeling, and emoting and, fundamentally, whether a photo will be taken at all. Every time Shakir pressed the button on the camera, turned as it was on himself and usually a less enthusiastic TWLCRM team member, he loudly proclaimed "selfie!" Even though these photos were not expressly taken to be shared on social media, Shakir eagerly categorized them as part of this broader phenomenon, this radical change in the politics of visibility and representation through photography and portraiture.

Shakir's people-centered images depart from both the political dynamics and the aesthetic norms of conventional archaeological photography. They portray different people—more people—as well as more emotion and personality than the pictures taken for scientific recording purposes during an excavation. Importantly, they are also very different in their content and composition from the photos taken by Agelah. The participants in this project used the camera to capture and communicate very distinctive aspects of the excavation process. Each person had an individual view to contribute.

An examination of the photographs created by a third participant in the inclusive photographic recording experiment at the Temple of the Winged Lions provides further compelling evidence for this argument. Ahmad al-Mowasa was uninterested—resistant, even—in using the camera at all. "I don't like to take photos," he told me as we looked at the assortment of photos Agelah had taken on the first day I brought the camera to the excavation. "Sometimes I don't mind taking them of nature and the landscape, but I don't like to take photos of people. I even delete photos of my son. I don't want the memories."

Ahmad's initial indifference, though, only lasted a few days before he found his own use for the camera. During a tea break one morning, he looked across the wadi and noticed a bulldozer driving over the plateau next to the Great Temple. For the first time, he vocalized explicit interest in creating a photograph. When he noticed the bulldozer, he immediately exclaimed "they shouldn't be doing that! There are ruins under there! Take a picture of it!" he directed me.

FIGURE 6.4. *Photos by Ahmad al-Mowasa of a bulldozer at the Great Temple in Petra*

I turned on the camera, zoomed in, and snapped a photo of the bulldozer. When I showed the photo to him, though, he shook his head. The bulldozer wasn't in the right place; the picture didn't show the conservation problem he saw and wanted to document. He took the camera, adjusted the zoom, and waited until the bulldozer was in the position where it was causing potential damage, then he took a series of photos showing the problem that had made him take notice from a distance (figure 6.4).

Ahmad had worked on the excavations at the Great Temple in the 1990s and knew the weak spots around the monument. He was therefore able to see where and how the bulldozer posed a threat to the remains it was driving over in a way I could not. His photographs represent a union between his archaeological experience and his personal dedication to preserving and caring for this landscape. In the weeks after he created these photographs, Ahmad showed them to several people he thought would be interested: our project directors, park rangers, other members of the Bedouin community. They were evidence, a clear illustration of improper management of the archaeological resources, whether through lack of oversight or a lack of knowledge on the part of the bulldozer driver. Ahmad's photos have a clear purpose behind them: to draw attention to and raise awareness of cavalier and potentially destructive handling of Petra's archaeological remains.

Each of the TWLCRM team members exploited the same camera to different ends. The collections of photos each member produced contribute distinct visions of the archaeological process, visions that marry their local knowledge and excavation training, visions that challenge the conventional politics of representation in archaeological photography, but, most of all, fundamentally creative visions that correspond to their personal experiences and interest in archaeology. Each individual curated his or her own distinct genre of archaeological photography during this eight-week experiment, demonstrating the adaptive power of photography and its capacity to evince unique and unusual perspectives even within the same constraints of time, place, and equipment.

The photographs created by the TWLCRM team demonstrate the flexibility of photography as a recording method that can document different information and perspectives. They suggest as well that photographs by local team members will depart meaningfully in both intention and content from the photographs created by archaeological researchers.

At Çatalhöyük, a comparison can be drawn directly between the photography of site workers and that of a scientific excavation team. The photographs created by the Çatalhöyük site workers during the six weeks they passed around the camera can be viewed alongside the massive archive of photos the excavation team has built over twenty years of excavation. This comparison, moreover, must be considered in the context of the question: How well do the perspectives provided by the site workers' photography reflect the unique, specific perception and knowledge of the excavation process they have conveyed through oral history interviews?

In most ways, the expertise expressed by the site workers who have been employed on the excavation at Çatalhöyük overlaps a great deal with that presented by the archaeological researchers in the written site records. In oral history interviews, local laborers at Çatalhöyük tend to recall the same sorts of finds and archaeological research approaches detailed in the written archive from the project. For any recording strategy employed at this site to be truly reflective of the locally hired site workers' perspectives of the excavation, therefore, it should accommodate and reveal this resonance.

Indeed, some of the photos taken by the four excavation workers who participated in the 2015 experiment replicate the content, framing, and composition of photos taken by excavators and the site photographer at Çatalhöyük, Jason Quinlan. There are landscapes, for instance, depicting the North Shelter and the surrounding agricultural plains that have obvious parallels (e.g., figure 6.5). The site workers' photos of pits, buildings, and wall paintings are often taken from the same angles, filling the frame in the same way and containing identical colors (e.g., figure 6.6). Often, even the images they captured of people working—despite depicting different individuals in different places at different times—remake earlier photos in the project's photographic archive (e.g., figures 6.7, 6.8).

A comparison of former and current site workers' memories of the excavation to the written record created by the excavation team has illustrated visually and mathematically the amount of corresponding, shared knowledge between the two groups. With the camera, the four locally hired excavation workers assert their equal insight into the excavation process and the common perspective on the site, its surroundings, the work going on there, and the features being excavated.

FIGURE 6.5. *Very similar photos of the North Shelter. (*Left*): Hüseyin Yaşlı, 2015;* (*right*): *Jason Quinlan, 2010.*

FIGURE 6.6. *Very similarly composed photos of two different buildings in the north area of excavation. (*Left*): Osman Yaşlı, 2015; (*right*): Jason Quinlan, 2006.*

FIGURE 6.7. *Very similar photos of students excavating pits in the Team Poznań Connect (TPC) area. (*Left*): Mevlut Sivas and Lokman Yaşlı, 2015; (*right*): Patrycja Filipowicz, 2013.*

FIGURE 6.8. *Very similar photos of excavators working carefully, shot from overhead. (Left): Mevlut Sivas and Lokman Yaşlı, 2015; (right): D.E., 2006.*

Still, despite the similarities between the written record from the excavation and the oral history recalled by the site workers, site workers' access to expertise has limitations. The site workers at Çatalhöyük have not experienced total integration into all aspects of the excavation; interpretation and analysis was a notable area in which they had less knowledge and experience than the members of the research team. The photographs they created reveal a similar limitation in the degree to which they embody and replicate the photographic perspective of the researchers and the site photographer. One significant and consistent difference in the images created by the site workers versus those made by the research team members is that the former lack many of the hallmarks of scientific photography—the cleaned-up site, careful brushing, moving the tools out of the limits of the frame, the scale, the white board, the north arrow, the right angles and perfect overhead shots (figure 6.9).

The way archaeological photographs are cleansed of people, equipment, and excess dirt has been widely critiqued as a means of making photographs seem like objective, positivist records (Bohrer 2011; Perry 2009; Tringham 2010; Van Dyke 2006). Ironically, all the careful curation of scientific archaeological photos—delicately placing the scale and north arrow, brushing away one's footprints that mar the freshly swept surface—is intended to mask the markings of the people who have worked to make the photographic subject look the way it does. The photograph, thus sanitized, makes the archaeological remains look discovered rather than dug, interpreted, and thoughtfully represented. As Jonathan Bateman (2005: 194) states, "The formalized photograph of an excavated trench excludes the people who made it and the tool with which it was made. It is presented as archaeological reality, unhindered by the means and technology of its production."

FIGURE 6.9. *Photos illustrating the scientific signatures present in the excavation team's photos at Çatalhöyük but absent from the site workers' photos. (*Upper left*): photo of a pit in the TPC area, taken by Zekeriya Sivas in 2015, without a scale or north arrow; (*upper right*): photo of a pit in the South Area, taken by E.A.L in 2004, with a scale and north arrow; (*lower left*): overview photo of the TPC area, taken by Mevlut Sivas and Lokman Yaşlı in 2015, with equipment and bags around the edges; (*lower right*): overview photo of the TPC area, taken by Marta Perlinska in 2014, cleaned up and absent of equipment.*

The photographs made by the site workers at Çatalhöyük provide a counterpoint to that partial view, resulting in a more complete and multidimensional visual record of the archaeological work. Their photos include the debris that inevitably and relentlessly blows into the pits and cracks in the open excavation area, the bags and buckets piled at the edge of the trench, the tops of heads and shoulders of people working in buildings or trenches just beyond. These photographs include the human dimension of the excavation, showing how the archaeological site is transformed into the state in which it appears in the picture, complementing the more conventional visual documentation created especially for a systematic and thorough scientific record and eventual publication.

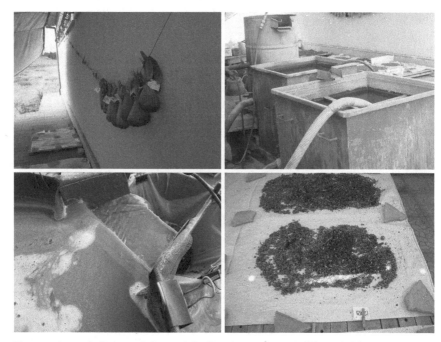

FIGURE 6.10. *Collection of photos of the flotation equipment.* (Upper left): *bags of heavy residue hanging to dry, taken by Zekeriya Sivas;* (upper right): *flotation machine, taken by Hüseyin Yaşlı;* (lower left): *water moving through flotation machine, taken by Zekeriya Sivas;* (lower right): *photo of heavy residue laid out to dry, taken by Zekeriya Sivas.*

There are some subjects as well that the site workers who participated in this experiment photographed not just in a different way but for the first time ever. One consistent category of photos contributed by site workers that is dramatically underrepresented in the project's existing photographic archive includes pictures of equipment alone, with special documentation of the sieve and the stages of the flotation machine (figure 6.10).

These photos represent a direct expression of the exclusive knowledge site workers possess in contradistinction to that of the archaeologists at Çatalhöyük. They provide insight into objects, places, and spaces that site workers predominantly occupy. These images fill out the positions and perspectives represented by the visual documentation of the project. They help to create a record that better, more inclusively encompasses the viewpoints and experiences of all who participate in creating archaeological knowledge at Çatalhöyük.

This emphasis on objects was a broader theme across the pictures taken by the site workers at Çatalhöyük during this period. In many of their photographs, even the ones that prominently feature individuals or groups of people, it is very difficult to confidently assert who or what is the main subject (figure 6.11). Their photos are often ostensibly "of" a person, but that person is so de-centered in the frame, so overshadowed by the objects or archaeological remains filling the space around him or her, so underexposed or overexposed, that calling this person the subject of the photograph feels like missing the point of the picture. On the other hand, the people in these pictures are not captured by accident; their bodies and actions are fully accommodated within the limits of the frame. To say that the photos are really "of" the archaeological contexts that take up the majority of the photograph equally feels like a dismissal of the thoughtful choice to compose the photograph in a way that includes the people in the image and the work they are performing.

Part of the difficulty in discerning the main subject of the photos in figure 6.11 is that they do not fit comfortably within the two firm, segregated conventional categories of archaeological photos discussed by Jonathan Bateman (2005) and Ruth Tringham (2010): the serious photographs of archaeological remains, for purposes of publication; and the more fun, candid, human-centered photographs of people working, smiling, and posing, which are restricted for personal purposes, social media, or the occasional informal PowerPoint. The equipment photos taken by the site workers also do not slot easily into either one of these categories.

This reflects a more abstract but significant contribution to the photographic archive that locally hired laborers are poised to make: the site workers are overall less constricted by the prevailing categories of archaeological photography other research team members tend to re-create because of their disciplinary training as archaeologists. The decision to de-emphasize the person in the frame demonstrates the lack of a need to create a photo for either the academic scientific endeavor or emotional, personal memory making. While many of the site workers' photos stunningly re-create the viewpoints and stances exhibited in the photos previously created at Çatalhöyük, illustrating their knowledge and awareness of how the archaeological team usually takes pictures of the people, places, and things on the excavation, site workers also created photographs that reflect their willingness to step away from the conventions they have observed and build alternative categories of photographic documentation.

The images produced by the four locally hired excavation workers at Çatalhöyük during this trial program reflect well the themes that emerged

FIGURE 6.11. *Four photos showing the de-centering of people that emerged as a theme across the photos created by site workers at Çatalhöyük. (*Upper left*): by Mevlut Sivas and Lokman Yaşlı; (*upper right*): by Mevlut Sivas and Lokman Yaşlı; (*lower left*): by Osman Yaşlı; (*lower right*): by Osman Yaşlı.*

from comparing site workers' oral histories to the excavation archive on this project. On the whole, there is a great deal of overlap and comparability. The site workers expressed their intimate knowledge, expertise, and archaeological professionalism through photography by replicating the photographic perspectives archaeologists at Çatalhöyük conventionally use. But in some ways as well, the site workers departed from the conventions of archaeological photography—their photos include the tools, weeds, footprints, and other marks of human presence and active creation going on at the excavation. They also demonstrate a desire to create new kinds of images, ones that disrupt the expected categories of archaeological photography—pictures of equipment and of people without highlighting or focusing on them. The site workers' experience of the archaeological project is not isometric with that of the archaeological research team members, and the photos speak to this reality, illustrating preponderant similarity but not mimicry or duplication.

As I reviewed the photographs that have been taken at Çatalhöyük, I was struck by the number of photos in the archive of three of the men who participated in this trial. Their physical contributions to the excavation at the site are not invisible; there are posed and candid shots, pictures in which they are smiling, relaxing, and laughing as well as shoveling, straining, and sweating. But it was impossible to get a sense of what these men were experiencing, seeing, learning, or thinking from the photographs. They had not contributed their own documentation to the Çatalhöyük record, despite the investment the project has put into community engagement more generally since its early seasons. On a fundamental level, the site workers' participation in making photos fills a political gap, one of representation, in which they can be looked at but their own views have not been invited or incorporated.

Photography therefore represents a flexible medium for encouraging new and alternative perspectives on the archaeological process, one that corresponds to the nature of expertise site workers possess. It aids in creating a comprehensive, multidimensional vision of the research process, an essential component of building scientific knowledge, while also performing a role in redefining the politics of representation to include locally hired laborers not just as subject matter for photos but also as the creative producers of those photos. The labor relations and the construction of knowledge in archaeology are, after all, intertwined with one another. The promise of any strategy for inclusive recording lies in its effect on them both.

Conclusion

"Look," said Arbayah Juma'a Eid, or, as he introduced himself to me, Spring Friday Christmas. "There's been a lot of work in excavation. We've led it. We know it."

Arbayah's "there" refers specifically to Petra, and his "we" is the Bedouin tribes living near the site, but the sentiment stands for any setting where there has been a lot of archaeological work. Residents of Küçükköy have led a lot of work in excavation, and they know it. The Sherqati villagers from Iraq have led a lot of work in excavation, and they know it. Men from the Qufti community in Egypt have led a lot of work in excavation. They know it.

To some extent, archaeologists have known for some time that these people know it. Since the early nineteenth-century excavations in the Middle East, archaeologists have written about how skillful local laborers are at excavation, at recovering fragile artifacts safely, at knowing where to dig next, and at predicting what will be found. Sir Austen Henry Layard's (1856: 75) famous account of Nineveh and its remains mentions that "a variety of original suggestions and ideas were supplied by my workmen." Fifty years later, William Matthew Flinders Petrie (1904: 22) wrote that "a gang of well-trained men need hardly any direction, especially in cemetery work; and their observations and knowledge should always be listened to, and will often determine matters."

But over the decades of the discipline's development, even as archaeologists penned this praise of site

DOI: 10.5876/9781646421152.c007

154

workers' abilities and expertise, they simultaneously participated in processes and systems that divested those site workers and their communities from benefiting from the archaeological remains or the work done there. In the nineteenth and twentieth centuries, the most beautiful artifacts recovered through excavation and even entire sections of massive monuments were shipped to foreign museums, ultimately directing both tourism revenue and political prestige away from the places from which they were taken. The residents of Middle Eastern nations who had undertaken higher education and training in archaeology were blocked for decades from achieving representation or control over the management of antiquities in these countries by foreign archaeologists representing colonial powers. At the site-specific level, project directors often paid minimal wages to locally hired laborers, whose specific contributions and "original suggestions and ideas" were meanwhile almost never directly expressed or attributed in publications. For the majority of the history of archaeology, locally hired laborers have not received intellectual recognition or significant monetary remuneration for the role they have played in archaeological excavation and knowledge production.

Philip C. Hammond's excavation at the Temple of the Winged Lions, beginning in 1974, took place after more than a century of establishing such dynamics between archaeologists and site workers. Even as the archaeological enterprises led by foreign archaeologists became increasingly distant in time from colonial projects, the devaluation of site workers' contributions remained, and the labor relations sustaining this undervaluing continued to be consistently reproduced. The local labor force on Hammond's project was structured according to the norms and expectations for archaeological projects in the 1970s, which continued to distance locally hired site workers from the material and intellectual products of the archaeological research process. The memories recorded and remembered by all involved in the Hammond excavations evince the overall friction that developed out of this organization of labor. The archaeologists describe frustration with site workers arriving to work late and striking for more pay; in turn, former excavation laborers I spoke with disliked the strict treatment they experienced on the site, saying they were treated like "slaves" or "goats." They criticized as well the way they were ordered outside the trenches whenever the outlines of buried objects were identified in freshly exposed sand. They felt this reflected a lack of trust in their honesty—a feeling that was, in fact, substantiated by conversations with the person who initiated this practice and one that reflects centuries-old anxieties on the part of archaeologists working in the Middle East. Meanwhile, the precarity of the Bedouin workers in Petra was exacerbated by a general lack of other employment opportunities in the area, forcing them to work for minimal wages and under these hostile and unprotected conditions.

Beginning in the late 1980s and into the 1990s, more than a decade after the inception of the original excavation at the Temple of the Winged Lions, a discourse began to crystallize within global archaeology concerning the responsibilities archaeologists have toward the communities that live on and around archaeological sites. An early project to commit to applying the theoretical concepts and practical methods proposed in these expanding discussions on public engagement in archaeology was the renewed excavation at Çatalhöyük led by Ian Hodder starting in 1993. In these excavations, relations between foreign researchers and locally hired laborers took on a different form from the normative organizations on previous archaeological projects in the region. This is clear from the diary entries of archaeologists on the excavation, who gave the names of specific site workers to whom they felt closest or whose extra efforts they most appreciated; they also told stories of warm memories and moments shared with local community members. My conversations with former site workers at Çatalhöyük overwhelmingly described the same sorts of relationships. Site workers reported enjoying learning about the archaeological assemblage from members of the team who reached out to answer their questions and teach them about the excavation. Site workers at Çatalhöyük also had bargaining powers not available to the Bedouin workers in Petra and local workers in many other Middle Eastern contexts by virtue of a stable agricultural industry in the region. They did not have to work in archaeology, so those who did were there because they wanted to be, because they could afford the potential pay cut, and because they had argued for conditions that were amenable to them.

The early excavations at the Temple of the Winged Lions and the later ones at Çatalhöyük are situated in different times and disciplinary moments, and their labor is structured according to different principles and priorities. They serve as two distinct paradigms that can be used to study and understand local labor in archaeology, to look closely at the knowledge and skills site workers are able to possess, and to answer for the first time: What expertise do locally hired laborers who have worked extensively at major archaeological sites in the Middle East develop? How does this expertise compare to the information archaeologists traditionally record? Do community engagement strategies, which are quickly becoming increasingly standard in archaeology, have any effect on this comparison?

The evidence presented here demonstrates that locally hired archaeological laborers, working in different places and at different times, do possess undeniable archaeological expertise. It also illustrates that community engagement strategies, to the extent that they transform the relationships between excavation team members, do have an impact on the archaeological expertise locally hired laborers possess. Specifically, prioritizing community outreach in the vein of the Çatalhöyük Research Project encourages an alignment between locally hired workers' knowledge of archaeological finds and methods and that of the foreign researchers. The positive relationships described by both of these groups are indicative not simply of a happy work environment but also of a fluid and dialogic epistemological process—at least compared to the 1974–2005 Temple of the Winged Lions excavation. The locally hired laborers who worked on this project recalled information unlike that recorded by the excavation supervisors who kept the field notebooks documenting the excavation findings. But this, too, is expertise. The site workers' recollections and shared oral histories form a complementary archive to the excavation documentation, which is as informative, partial, and flawed as any data set.

As I heard and quantified these differences between the two archaeological sites, I found myself asking which of the models more correctly constitutes "expertise." Is it better for the locally hired workers to function as a microcosm of the overall excavation team, possessing the same range of skills and having the same recollections of the archaeological assemblage as what is recorded in the multimedia archive? Or is it a clearer representation of expertise to show that archaeological workers know something additional to and different from what archaeologists are already recording? The former is perhaps more effective at convincing an audience of archaeologists that what Arbayah Juma'a Eid said is true—site workers "know" archaeology in ways that are familiar and impressive and likely surprising. But the case for why disciplinary practice should be transformed to accommodate site workers' expertise is harder to make if they are likely to repeat the information collected by archaeologists themselves. If locally hired site workers know new information about archaeological objects and excavation strategies used, then it is easier to show why they should be more active participants in all (analytical and manual) aspects of the excavation process. But I anticipated that it would be harder to make this different array of knowledge and skills legible as expertise—particularly given the site workers' accounts of their previous difficulties with making their contributions apparent to archaeologists in ways they wouldn't be punished for.

The truth is that both of these forms of expertise are essential to the scientific process of archaeology. Science aims at consensus building, which requires the agreement of more and more experts who understand the questions being asked and how they might be answered. Some locally hired site workers' ability to lend further support and confirmation to the conclusions generated through the fieldwork process has an unmistakably vital role to play in that process. Science, at the same time, thrives on the formulation of new hypotheses, new strategies for evaluating these hypotheses, new sources of evidence, and new ways of studying this evidence. The expertise of other locally hired site workers that diverges from the expertise of the foreign archaeological team is crucial in this generative character of the knowledge production process.

In any case, my conversations with site workers at both sites have shown that while community engagement strategies like those at Çatalhöyük have shaped the nature of the scientific knowledge locally hired site workers possess, they have not dramatically expanded site workers' opportunities to contribute that knowledge. The site workers at Çatalhöyük, like those in Petra, knew relatively little about the analysis and interpretation that could be performed at the site and had very few stories about participating in these processes themselves. Instead, they saw their main contributions to the archaeological research projects in terms of the ways they could act as proxy Neolithic subjects, reliving the foodways and lifestyles of the ancient inhabitants of the archaeological site. They disavowed, on the other hand, the advanced scientific knowledge they simultaneously revealed. They would in the same breath describe the technical engineering of the flotation, then emphasize their lack of desire to know anything about archaeology and shift the conversation to how they live with their herds of sheep just like Neolithic people did.

What disturbed me, as I built relationships with site workers in both of these locations and heard such different stories about the ways the two projects ran, was that the former Temple of the Winged Lions site workers did the same thing. They would tell me all about how Nabataean fineware was produced or how to tell the difference between destruction layers in Petra, then affirm that I was the archaeologist, I was the one with expertise, and they were just "simple Bedouin."

At both sites, regardless of whether community engagement was an ideological value of the project director, this performance of a lack of knowledge literally paid financially. At Çatalhöyük, it meant being cast in one of the many documentary films produced at the site over the twenty-five years of excavation there or being hired to participate in ethnoarchaeological and experimental archaeology projects. In Petra, it meant not being fired or being re-hired the subsequent field season or getting a word-of mouth recommendation between archaeologists, thereby increasing one's likelihood of finding further archaeological employment. I call this cross-site phenomenon "lucrative non-knowledge" to point to the ways site workers behave consistently and rationally, across different sites and different moments in the discipline's history, to maximize the financial benefit they can gain from archaeology. This pay, of course, is almost always low; archaeology around the world is hardly an objectively lucrative employment sector. But it may be steady or better than the alternative. And the frequent precarity of working on an archaeological site increases the necessity of maximizing one's opportunity for payment, even if it means exaggerating one's ignorance about archaeology in spite of years or decades of archaeological experience. In fact, in Petra, it is hard to imagine any of the men I got to know over the course of this project (except for two, who were hired as foremen) having been able to enjoy decades of archaeological work experience without downplaying the knowledge and skills they had mastered. Hence: lucrative. Hence: non-knowledge.

Lucrative non-knowledge is inculcated by a specific set of structural conditions—ones with roots in the deep origins of archaeology. It comes about through the implementation of labor management strategies that were initially developed when the discipline was closely married to a colonial interest in territorial expansion, when archaeology served to bolster fantasies of landscapes devoid of native inhabitants, and when the manual labor of archaeology was conceived as separable from the analytical or intellectual work of archaeological excavation. This is why community outreach values cannot disrupt the propagation of lucrative non-knowledge among locally hired workers in archaeology. And this is why lucrative non-knowledge continues to operate across the Middle East, in India, in southern Africa, and in Central and South America.

But these structures were built up in a particular historical context. The expectations of locally hired laborers and the models by which they are paid, hired, and fired are not natural or inevitable. Recent projects, especially in Honduras and Belize, show that these structural knowledge production dynamics are not unshakable. The continued interconnections within the practice of archaeology across these geographically disparate contexts may allow for the shifts at one site to affect others, to share ways archaeological labor conditions that have persisted for so long as to seem endemic to the discipline might be dismantled and rebuilt.

So how did archaeologists get here, and how do we get out? How do we dismantle the foundations of these labor management systems? To answer these questions, I refer once again to Petrie, who illustrates archaeology's internal dissonance about whether site workers do or do not perform vital, expert roles in the production of archaeological knowledge. Petrie (1904: 22, emphasis added), despite pronouncing that "a gang of well-trained men need hardly any direction," went on to specify a caveat: "the freshman from England is their inferior in everything *except in recording.*"

This is where a radical change can be made, something that might shift the politics and labor relations of the archaeological process so that site workers' expertise can be recognized, valued, and even incorporated directly into the knowledge production process. The division Petrie describes between well-trained workers offering their observations and being heard versus their participation in recording is precisely the crystallized belief system underpinning the economic dimensions of the labor structures at the Temple of the Winged Lions, at Çatalhöyük, at archaeological sites throughout the Middle East and around the world. If this expectation—that site workers cannot record—is undone in archaeology, then it will be difficult to see them as unskilled workers or as solely manual laborers or as simple traditional villagers. More to the point, it will be difficult to pay them to be unskilled or unknowledgeable.

I argue that flexible and creative media like drawing, storytelling, video recording, and photography represent inclusive recording strategies that can accommodate the unique subjectivities and stances site workers possess on archaeological sites. I have demonstrated how adaptable photography in particular is to diverse individual viewpoints and how well it reflects the same relationships that exist between the expertise of the archaeological team and that of local laborers. Multimedia recording methods have the potential to represent the real, specific knowledge and viewpoints site workers enjoy on the archaeological process. They perform the work of dissociating site workers from the defined, singular categories of equipment that circumscribe and instrumentalize their role in the archaeological process. Involving locally-hired laborers in recording broadens the range of labor for which site workers are hired, making not only physical labor lucrative but also intellectual participation in the production of knowledge.

What is more, those who participated in the photographic experiment were happy to contribute to the archaeological endeavor in this way. They embraced the transformation of their work into being both physical and mental. At the same time, though, these experiments took place on projects on which site workers had either bargained for their wages or where the project was committed to paying benefits to those who worked for an extended amount of time (incidentally, the same people who participated in the photography initiative). I do not want to mischaracterize this call for a transformation in archaeological labor management systems as a swell from the grassroots, as if site workers all around the world are demanding Canon point-and-shoots so they can lead an archaeological revolution. By far the majority of the site workers I spoke to expressed a desire to be paid more, to be paid steadily, to earn benefits, and to enjoy protection from the hazards of archaeological excavation. These are essential economic changes that represent half of the way archaeological labor management must be transformed to foster the free exchange of expertise rather than making non-knowledge lucrative.

But site workers also expressed their frustration with being excluded from the analytical and interpretive aspects of the archaeological project. They may be practicing lucrative non-knowledge because it is the best way of maximizing their financial benefit from an industry where such benefit is limited, but that doesn't mean it is what they want. More significant, a science in which some of the most experienced researchers are so disincentivized from sharing their expertise that they refuse to speak is bad science. Such a system eliminates the multivocality that is critical to knowledge accommodating all viewpoints. Such a system also takes away these groups' motivation and opportunity to be represented and heard as facts about the past are formulated. Substantive changes are needed in the arrangement of the archaeological process so the denial of one's expertise is no longer the best, most attractive, most financially rewarding option. Wages and protections for workers need to be increased. Workers must be consulted on the aspects of research design that affect their employment conditions; they are, after all, very frequently experts in how to make excavation more efficient and safer, having learned from past experiences. These forms of financial empowerment need to be aligned with a dramatic shift in the qualitative nature of the job for which archaeological site workers are hired, one that includes recording and other intellectual production activities. Archaeological site workers, in the Middle East and around the world, require fair pay for the entwined physical and intellectual work they contribute to the production of archaeological knowledge. Otherwise, archaeologists lose. We inevitably miss out on important insights regarding the archaeological evidence site workers have seen, handled, and discussed—insight that could lend further solidity to conclusions already being created about the past as well as insight that could transform these conclusions. If this kind of insight is not recorded in the context of the archaeological project, it may never be recorded at all.

On my last day in Petra, I went to lunch at my favorite restaurant. I stationed myself at my regular table by the window, working on my computer, appreciating the fast wi-fi and homemade flatbread. I had spoken with the owner, Sami, many times; he knew my go-to order and gave me a discount at every visit. There was no better place to go before moving my bags out of the house and driving north to Amman, to the airport and beyond.

"So what is your project about, exactly?" Sami asked as he delivered plates of muttabal, fattoush, and hummus to my table. I had told him before that I was researching the history of archaeological excavation in Petra, but for the first time I explained the details of my project. I said I was interested in talking to the people who had worked with Philip Hammond at the Temple of the Winged Lions, that I wanted to know what they remembered and felt about working on this project because I was interested in the expertise site workers gain from participating in excavation.

"Oh," he replied casually. "That's a very interesting project." Bending slightly to place a bowl of yellow lentil soup at my place, he went on. "You know, I worked for Hammond."

After three years of seeking out people who had worked on this project—using vague references in archives, extended kin networks and word of mouth, educated guesses about who in the local community had partici-pated in the greatest number of excavations, searching for specific individuals using only a first name, often to find they had not actually worked on the project—most of my leads had run dry. Plenty of people had moved away or passed away. I knew I hadn't found every single person who had worked at the Temple of the Winged Lions; I was reasonably certain I hadn't even spoken with all the people still living in the Petra area who had worked on this project. This person, though, was someone I considered a friend. I talked to Sami at least once a week. Yet the very topic I spent hours discussing with others each day had never come up in our conversations.

My last interview in Petra was over the phone with Sami, the day I went to the airport. It turned out that he had only worked on the project briefly. He mentioned some special artifacts and described as well what he learned about the various types of pottery archaeologists find in Petra. We spoke for nearly an hour and I closed, as usual, by inviting any questions he had about my proj-ect. The interview format was familiar by then, and this one in particular was easy since I was talking to someone with whom I had become friends. It felt like a tidy narrative coda, to end my years of research in Petra by discovering that someone I had seen nearly every day during the fourteen months I lived there belonged on my quite specific list of oral history interviewees.

When I hung up after talking with him, though, my dominant feeling was one of irresolution. For some reason, Sami hadn't thought, in the years I had known him, that I would want to hear about his own archaeological expe-rience. Even if he hadn't known that I was researching the project he had worked for, he didn't think it was worth even mentioning to me because he was simply a "goofah boy" (again, that identification of human as equipment).

But he had seen and learned things on the archaeological project—even as a pre-teen carrying goofahs—that should have been recorded in the archaeological record. He should have been credited in that record and especially in publications. Fundamentally, the labor conditions should have been such that Sami could inscribe the observations he made and the ideas he came up with in the archaeological record. He should have been paid for this aspect of the job, too, so there was no doubt in his mind that he had contributed to the project.

My conversation with Sami was friendly. He was not demanding massive structural economic changes in the archaeological industry as some others have and as I advocate for. This, though, only furthered my sense of irresolution. Sami had no qualms about sharing what he knew and could remember about the archaeological project he had worked on more than twenty years prior. No one, simply, had ever asked him. The things he knew and had seen would slip away from the archaeological record and out of reach from a discipline that emphasizes the importance of thorough recording and the unrepeatable nature of archaeological excavation. His memories now are out of context—memories regarding a discipline in which provenance is of the utmost importance. If he hadn't made his happenstance remark about working for Hammond or if I hadn't gone to his restaurant for my last lunch in Petra, I would never have recorded his memories. This after more than a year of searching for people exactly like him.

After interviewing Sami, I could only think at first of how many other people I had never spoken to whose knowledge and observations would never be added to the body of knowledge about the Temple of the Winged Lions or about Nabataean life in Petra. But I started to visualize how expansive the network of archaeological practice is, how global the disciplinary history is, how similarly fieldwork is structured around the world. Sami's memories of his two summers as a goofah boy at this one archaeological site in southern Jordan might be a loss the discipline is willing to accept, but the scale of the loss of information about archaeological sites anywhere locally hired laborers are reward exclusively for their physical labor is immense.

By continuing to re-create entrenched systems of archaeological labor management, archaeologists as producers of knowledge deny contributions from experts whose observations, perceptions, hypotheses, and ideas have the potential to transform our understanding of the past. Instead, if archaeologists can involve local community members in inclusive multimedia documentation strategies, the work and labor structures of the archaeology excavation can be disrupted and changed so local laborers' expertise, instead of their performances of non-knowledge, can become economically valuable. Site workers' expertise adds novel understandings of archaeological assemblages, excavation procedures, and the past. They must be paid to contribute these diverse, informed perspectives because there's been a lot of work in excavation, and they've led it. They know it.

INTRODUCTION

1. Although evidence suggests that the city and the region were occupied continuously from Paleolithic times until the present (Bienert and Gebel 2004; Gebel 2003; Kirkbride 1968; Knodell et al. 2017; Mickel and Knodell 2015).

2. Like Petra, however, archaeological evidence exists of the use of the site by later communities and cultural groups (Cottica et al. 2012; Moore 2014; Moore and Gamble 2015).

3. 1 JD was equal to $3.15USD in 1975 (Department of the Treasury 1975: 2).

4. During Ramadan, many Muslims fast during the daytime. For the workers at Çatalhöyük, this made it impossible or difficult to work, so they arranged to have reduced work hours, work replacements, or increased salaries if they were to choose not to fast and to work instead. Bayram, called Eid al-Adha in Arabic, is a days-long holiday where families come together to celebrate the end of Ramadan. Workers at Çatalhöyük negotiated each year for how many vacation days they had to celebrate Bayram.

5. I speak Arabic and conducted these interviews with only a research assistant who made the necessary introductions. The community at Çatalhöyük speaks a very local and specific dialect of Turkish, so I had an interpreter there to help me ask questions and understand interviewees' responses. The conversation extracts presented in this book are a mixture of my own translations from Arabic, translations by a Turkish interpreter, and direct transcription of English-language interviews, which accounts for the dissimilarity in grammar and syntax across interview transcriptions.

CHAPTER 1: LOCAL COMMUNITIES, LABOR, AND LABORATORIES

1. In the last few years, the Turkish government has reversed this historical trend and cut down dramatically on the number of excavation permits issued to foreign archaeologists (Erbil 2016). It has also instituted the 51 percent rule, in which more than half of the members of any excavation team must be Turkish nationals. These policies are likely to have major ramifications for the themes discussed in this book but also serve to further illustrate the entanglement of archaeology with politics and nationalism.

2. Even though this word literally translates to "sharing," it reflects a practice that historically tended to benefit foreign countries rather than the host nations of archaeological research. See Abdi (2001); Goode (2007); Kersel (2015); Majd (2003).

3. With the notable exception of Dorothy Garrod, who employed large teams of Palestinian women for at least some work normally done by men (Smith et al. 1997).

4. Although see Tansey (2008: 91), who locates a shift in British medical research after World War II, where technicians increasingly began "to work with (rather than for) scientists, to get their contributions explicitly acknowledged, and to benefit from day-release and other training courses."

5. Knorr Cetina's (1999) landmark laboratory study offered the concept of "epistemic cultures," the range of object relations, social behaviors, norms, and historical developments that determine what serves as fact or expertise in a given scientific research context. See also Gilbert and Mulkay (1984: 40), who emphasize "the existence of different social contexts in science" to show that scientists make highly selective and particular decisions about how to interpret evidence.

6. An Arabic dish made with beans.

CHAPTER 2: SITE WORKERS AS SPECIALISTS, SITE WORKERS AS SUPPORTERS

1. This conversation was in English, which was Nawaf's choice, but almost all interviews in Petra were conducted in Arabic by me. In Petra, I often had a research assistant but not an interpreter. The TWLCRM project appointed this research assistant, Eman Abdessalam, who grew up in Petra, to help me locate people once we had learned that they worked with Hammond. After she introduced me as her colleague to an individual we had identified, I conducted the interviews myself, mostly in Arabic but sometimes in English, depending on the interviewee's preference.

2. With the permission of the individuals mentioned here, most names have not been changed, as one of the central goals of this project is to credit site workers for the expertise they contribute to the archaeological record.

3. Dushara is actually another principal god of the Nabataeans but is often used generically by members of the local community to refer to any deity in the Nabatean pantheon, as well as to this specific artifact.

4. Stored at the American Center of Oriental Research in Amman, Jordan, along with the photographic records from Hammond's excavation. Because I could not obtain permission from them, the names of the participants in Hammond's project responsible for creating this archival record have been changed here.

5. Quotes from the AEP site notebooks are reprinted courtesy of the American Center of Oriental Research, but the names of the notebook authors have been changed and page numbers cannot be given, as this might identify the authors. The site notebook authors—some of whom are still active in the field—did not give informed consent to be quoted in this project. Furthermore, my goal is to illustrate normative practices in labor management and knowledge production, not to indict particular individuals.

6. Rubber buckets used for moving soil in excavations in Jordan.

7. The house inside the Petra Archaeological Park used as the headquarters for Hammond's excavation for several years.

8. In Turkey, all interviews were entirely in Turkish, which I speak but in which I am not fluent. To thoroughly understand the nuances of the local dialect spoken by those who live near Çatalhöyük, I had interpreters helping me not only to meet interviewees but also to translate all the questions and answers. These interpreters—Numan Arslan, Cansu Kurt, Duygu Ertemin, and Tunç İlada—were fellow members of the Çatalhöyük Research Project who volunteered to help me with this translation. The conversation extracts presented in this book are a mixture of my own translations from Arabic, translations by a Turkish interpreter, and direct transcription of English-language interviews, which accounts for the dissimilarity in the grammar and syntax across interview transcriptions.

9. Burcu Tung, an archaeologist involved in the Çatalhöyük project from 2012 on, who became the co-field director of the project.

10. Referring to Mirjana Stevanović and Ruth Tringham, who directed the University of California, Berkeley excavations at Çatalhöyük.

11. These diaries are visible to the rest of the excavation team during the field season and are published online at the end of each season. They are available for browsing at http://www.catalhoyuk.com/database/catal/diarybrowse.asp.

12. Most of this massive archive is available online, hosted on the Çatalhöyük project website, www.catalhoyuk.com. Accordingly, the names of the Çatalhöyük team members that appear here are unchanged from those on the website, in association with the records I am studying.

13. Mathematically, it is the fraction of edges that fall within the groups of the graph when it is partitioned minus the fraction of edges that we would expect to

fall within these groups if the links were distributed randomly throughout the graph (Newman 2006). Modularity can fall anywhere from -0.5 to 1, with higher, positive values indicating that the division of the graph sorts the network into measurable and inherent community sub-structures.

14. At 0.128, calculated according to the algorithm presented by Blondel and colleagues (2008), given a resolution of 0.85, using edge weights, randomized.

15. It has also been given the identification number 22130.H1.

16. The lack of employment opportunities for women at Çatalhöyük meant that hiring women on the excavation challenged social norms and cultural expectations, leading to tensions and rifts with the community in the early years of the project (see Hodder 2000).

CHAPTER 3: ACCESS TO INTERPRETATION

1. A stewed tomato dish, literally translated to "frying pan of tomatoes"

2. Even though Cansu is Turkish and might therefore be able to debate this woman's idea without necessarily embodying the problematic foreign versus local dynamic I am critiquing, I maintain still that for Cansu to simply deny the site worker's hypothesis out of hand would contradict the tenets of multivocality the Çatalhöyük Research Project prioritizes. The expression of multivocality necessitates encouraging a diversity of viewpoints and, most essentially, fostering direct dialogue *between* those viewpoints so that those who hold differing ideas respond to one another (Joyce 2002). On the issue of whether archaeologists and researchers who are citizens of countries that have traditionally experienced colonialism and oppression from foreign nations can in turn disenfranchise local communities in their own countries, Randall H. McGuire (2008) discusses the idea of "double colonialism." In the Mexican context he examines, there is a colonial archaeological program of Americans working in Latin America but a second colonialism of middle-class Americans *and* Mexicans studying marginalized indigenous peoples. It is precisely for this reason that my analysis here focuses on how locally hired laborers respond to each others' theories that are impossible to correlate with the archaeological evidence. Site workers occupy a unique position in the system of inequality created through the long-standing systems of archaeological labor management, one that cannot be rectified only by yielding interpretive authority to other scientists from the country in which research is being conducted.

CHAPTER 4: LUCRATIVE NON-KNOWLEDGE

1. The amount of this salary depended on the work one did and changed each year. It was determined in negotiation with the site workers.

2. A sitting room, used especially to welcome guests.

CHAPTER 6: INCLUSIVE RECORDING

1. This publication was an update of a 1992 text in which Landow initially made these claims at the height of optimism around the internet's democratic potential. While skepticism regarding these possibilities has increased, 2006 also represents the year that Facebook, after having been available to college and high school students for two years, became open to anyone with a valid email address. New forms of social connection still seemed possible at this point in time, twelve years before Mark Zuckerberg would be brought to testify before the US Congress about issues of user privacy and national security.

2. This is, of course, not everyone; but when 84 percent of the world had access to a mobile broadband connection as of 2016 (International Telecommunications Union 2016), I argue that this is an example of scientific practice that is more democratic than what has been practiced traditionally.

3. At the Temple of the Winged Lions project in Petra, we used a Canon Powershot A1400; in Çatalhöyük, we used a Nikon Coolpix P2. These models were chosen because they were easy to use, relatively inexpensive, and easily available point-and-shoot cameras.

References

Abdi, Kamyar. 2001. "Nationalism, Politics, and the Development of Archaeology in Iran." *American Journal of Archaeology* 105 (1): 51–76.

Abdi, Kamyar. 2008. "From Pan-Arabism to Saddam Hussein's Cult of Personality: Ancient Mesopotamia and Iraqi National Ideology." *Journal of Social Archaeology* 8 (1): 3–36.

Abu El-Haj, Nadia. 2001. *Facts on the Ground: Archaeological Practice and Territorial Self-Fashioning in Israeli Society.* Chicago: University of Chicago Press.

Albright, William Foxwell. 1954. *The Archaeology of Palestine.* 3rd ed. Melbourne: Penguin Books.

Alhasanat, Sami. 2010. "Sociocultural Impacts of Tourism on the Local Community at Petra, Jordan." *European Journal of Scientific Research* 44 (3): 374–386.

Andresen, Jens, and Torsten Madsen. 1992. "Data Structures for Excavation Recording: A Case of Complex Information Management." In *Sites and Monuments: National Archaeological Records*, edited by Carsten U. Larsen, 49–67. Copenhagen: National Museum of Denmark.

Ansari, Ali M., 2012. *The Politics of Nationalism in Modern Iran.* Cambridge: Cambridge University Press.

Asouti, Eleni, Aylan Erkal, Andy Fairbairn, Christine Hastorf, Amanda Kennedy, Julie Near, and Arlene Miller Rosen. 1999. *Archaeobotany and Related Plant Studies.* Çatalhöyük 1999 Archive Report. http://www.catalhoyuk .com:8080/archive_reports/1999/ar99_07.html.

DOI: 10.5876/9781646421152.c008

Atakuman, Çiğdem. 2008. "Cradle or Crucible: Anatolia and Archaeology in the Early Years of the Turkish Republic (1923–1938)." *Journal of Social Archaeology* 8 (2): 214–235.

Atalay, Sonya. 2010. " 'We Don't Talk about Çatalhöyük, We Live It': Sustainable Archaeological Practice through Community-Based Participatory Research." *World Archaeology* 42 (3): 418–429.

Atalay, Sonya. 2012. *Community-Based Archaeology: Research with, by, and for Indigenous and Local Communities.* Berkeley: University of California Press.

Bahrani, Zainab. 1998. "Conjuring Mesopotamia: Imaginative Geography and a World Past." In *Archaeology under Fire: Nationalism, Politics, and Heritage in the Eastern Mediterranean and Middle East*, edited by Lynn Meskell, 159–174. London: Routledge.

Banning, Edward B., and Philip Hitchings. 2015. "Digital Archaeological Survey: Using iPads in Archaeological Survey in Wadi Quseiba, Northern Jordan." *SAA Archaeological Record* 15 (4): 31–36.

Baram, Uzi, and Yorke M. Rowan. 2004. "Archaeology after Nationalism: Globalization and the Consumption of the Past." In *Marketing Heritage: Archaeology and the Consumption of the Past*, edited by Yorke M. Rowan and Uzi Baram, 3–23. Walnut Creek, CA: Altamira.

Barker, Philip. 1993. *Techniques of Archaeological Excavation.* 3rd ed. London: B. T. Batsford Ltd.

Barley, Stephen, and Beth Bechky. 1993. *In the Back Rooms of Science: The Work of Technicians in Science Labs.* Philadelphia: National Center for Educational Quality in the Workforce.

Bartu, Ayfer. 2000. "Where Is Çatalhöyük? Multiple Sites in the Construction of an Archaeological Site." In *Towards Reflexive Method in Archaeology: The Example at Çatalhöyük*, edited by Ian Hodder, 101–110. Cambridge: McDonald Institute for Archaeological Research.

Bateman, Jonathan. 2005. "Wearing Juninho's Shirt: Record and Negotiation." In *Excavation Photographs in Envisioning the Past: Archaeology and the Image*, edited by Sam Smiles and Stephanie Moser, 192–203. Malden, MA: Blackwell.

Beckers, Brian, and Brigitta Schütt. 2013. "The Chronology of Ancient Agricultural Terraces in the Environs of Petra." In *Men on the Rocks: The Formation of Nabataean Petra*, edited by Stephan G. Schmid and Michel Mouton, 313–322. Berlin: Logos Verlag.

Ben-Yehuda, Nachman. 2002. *Sacrificing Truth: Archaeology and the Myth of Masada.* Amherst, MA: Humanity Books.

Bender, Barbara, Sue Hamilton, and Christopher Tilley. 1997. "Leskernick: Stone Worlds, Alternative Narratives, Nested Landscapes." *Proceedings of the Prehistoric Society* 63: 147–178.

Benjamin, Walter. 1980. "A Short History of Photography." In *Classic Essays on Photography*, edited by Alan Trachtenberg, 199–216. New Haven, CT: Leete's Island Books.

Berggren, Åsa. 2009. "Evaluation of a Reflexive Attempt: The Citytunnel Project in Retrospect." *Archaeological Review from Cambridge* 24 (1): 23–37.

Berggren, Åsa, Nicolo Dell'Unto, Maurizio Forte, Scott D. Haddow, Ian Hodder, Justine Issavi, Nicola Lercari, Camilla Mazzuccato, Allison Mickel, and James Taylor. 2015. "Revisiting Reflexive Archaeology at Çatalhöyük: Integrating Digital and 3D Technologies at the Trowel's Edge." *Antiquity* 89 (344): 433–448.

Berggren, Åsa, and Ian Hodder. 2003. "Social Practice, Method, and Some Problems of Field Archaeology." *American Antiquity* 68 (3): 421–434.

Bernhardsson, Magnus Thorkell. 2005. *Reclaiming a Plundered Past: Archaeology and Nation-Building in Modern Iraq*. Austin: University of Texas Press.

Bienert, Hans-Dieter, and Hans Georg K. Gebel. 2004. "Summary on Ba'ja 1997, and Insights from the Later Seasons." In *Central Settlements in Jordan*, edited by Hans-Dieter Bienert, Hans Georg K. Gebel, and Reinder Neef, 119–144. Berlin: Ex Oriente.

Bille, Mikkel. 2009. "Negotiating Protection: Bedouin Material Culture and Heritage in Jordan." PhD thesis, University College London, UK.

Bille, Mikkel. 2012. "Assembling Heritage: Investigating the UNESCO Proclamation of Bedouin Intangible Heritage in Jordan." *International Journal of Heritage Studies* 18 (2): 107–123.

Bille, Mikkel. 2013. "The Samer, the Saint, and the Shaman: Ordering Bedouin Heritage in Jordan." In *Politics of Worship in the Contemporary Middle East: Sainthood in Fragile States*, edited by Andreas Bandak and Mikkel Bille, 101–126. Leiden: Brill.

Bliss, Frederick Jones. 1906. *The Development of Palestine Exploration*. London: Hodder amd Stoughton.

Blok, Aad, and Greg Downey, eds. 2003. *Uncovering Labour in Information Revolutions, 1750–2000*. Cambridge: Cambridge University Press.

Blondel, Vincent D., Jean-Loup Guillaume, Renaud Lambiotte, and Etienne Lefebvre. 2008. "Fast Unfolding of Communities in Large Networks." *Journal of Statistical Mechanics: Theory and Experiment* (10): P1000–P1008.

Bohrer, Frederick N. 2011. *Photography and Archaeology*. London: Reaktion Books.

Bonacchi, Chiara. 2012. *Archaeology and Digital Communication: Towards Strategies of Public Engagement*. London: Archetype.

Bonacchi, Chiara, Andrew Bevan, Daniel Pett, Adi Keinan-Schoonbaert, Rachael Sparks, Jennifer Wexler, and Neil Wilkin. 2014. "Crowd-Sourced Archaeological Research: The MicroPasts Project." *Archaeology International* 17: 61–68.

Borgatti, Stephen P. 2005. "Centrality and Network Flow." *Social Networks* 27 (1): 55–71.

Brand, Laurie A. 2000. "Resettling, Reconstructing, and Restor(y)ing: Archaeology and Tourism in Umm Qays." *Middle East Report* 216: 28–31.

Breasted, James Henry. 1926. "JB to Mrs. Rockefeller." Letter, folder Tutankhamun: Important Letters and Notes, JHB, OI Archives, University of Chicago, IL.

Breglia, Lisa C. 2005. "Keeping World Heritage in the Family: A Genealogy of Maya Labour at Chichén Itzá." *International Journal of Heritage Studies* 11 (5): 385–398.

Breglia, Lisa C. 2006. *Monumental Ambivalence: The Politics of Heritage.* Austin: University of Texas Press.

Brodie, Neil, Morag M. Kersel, Christina Luke, and Kathryn Walker Tubb, eds. 2006. *Archaeology, Cultural Heritage, and the Antiquities Trade.* Gainesville: University of Florida Press.

Brovarski, Edward. 1996. "Epigraphic and Archaeological Documentation of Old Kingdom Tombs and Monuments at Giza and Saqqara." In *The American Discovery of Ancient Egypt*, edited by Nancy Thomas, 25–44. Los Angeles: Los Angeles County Museum of Art.

Brown, Tony, Sean Hawken, Frances Griffith, Lucy Franklin, and Charlotte Hawkins. 2004. "Science, Landscape Archaeology, and Public Participation: The Community Landscape Project, Devon, UK." *Public Archaeology* 3 (4): 217–226.

Brunhouse, Robert Levere. 1971. *Sylvanus G. Morley and the World of the Ancient Mayas.* Norman: University of Oklahoma Press.

Burch, Jonathon. 2013. "In Turkey's Pious Heartland, Protests Seem World Away." *Reuters*, June 21. https://www.reuters.com/article/us-turkey-protests-heartland/in-turkeys-pious-heartland-protests-seem-world-away-idUSBRE95K0AF20130621.

Burckhardt, Johann Ludwig. 1822. *Travels in Nubia.* London: John Murray.

Burri, Regula Valérie, and Joseph Dumit. 2008. "Social Studies of Scientific Imaging and Visualization." In *The Handbook of Science and Technology Studies*, edited by Edward J. Hackett, Olga Amsterdamska, Michael Lynch, and Judy Wajcman, 297–318. 3rd ed. Cambridge: Massachusetts Institute of Technology Press.

Caraher, William. 2019. "Slow Archaeology, Punk Archaeology, and the 'Archaeology of Care.'" *European Journal of Archaeology* 22 (3): 372–385.

Carver, Geoff. 2010. "Doku-Porn: Visualising Stratigraphy." In *Unquiet Pasts: Risk Society, Lived Cultural Heritage, Re-Designing Reflexivity*, edited by Stephanie Koerner and Ian Russell, 109–122. Oxon, UK: Routledge.

Castañeda, Quetzil E. 1996. *In the Museum of Maya Culture: Touring Chichén Itzá.* Minneapolis: University of Minnesota Press.

Castañeda, Quetzil E. 2008. "The 'Ethnographic Turn' in Archaeology: Research Positioning and Reflexivity in Ethnographic Archaeologies." In *Ethnographic Archaeologies: Reflections on Stakeholders and Archaeological Practices*, edited by

Quetzil E. Castañeda and Christopher N. Matthews, 1–24. Lanham, MD: Altamira.

Ceram, Curt W. 1968. *Gods, Graves, and Scholars: The Story of Archaeology*. 2nd ed. New York: Knopf.

Chadha, Ashish. 2002. "Visions of Discipline: Sir Mortimer Wheeler and the Archaeological Method in India (1944–1948)." *Journal of Social Archaeology* 2 (3): 378–401.

Chakrabarti, Dilip Kumar. 1997. *Colonial Indology: Sociopolitics of the Ancient Indian Past*. New Delhi: Munshiram Manoharial.

Chirikure, Shadreck, and Gilbert Pwiti. 2008. "Community Involvement in Archaeology and Cultural Heritage Management: An Assessment from Case Studies in Southern Africa and Elsewhere." *Current Anthropology* 49 (3): 467–485.

Chrysanthi, Angeliki, Åsa Berggren, Rosamund Davies, Graeme P. Earl, and Jarrod Knibbe. 2016. "The Camera 'at the Trowel's Edge': Personal Video Recording in Archaeological Research." *Journal of Archaeological Method and Theory* 23: 238–270.

Claassen, Cheryl. 1994. *Women in Archaeology*. Philadelphia: University of Pennsylvania Press.

Clarke, D. V. 1978. "Excavation and Volunteers: A Cautionary Tale." *World Archaeology* 10 (1): 63–70.

CLC. 2013. Excavation Diary Entry. August 26. http://www.catalhoyuk.com/data base/catal/diaryrecord.asp?id=3169.

Colla, Elliott. 2007. *Conflicted Antiquities: Egyptology, Egyptomania, Egyptian Modernity*. Durham, NC: Duke University Press.

Colwell-Chanthaphonh, Chip, and T. J. Ferguson, eds. 2008. *Collaboration in Archaeological Practice: Engaging Descendant Communities*. Lanham, MD: Altamira.

Comer, Douglas C. 2012. *Tourism and Archaeological Heritage Management at Petra: Driver to Development or Destruction?* New York: Springer.

Conkey, Margaret W. 2003. "Has Feminism Changed Archaeology?" *Signs: Journal of Women in Culture and Society* 28 (3): 867–880.

Corbett, Elena. 2014. *Competitive Archaeology in Jordan: Narrating Identity from the Ottomans to the Hashemites*. Austin: University of Texas Press.

Cottica, Daniela, Lori D. Hager, and Başak Boz. 2012. "Post-Neolithic Use of Building 3 (Space 86), Space 88. and Space 89 at Çatalhöyük." In *Last House on the Hill: Bach Area Reports from Çatalhöyük, Turkey*, edited by Ruth Tringham and Mirjana Stevanović, 331–345. Monumenta Archaeologica 27. Los Angeles: Cotsen Institute of Archaeology Press.

Davies, Graham I. 1988. "British Archaeologists." In *Benchmarks in Time and Culture: An Introduction to Palestinian Archaeology*, edited by Joel F. Drinkard Jr., Gerald L. Mattingly, and J. Maxwell Miller, 37–62. Atlanta: Scholars Press.

Davis, Thomas W. 2004. *Shifting Sands: The Rise and Fall of Biblical Archaeology.* Oxford: Oxford University Press.

Department of the Treasury. 1975. *Treasury Reporting Rates of Exchange as of March 31, 1975.* https://www.gpo.gov/fdsys/pkg/GOVPUB-T63_100-50f9e65923794e5277e8 49ca5f182223/pdf/GOVPUB-T63_100-50f9e65923794e5277e849ca5f182223.pdf.

Dirks, Nicholas B. 1994. "Guiltless Spoliations: Picturesque Beauty, Colonial Knowledge, and Colin Mackenzie's Survey of India." In *Perceptions of South Asia's Visual Past,* edited by Catherine Ella Blanshard Asher and Thomas R. Metcalf, 211–232. New Delhi: American Institute of Indian Studies.

Dissard, Laurent, Melissa Rosenzweig, and Timothy Matney. 2011. "Beyond Ethics: Considerations in Problematizing Community Involvement and Outreach in Archaeological Practice." *Archaeological Review from Cambridge* 26 (2): 59–70.

Doan, Petra L. 2006. "Tourism Planning and Regional Instability: The Consequences of Rapid Expansion of the Tourism Sector in Jordan." *International Development Planning Review* 28 (3): 311–332.

Doing, Park. 2004. "'Lab Hands' and the 'Scarlet O': Epistemic Politics and (Scientific) Labor." *Social Studies of Science* 34 (3): 299–323.

Doing, Park. 2008. "Give Me a Laboratory and I Will Raise a Discipline: The Past, Present, and Future Politics of Laboratory Studies in STS." In *The Handbook of Science and Technology Studies,* edited by Edward J. Hackett, Olga Amsterdamska, Michael Lynch, and Judy Wajcman, 279–296. 3rd ed. Cambridge: Massachusetts Institute of Technology Press.

Douglas, Madeleine "Bear." 2014. "Evaluating Çatalhöyük: Economic and Ethnographic Approaches to Understanding the Impact of Cultural Heritage." In *Integrating Çatalhöyük: Themes from the 2000–2008 Seasons,* edited by Ian Hodder, 47–54. Ankara: British Institute of Archaeology.

Doyon, Wendy. 2014. "On Archaeological Labor in Modern Egypt." In *Histories of Egyptology: Interdisciplinary Measures,* edited by William Carruthers, 141–156. New York: Routledge.

Dufton, Andrew, and Stuart Eve. 2012. "Guerrilla Foursquare: A Digital Archaeological Appropriation of Commercial Location-Based Social Networking." CAA 2012 Proceedings of the 40th Conference in Computer Applications and Quantitative Methods in Archaeology. Southampton, UK, March 26–30.

Dural, Sadrettin. 2007. *Protecting Çatalhöyük: Memoir of an Archaeological Site Guard.* Walnut Creek, CA: Left Coast Press.

Dural, Sadrettin. 2015. *Life in Çatalhöyük 9000 Years Ago.* Konya, Turkey: Selcuk Universitesi.

Dyson, Robert H., Jr. 1968. "Early Work on the Acropolis at Susa: The Beginnings of Prehistory in Iran and Iraq." *Expedition* 10 (4): 21–31.

Edgeworth, Matt. 2003. *Acts of Discovery: An Ethnography of Archaeological Practice.* BAR International Series. Oxford: Archaeopress.

Edgeworth, Matt, ed. 2006. *Ethnographies of Archaeological Practice: Cultural Encounters, Material Transformations.* Lanham, MD: Altamira.

ER. 2006a. Excavation Diary Entry. July 22. http://www.catalhoyuk.com/database /catal/diaryrecord.asp?id=853.

ER. 2006b. Excavation Diary Entry. July 24. http://www.catalhoyuk.com/database /catal/diaryrecord.asp?id=954.

Erbil, Ömer. 2016. "Austrian Archaeological Excavations in Turkey Canceled amid Diplomatic Row." *Hurriyet Daily News.* September 7. http://www.hurriyetdaily news.com/austrian-archaeological-excavations-in-turkey-canceled-amid-diplo matic-row-103629.

Erickson-Gini, Tali. 2012. "Nabataean Agriculture: Myth and Reality." *Journal of Arid Environments* 86: 50–54.

Fagan, Brian. 2004. *The Rape of the Nile: Tomb Robbers, Tourists, and Archaeologists in Egypt.* 3rd ed. New York: Charles Scribner's.

Fee, Samuel B., David K. Pettegrew, and William R. Caraher. 2013. "Taking Mobile Computing to the Field." *Near Eastern Archaeology* 76 (1): 50–55.

Fergusson, James. 1848. *Picturesque Illustrations of Ancient Architecture in Hindostan.* London: J. Hogarth.

Fiema, Zbigniew T. 2003. "Roman Petra (AD 106–363): A Neglected Subject." *Zeitschrift Des Deutschen Palästina-Vereins (1953–)* H. 1: 38–58.

Fleming, Shannon. 2015. "Searching for the Jordanian Nation: Archaeology and the Fluidity of Nationalism." Master's thesis, Brandeis University, Waltham, MA.

Forte, Maurizio, Nicolo Dell'Unto, Justine Issavi, Llonel Onsurez, and Nicola Lercari. 2012. "3D Archaeology at Çatalhöyük." *International Journal of Heritage in the Digital Era* 1 (3): 351–378.

Fotiadis, Michael. 2013. "Naked Presence and Disciplinary Wording." In *Modernity's Classics*, edited by Sarah C. Humphreys and Rudolph G. Wagner, 293–313. Berlin Heidelberg: Springer-Verlag.

Frankfort, Henri. 1950. "Town Planning in Ancient Mesopotamia." *Town Planning Review* 21 (2): 98–115.

Galor, Katharina. 2017. *Finding Jerusalem: Archaeology between Science and Ideology.* Berkeley: University of California Press.

Gebel, Hans Georg K. 2003. "The Significance of Ba'Ja for Early Near Eastern Neolithic Research." *Occident and Orient: Newsletter of the German Protestant Institute of Archaeology in Amman* 8 (1): 17–19.

Gero, Joan M. 1994. "Excavation Bias and the Woman at Home Ideology." *Archeological Papers of the American Anthropological Association* 5 (1): 37–42.

Gero, Joan M. 1996. "Archaeological Practice and Gendered Encounters with Field Data." In *Gender and Archaeology*, edited by Rita P. Wright, 251–280. Philadelphia: University of Pennsylvania Press.

Gilbert, Nick, and Michael Mulkay. 1984. *Opening Pandora's Box: A Sociological Analysis of Scientists' Discourse.* Cambridge: Cambridge University Press.

Gillot, Laurence. 2010. "Towards a Socio-Political History of Archaeology in the Middle East: The Development of Archaeological Practice and Its Impacts on Local Communities in Syria." *Bulletin of the History of Archaeology* 20 (1): 4–17.

Giraudo, Rachel F., and Benjamin W. Porter. 2010. "Archaeotourism and the Crux of Development." *Anthropology News* 51 (8): 7–8.

"GlobalXplorer." 2017. https://www.globalxplorer.org/.

Goldstein, Lynne, Barbara Mills, Sarah Herr, Jo Burkholder, Leslie Aiello, and Christopher Thornton. 2017. *Society for American Archaeology Task Force on Gender Disparities in Archaeological Grant Submissions.* http://saa-gender.anthropology.msu.edu/wp-content/uploads/2017/05/SAA_TF_Gender_Disparities_Final_17April17.pdf.

Gomes, Denise Maria Cavalcante. 2006. "Amazonian Archaeology and Local Identities." In *Ethnographies of Archaeological Practice: Cultural Encounters, Material Transformations*, edited by Matt Edgeworth, 148–160. Lanham, MD: Altamira.

Goode, James F. 2007. *Negotiating for the Past: Archaeology, Nationalism, and Diplomacy in the Middle East, 1919–1941.* Austin: University of Texas Press.

Goodwin, John. 1955. "5.1.1995 Letter, Addressed to 'My Dear Everybody.'" University of Cape Town, South Africa.

Graham, M. Patrick. 1989. "The Discovery and Reconstruction of the Mesha Inscription." In *Studies in the Mesha Inscription and Moab*, edited by Andrew Dearman, 41–92. Atlanta: Scholars Press.

Gray, Matthew. 1998. "Economic Reform, Privatization, and Tourism in Egypt." *Middle Eastern Studies* 34 (2): 91–112.

Guha-Thakurta, Tapati. 2004. *Monuments, Objects, Histories: Institutions of Art in Colonial and Post-Colonial India.* New York: Columbia University Press.

Hall, Kathryn E. 2007. Excavation Diary Entry. June 25. http://www.catalhoyuk.com/database/catal/diaryrecord.asp?id=1137.

Hamilakis, Yannis. 2011. "Archaeological Ethnography: A Multitemporal Meeting Ground for Archaeology and Anthropology." *Annual Review of Anthropology* 40: 399–414.

Hamilakis, Yannis, and Aris Anagnostopoulos. 2009. "What Is Archaeological Ethnography?" *Public Archaeology* 8 (2–3): 65–87.

Hamilakis, Yannis, Aris Anagnostopoulos, and Fotis Ifantidis. 2009. "Postcards from the Edge of Time: Archaeology, Photography, Archaeological Ethnography (a Photo-Essay)." *Public Archaeology* 8 (2–3): 283–309.

Hamilton, Carolyn. 2000. "Faultlines: The Construction of Archaeological Knowledge at Çatalhöyük." In *Towards Reflexive Method in Archaeology: The Example at Çatalhöyük*, edited by Ian Hodder, 119–128. Cambridge: McDonald Institute for Archaeological Research.

Hammond, Philip C. 1965. *The Excavation of the Main Theater at Petra, 1961–1962: Final Report*. London: Bernard Quaritch Ltd.

Hammond, Philip C. 1976. "American Expedition to Petra: Interim Report." Unpublished report. ACOR Library, Amman, Jordan.

Hammond, Philip C. 1992. "A Proposal for the Reconstruction of the Temple of the Winged Lions, Petra, the Hashemite Kingdom of Jordan." Unpublished report. ACOR Library, Amman, Jordan.

Hammond, Philip C. 1996. *The Temple of the Winged Lions: Petra, Jordan 1974–1990*. Fountain Hills, AZ: Petra.

Handler, Richard. 2008. "A Dangerously Elusive Method: Disciplines, Histories, and the Limits of Reflexivity." In *Ethnographic Archaeologies: Reflections on Stakeholders and Archaeological Practices*, edited by Quetzil E. Castañeda and Christopher N. Matthews, 95–118. Lanham, MD: Altamira.

Hazbun, Waleed. 2008. *Beaches, Ruins, Resorts: The Politics of Tourism in the Arab World*. Minneapolis: University of Minnesota Press.

Hazbun, Waleed. 2010. "Revising Itineraries of Tourism and Tourism Studies in the Middle East and North Africa." *Journal of Tourism and Cultural Change* 8 (4): 225–239.

Herzfeld, Michael. 2004. *The Body Impolitic: Artisans and Artifice in the Global Hierarchy of Value*. Chicago: University of Chicago Press.

Hester, Thomas R., Harry J. Shafer, and Kenneth L. Feder, eds. 2009. *Field Methods in Archaeology*. 7th ed. Walnut Creek, CA: Left Coast Press.

Hodder, Ian. 1989. "Writing Archaeology: Site Reports in Context." *Antiquity* 63 (239): 268–274.

Hodder, Ian. 1999. *The Archaeological Process: An Introduction*. Oxford: Blackwell.

Hodder, Ian, ed. 2000. *Towards Reflexive Method in Archaeology: The Example at Çatalhöyük*. Cambridge: McDonald Institute for Archaeological Research.

Hodder, Ian, ed. 2005. *Çatalhöyük Perspectives: Reports from the 1995–99 Seasons*. Cambridge: McDonald Institute for Archaeological Research.

Hollowell, Julie, and George P. Nicholas. 2008. "A Critical Assessment of Ethnography in Archaeology." In *Ethnographic Archaeologies: Reflections on Stakeholders and Archaeological Practices*, edited by Quetzil E. Castañeda and Christopher N. Matthews, 63–94. Lanham, MD: Altamira.

Hollowell, Julie, and George P. Nicholas. 2009. "Using Ethnographic Methods to Articulate Community-Based Conceptions of Cultural Heritage Management." *Public Archaeology* 8 (2–3): 141–160.

Howland, Matthew D., Falko Kuester, and Thomas E. Levy. 2014. "Structure from Motion: Twenty-First Century Field Recording with 3D Technology." *Near Eastern Archaeology* 77 (3): 187–191.

International Telecommunications Union. 2016. *Measuring the Information Society Report*. Geneva: Place des Nations.

Jasanoff, Sheila. 1998. "The Eye of Everyman Witnessing DNA in the Simpson Trial." *Social Studies of Science* 28 (5–6): 713–740.

Johnson-Roehr, Susan. 2008. "The Archaeological Survey of India and Communal Violence in Post-Independence India." *International Journal of Heritage Studies* 14 (6): 506–523.

Joyce, Rosemary A. 2002. *The Languages of Archaeology: Dialogue, Narrative, and Writing*. Oxford: Blackwell.

JT. 2016. "More Suspects in Wadi Musa 'Land Sale Fraud' Detained." *Jordan Times*. March 14. http://www.jordantimes.com/news/local/more-suspects-wadi-musa -land-sale-fraud%E2%80%99-detained.

Kansa, Eric C., Sarah Whitcher Kansa, and Ethan Watrall, eds. 2011. *Archaeology 2.0: New Approaches to Communication and Collaboration*. Los Angeles: Cotsen Institute of Archaeology Press.

Katsamudanga, Seke. 2015. "Consuming the Past: Public Perceptions towards the Discipline of Archaeology in Zimbabwe." *Public Archaeology* 14 (3): 172–190.

Kendall, Timothy. 1996. "The American Discovery of Meroitic Nubia and the Sudan." In *The American Discovery of Ancient Egypt*, edited by Nancy Thomas, 151–168. Los Angeles: Los Angeles County Museum of Art.

Kersel, Morag M. 2007. "Transcending Borders: Objects on the Move." *Archaeologies* 3 (2): 81–98.

Kersel, Morag M. 2011. "When Communities Collide: Competing Claims for Archaeological Objects in the Market Place." *Archaeologies* 7 (3): 518–537.

Kersel, Morag M. 2015. "Storage Wars: Solving the Archaeological Curation Crisis?" *Journal of Eastern Mediterranean Archaeology and Heritage Studies* 3 (1): 42–54.

Kirkbride, Diana. 1968. "Beidha: Early Neolithic Village Life South of the Dead Sea." *Antiquity* 42 (168): 263–274.

Knodell, Alex R., Susan E. Alcock, Christopher A. Tuttle, Christian F. Cloke, Tali Erickson-Gini, Cecelia Feldman, Gary O. Rollefson, Micaela Sinibaldi, Thomas M. Urban, and Clive Vella. 2017. "The Brown University Petra Archaeological Project: Landscape Archaeology in the Northern Hinterland of Petra, Jordan." *American Journal of Archaeology* 121 (4): 621–683.

Knorr Cetina, Karin. 1981. *The Manufacture of Knowledge*. Oxford: Pergamon.

Knorr Cetina, Karin. 1999. *Epistemic Cultures: How the Sciences Make Knowledge*. Cambridge: Harvard University Press.

Kooring, Deborah, and Steven R. Simms. 1996. "The Bedul Bedouin of Petra, Jordan: Traditions, Tourism, and an Uncertain Future." *Cultural Survival Quarterly* 19 (4): 22–30.

Kouki, Paula. 2009. "Archaeological Evidence of Land Tenure in the Petra Region, Jordan: Nabataean–Early Roman to Late Byzantine." *Journal of Mediterranean Archaeology* 22 (1): 29–56.

Kouki, Paula. 2012. "Changing Times, Continuing Traditions: The Transfer of Religious Traditions at Jabal Harun." In *Archaeology of Social Relations: Ten Case Studies by Finnish Archaeologists*, edited by Tiina Äikäs, Sanna Lipkin, and Anna-Kaisa Salmi, 103–118. Oulu, Finland: University of Oulu.

Lahiri, Nayanjot. 2000. "Archaeology and Identity in Colonial India." *Antiquity* 74 (285): 687–692.

Landels, John Gray. 1978. *Engineering in the Ancient World*. Berkeley: University of California Press.

Landow, George P. 2006. *Hypertext 3.0: Critical Theory and New Media in an Era of Globalization*. Baltimore: Johns Hopkins University Press.

Lane, Paul. 2011. "Possibilities for a Postcolonial Archaeology in Sub-Saharan Africa: Indigenous and Usable Pasts." *World Archaeology* 43 (1): 7–25.

Larsen, Mogens Trolle. 1996. *The Conquest of Assyria: Excavations in an Antique Land 1840–1869*. London: Routledge.

Larsson, Åsa M. 2013. "Participate or Perish: Why Archaeology Must Gain Confidence." *Archaeological Dialogues* 20 (1): 29–35.

Latour, Bruno. 1987. *Science in Action: How to Follow Scientists and Engineers through Society*. Cambridge: Harvard University Press.

Latour, Bruno, and Steve A. Woolgar. 1979. *Laboratory Life: The Construction of Scientific Facts*. Princeton, NJ: Princeton University Press.

Layard, Austen Henry. 1849. *Nineveh and Its Remains*. London: John Murray.

Layard, Austen Henry. 1853. *Discoveries among the Ruins of Nineveh and Babylon*. London: Harper and Bros.

Layard, Austen Henry. 1887. *Early Adventures in Persia, Susiana, and Babylonia*. London: John Murray.

Lazar, Irena, Tina Kompare, Heleen van Londen, and Tine Schenk. 2014. "The Archaeologist of the Future Is Likely to Be a Woman: Age and Gender Patterns in European Archaeology." *Archaeologies* 10 (3): 257–280.

Leighton, Mary. 2016. "Indigenous Archaeological Field Technicians at Tiwanaku, Bolivia: A Hybrid Form of Scientific Labor." *American Anthropologist* 118 (4): 742–754.

Leone, Mark P. 2008. "The Foundations of Archaeology." In *Ethnographic Archaeologies: Reflections on Stakeholders and Archaeological Practices*, edited by Quetzil E. Castañeda and Christopher N. Matthews, 119–138. Lanham, MD: Altamira.

Lightfoot, Kent G. 2006. "Rethinking Archaeological Field Methods." *News from Native California* 19 (3): 21–24.

Lightfoot, Kent G. 2008. "Collaborative Research Programs: Implications for the Practice of North American Archaeology." In *Collaborating at the Trowel's Edge: Teaching and Learning in Indigenous Archaeology*, edited by Stephen W. Silliman, 211–227. Tucson: University of Arizona Press.

Little, Barbara J., and Paul A. Shackel, eds. 2007. *Archaeology as a Tool of Civic Engagement*. Lanham, MD: Altamira.

Little, Barbara J., and Larry J. Zimmerman. 2010. "In the Public Interest: Creating a More Activist, Civically-Engaged Archaeology." In *Voices in American Archaeology*, edited by Wendy Ashmore, Dorothy T. Lippert, and Barbara J. Mills, 131–159. Washington, DC: Society for American Archaeology Press.

Lloyd, Seton. 1963. *Mounds of the Near East*. Edinburgh: Edinburgh University Press.

Loud, Gordon. 1936. "An Architectural Formula for Assyrian Planning Based on the Results of Excavations at Khorsabad." *Revue d'Assyriologie Et d'Archéologie Orientale* 33 (3): 153–160.

Loud, Gordon, and Charles B. Altman. 1938. "Khorsabad, Part II: The Citadel and the Town." *Oriental Institute Publications* 40: 42–43.

Lucas, Gavin. 2001. *Critical Approaches to Fieldwork: Contemporary and Historical Archaeological Practice*. London: Routledge.

Luke, Christina, and Morag M. Kersel. 2013. *US Cultural Diplomacy and Archaeology: Soft Power, Hard Heritage*. New York: Routledge.

Lyons, Natasha, and Kisha Supernant. 2020. "Introduction to an Archaeology of the Heart." In *Archaeologies of the Heart and Emotion*, edited by Kisha Supernant, Jane Baxter, Natasha Lyons, and Sonya Atalay, 1–19. New York: Springer International.

Lyons, Natasha, Kisha Supernant, and John R. Welch. 2019. "What Are the Prospects for an Archaeology of Heart?" *SAA Archaeological Record* 19 (2): 6–9.

Majd, Mohammad Gholi. 2003. *The Great American Plunder of Persia's Antiquities 1925–1941*. Lanham, MD: University Press of America.

Maldonado, Doris Julissa. 2011. "Reconfiguring Archaeological Practice: Lessons from Currusté, Honduras." PhD dissertation, University of California, Berkeley.

Maler, Teobert. 1932. *Impresiones De Viaje a Las Ruinas De Cobá y Chichén Itzá*. Merida: J. E. Rosado.

Marshall, Yvonne, Sasha Roseneil, and Kayt Armstrong. 2009. "Situating the Greenham Archaeology: An Autoethnography of a Feminist Project." *Public Archaeology* 8 (2–3): 225–245.

Martin, Louise, and Nerissa Russell. 1997. *Animal Bone Report*. Çatalhöyük 1997 Archive Report. http://www.catalhoyuk.com:8080/archive_reports/1997/ar97_14.html.

Marx, Karl. 1906. *Capital.* Vol. 1. Chicago: Kerr.

Marx, Karl. 2012 [1844]. *Economic and Philosophic Manuscripts of 1844.* Mineola, NY: Courier Dover.

Marx, Karl, and Friedrich Engels. 1848. *Manifesto of the Communist Party.* London: Workers' Educational Association.

Marx, Karl, and Friedrich Engels. 1959 [1845]. *The German Ideology.* Amherst, NY: Prometheus Books.

Masry, Abdullah H. 1981. "Traditions of Archeological Research in the Near East." *World Archaeology* 13 (2): 222–239.

Massad, Joseph A. 2001. *Colonial Effects: The Making of National Identity in Jordan.* New York: Columbia University Press.

Matsuda, David. 1998. "The Ethics of Archaeology, Subsistence Digging, and Artifact Looting in Latin America: Point Muted Counterpoint." *International Journal of Cultural Property* 7 (1): 87–97.

Matthews, Wendy, Christine Hastorf, and Begumşen Ergenekon. 2000. "Ethnoarchaeology: Studies in Local Villages Aimed at Understanding Aspects of the Neolithic Site." In *Towards Reflexive Method in Archaeology: The Example at Çatalhöyük.*, edited by Ian Hodder, 177–188. Cambridge: McDonald Institute for Archaeological Research.

McAnany, Patricia A. 2016. *Maya Cultural Heritage: How Archaeologists and Indigenous Communities Engage the Past.* London: Rowman and Littlefield.

McAnany, Patricia A., and Sarah M. Rowe. 2015. "Re-Visiting the Field: Collaborative Archaeology as Paradigm Shift." *Journal of Field Archaeology* 40 (5): 499–507.

McGuire, Randall H. 2008. *Archaeology as Political Action.* Berkeley: University of California Press.

Mellaart, James. 1967. *Çatal Hüyük: A Neolithic Town in Anatolia.* London: Thames and Hudson.

Merriman, Nick. 2002. "Archaeology, Heritage, and Interpretation." In *Archaeology: The Widening Debate*, edited by Barry W. Cunliffe and Colin Renfrew, 541–566. Oxford: Oxford University Press.

Merriman, Nick, ed. 2004. *Public Archaeology.* London: Routledge.

Meskell, Lynn. 2005a. "Archaeological Ethnography: Conversations around Kruger National Park." *Archaeologies: Journal of the World Archaeology Congress* 1: 81–100.

Meskell, Lynn. 2005b. "Sites of Violence: Terrorism, Tourism, and Heritage in the Archaeological Present." In *Embedding Ethics*, edited by Lynn Meskell and Peter Pels, 123–146. Oxford: Berg.

Mickel, Allison, and Alex R. Knodell. 2015. "We Wanted to Take Real Information: Public Engagement and Regional Survey at Petra, Jordan." *World Archaeology* 47 (2): 239–260.

Mol, Annemarie, and John Law. 1994. "Regions, Networks, and Fluids: Anaemia and Social Topology." *Social Studies of Science* 24 (4): 641–671.

Moore, Sophie. 2014. "Burials and Identities at Historic Period Çatalhöyük." *Heritage Turkey* 4: 29.

Moore, Sophie, and Michelle Gamble. 2015. "Bodies of Evidence: The Historic Cemeteries of Çatalhöyük." *Heritage Turkey* 5: 13–14.

Moorey, Peter Roger Stuart. 1991. *A Century of Biblical Archaeology*. Louisville: Westminster/John Knox.

Morgan, Colleen, and Stuart Eve. 2012. "DIY and Digital Archaeology: What Are You Doing to Participate?" *World Archaeology* 44 (4): 521–537.

Morris, Earl. 1931. *The Temple of the Warriors at Chichén Itzá*. Washington, DC: Carnegie Institute of Washington.

Moscrop, John James. 2000. *Measuring Jerusalem: The Palestine Exploration Fund and British Interests in the Holy Land*. London: Leicester University Press.

Moser, Stephanie. 2007. "On Disciplinary Culture: Archaeology as Fieldwork and Its Gendered Associations." *Journal of Archaeological Method and Theory* 14 (3): 235–263.

Moser, Stephanie, Darren Glazier, James E. Phillips, Lamya Nasser el Nemr, Mohammed Saleh Mousa, Rascha Nasr Aiesh, Susan Richardson, Andrew Conner, and Michael Seymour. 2002. "Transforming Archaeology through Practice: Strategies for Collaborative Archaeology and the Community Archaeology Project at Quseir, Egypt." *World Archaeology* 34 (2): 220–248.

Muringaniza, Joseph. 1998. "Community Participation in Archaeological Heritage Management in Zimbabwe: The Case of Old Bulawayo." Master of Philosophy dissertation, Cambridge University, UK.

Nakamura, Carolyn, Lindsay Der, and Lynn Meskell. 2014. *Çatalhöyük Figurines Report*. Çatalhöyük 2014 Archive Report. http://www.catalhoyuk.com/sites/default /files/media/pdf/Archive_Report_2014_0.pdf.

Nasarat, Mohammed, Fawzi Abu Danah, and Slameh Naimat. 2012. "Agriculture in Sixth-Century Petra and Its Hinterland: The Evidence from the Petra Papyri." *Arabian Archaeology and Epigraphy* 23 (1): 105–115.

Nassaney, Michael S., and Mary Ann Levine, eds. 2009. *Archaeology and Community Service Learning*. Gainesville: University Press of Florida.

Ndoro, Webber. 2001. "Your Monument Our Shrine: The Preservation of Great Zimbabwe." PhD thesis, Uppsala University, Uppsala, Sweden.

Nelson, Margaret C., Sarah M. Nelson, and Alison Wylie, eds. 1994. *Equity Issues for Women in Archaeology*. Washington, DC: Archeological Papers of the American Anthropological Association.

Newman, Mark E.J. 2006. "Modularity and Community Structure in Networks." *Proceedings of the National Academy of Sciences* 103 (23): 8577–8582.

Nicholas, George P. 2008. "Melding Science and Community Values: Indigenous Archaeology Programs and the Negotiation of Cultural Differences." In *Collaborating at the Trowel's Edge: Teaching and Learning in Indigenous Archaeology*, edited by Stephen W. Silliman, 228–250. Tucson: University of Arizona Press.

O'Connor, David B. 1996. "The American Archaeological Focus on Ancient Palaces and Temples of the New Kingdom." In *The American Discovery of Ancient Egypt*, edited by Nancy Thomas, 79–96. Los Angeles: Los Angeles County Museum of Art.

O'Connor, David B. 2011. *Abydos: Egypt's First Pharaohs and the Cult of Osiris*. London: Thames and Hudson.

Özdoğan, Mehmet. 1998. "Ideology and Archaeology in Turkey." In *Archaeology under Fire: Nationalism, Politics, and Heritage in the Eastern Mediterranean and Middle East*, edited by Lynn Meskell, 111–123. London: Routledge.

Paddayya, K. 2002. "The Expanding Horizons of Indian Archaeology." *Bulletin of the Deccan College Research Institute* 62: 291–309.

Parcak, Sarah, David Gathings, Chase Childs, Greg Mumford, and Eric Cline. 2016. "Satellite Evidence of Archaeological Site Looting in Egypt: 2002–2013." *Antiquity* 90 (349): 188–205.

Parkington, John. 2006. *Shorelines, Strandlopers, and Shell Middens: Archaeology of the Cape Coast*. Cape Town, South Africa: Krakadouw Trust.

Pavel, Catalin. 2010. *Describing and Interpreting the Past: European and American Approaches to the Written Record of the Excavation*. Bucuresti, Romania: Editura Universitatii Din Bucuresti.

Paynter, Robert. 1983. "Field or Factory? Concerning the Degradation of Archaeological Labor." In *The Socio-Politics of Archaeology*, edited by Joan M. Gero, David M. Lacy, and Michael L. Blakey, 31–50. Amherst: University of Massachusetts Press.

Perry, Sara. 2009. "Fractured Media: Challenging the Dimensions of Archaeology's Typical Visual Modes of Engagement." *Archaeologies: Journal of the World Archaeology Congress* 5 (3): 389–415.

Perry, Sara. 2019. "The Enchantment of the Archaeological Record." *European Journal of Archaeology* 22 (3): 354–371.

Petrie, William Matthew Flinders. 1904. *Methods and Aims in Archaeology*. London: Macmillan.

Pollock, Susan. 2003. "The Looting of the Iraq Museum: Thoughts on Archaeology in a Time of Crisis." *Public Archaeology* 3 (2): 117–124.

Porter, Richard, and Simon Aspinall. 2010. *Birds of the Middle East*. 2nd ed. London: Christopher Helm.

Quirke, Stephen. 2010. *Hidden Hands: Egyptian Workforces in Petrie Excavation Archives 1880–1924*. London: Duckworth.

Reid, Donald Malcolm. 2002. *Whose Pharaohs? Archaeology, Museums, and Egyptian National Identity from Napoleon to World War I*. Berkeley: University of California Press.

Reisner, George Andrew. 1919. "19 June 1919, Reisner to Fairbanks." Letter, George A. Reisner Papers, American Archives of Art, Smithsonian Institution, Washington, DC.

Remondino, Fabio, and Stefano Campana, eds. 2014. *3D Recording and Modelling in Archaeology and Cultural Heritage: Theory and Best Practices*. Oxford: Archaeopress.

Roveland, Blythe E. 2006. "Reflecting upon Archaeological Practice: Multiple Visions of a Late Paleolithic Site in Germany." In *Ethnographies of Archaeological Practice: Cultural Encounters, Material Transformations*, edited by Matt Edgeworth, 56–67. Lanham, MD: Altamira.

Russell, Kenneth W. 1993. "Ethnohistory of the Bedul Bedouin of Petra." *Annual of the Department of Antiquities of Jordan* 37: 15–35.

Russell, Nick C., Elizabeth M. Tansey, and Pamela V. Lear. 2000. "Missing Links in the History and Practice of Science: Teams, Technicians, and Technical Work." *History of Science* 38 (2): 237–241.

Sabloff, Jeremy A. 2009. "How Can Archaeologists Usefully Contribute to Public Policy Considerations?" *Archaeological Dialogues* 16 (2): 169–171.

Sayej, Ghattas Jeries. 2013. "Can Archaeologists Intervene in Public Debate on Urgent Questions of a Social, Cultural, or Political Nature? A Reflection on the Israeli-Palestinian Archaeology Working Group (IPAWG)." *Archaeological Dialogues* 20 (1): 47–58.

Schlegel, Valerie. 2014. "Breaking In: Women's Representation in Archaeology." *ASOR Blog*. http://www.asor.org/blog/2014/03/21/breaking-in-womens-representation-in-archaeology/.

Segobye, Alinah Kelo. 2005. "The Revolution Will Be Televised: African Archaeology Education and the Challenge of Public Archaeology—Some Examples from Southern Africa." *Archaeologies* 1 (2): 33–45.

Senft, Theresa M., and Nancy K. Baym. 2015. "What Does the Selfie Say? Investigating a Global Phenomenon." *International Journal of Communication* 9: 1588–1606.

Shankland, David. 1999a. "Ethno-Archaeology at Küçükköy." *Anatolian Archaeology* 5: 23–24.

Shankland, David. 1999b. "Integrating the Past: Folklore, Mounds, and People at Çatalhöyük." In *Archaeology and Folklore*, edited by Amy Gazin-Schwartz and Cornelius Holtorf, 139–157. London: Routledge.

Shanks, Michael. 1997. "Photography and Archaeology." In *The Cultural Life of Images: Visual Representation in Archaeology*, edited by Brian Leigh Molyneaux, 73–107. London: Routledge.

Shanks, Michael, and Randall H. McGuire. 1996. "The Craft of Archaeology." *American Antiquity* 61 (1): 75–88.

Shapin, Steven. 1989. "The Invisible Technician." *American Scientist* 77 (6): 554–563.

Shapin, Steven, and Simon Schaffer. 1985. *Leviathan and the Air-Pump: Hobbes, Boyle, and the Experimental Life*. Princeton, NJ: Princeton University Press.

Shepherd, Nick. 2003. "When the Hand That Holds the Trowel Is Black: Disciplinary Practices of Self-Representation and the Issue of Native Labour in Archaeology." *Journal of Social Archaeology* 3 (3): 334–352.

Shoup, John Austin. 1985. "The Impact of Tourism on the Bedouin of Petra." *Middle East Journal* 39 (2): 277–291.

Silliman, Stephen W., ed. 2008. *Collaborating at the Trowel's Edge: Teaching and Learning in Indigenous Archaeology*. Tucson: University of Arizona Press.

Simpson, Faye. 2008. "Community Archaeology under Scrutiny." *Conservation and Management of Archaeological Sites* 10 (1): 3–16.

Simpson, Faye, and Howard Williams. 2008. "Evaluating Community Archaeology in the UK." *Public Archaeology* 7 (2): 69–90.

Smith, Kimbra L. 2005. "Looting and the Politics of Archaeological Knowledge in Northern Peru." *Ethnos* 70 (2): 149–170.

Smith, Pamela J., Jane Callander, Paul G. Bahn, and Genevi Pinçlon. "Dorothy Garrod in Words and Pictures." *Antiquity* 71 (272): 265–270.

Steele, Caroline. 2005. "Who Has Not Eaten Cherries with the Devil? Archaeology under Challenge." In *Archaeologies of the Middle East: Critical Perspectives*, edited by Susan Pollock and Reinhard Bernbeck, 45–65. Malden, MA: Blackwell.

Stephen, Jesse W., and Colleen Morgan. 2014. "Faces of Archaeology: A Photographic Portrait Study from the Seventh World Archaeological Congress." *Archaeologies* 10 (2): 194–206.

Stevanović, Mirjana. 1999. *Report on Experimental Archaeology at Çatalhöyük*. Çatalhöyük 1999 Archive Report. http://www.catalhoyuk.com:8080/archive_reports/1999/ar99_20.html.

Stoffle, Richard W., María Nieves Zedeño, and David B. Halmo, eds. 2001. *American Indians and the Nevada Test Site: A Model of Research and Consultation*. Washington, DC: US Government Printing Office.

Stone, Peter G., and Joanna Farchack Bajjaly. 2008. *The Destruction of Cultural Heritage in Iraq*. Woodbridge, GB: Boydell.

Stottman, M. Jay, ed. 2010. *Archaeologists as Activists: Can Archaeologists Change the World*. Tuscaloosa: University of Alabama Press.

Swain, Hedley. 1997. "Mirroring Reality? Images of Archaeologists." *The Archaeologist* 30: 16–17.

Tansey, Elizabeth M. 2008. "Keeping the Culture Alive: The Laboratory Technician in Mid-Twentieth-Century British Medical Research." *Notes and Records of the Royal Society* 62: 77–95.

Taruvinga, Pascall. 2007. "Community Participation and Rock Art Management in Zimbabwe." In *The Future of Africa's Past*, edited by Janette Deacon, 39–48. Nairobi: TARA.

Thomas, Nancy, ed. 1996. *The American Discovery of Ancient Egypt*. Los Angeles: Los Angeles County Museum of Art.

Tringham, Ruth. 2010. "Forgetting and Remembering: The Digital Experience and Digital Data." In *Archaeology and Memory*, edited by Dušan Borić, 68–105. Oxford: Oxbow Books.

Tuttle, Christopher A. 2013. "Preserving Petra Sustainably (One Step at a Time): The Temple of the Winged Lions Cultural Resource Management Initiative as a Step Forward." *Journal of Eastern Mediterranean Archaeology and Heritage Studies* 1 (1): 1–23.

TWLCRM (Temple of the Winged Lions Cultural Resource Management). n.d. "Petra Temple of the Winged Lions Cultural Resource Management—TWL CRM." https://www.facebook.com/TWLCRM/.

Van Dyke, Ruth M. 2006. "Seeing the Past: Visual Media in Archaeology." *American Anthropologist* 108 (2): 370–375.

Vann, Katie. 2004. "On the Valorization of Informatic Labour." *Ephemera* 4 (3): 246–266.

Vann, Katie, and Geoffrey C. Bowker. 2006. "Interest in Production: On the Configuration of Technology-Bearing Labors for Epistemic IT." In *New Infrastructures for Knowledge Production: Understanding E-Science*, edited by Christine Hine, 71–97. Hershey, PA: Information Science Publishing.

Vella, Clive, Emanuela Bocancea, Thomas M. Urban, Alex R. Knodell, Christopher A. Tuttle, and Susan E. Alcock. 2015. "Looting and Vandalism around a World Heritage Site: Documenting Modern Damage to Archaeological Heritage in Petra's Hinterland." *Journal of Field Archaeology* 40 (2): 221–235.

Warfield, Katie. 2014. "Making Selfies/Making Self: Digital Subjectivities in the Selfie." Paper presented at the Fifth Annual Conference on the Image and the Image Knowledge Community. Freie Universität, Berlin, Germany, October 29–30.

Wheeler, Mortimer. 1954. *Archaeology from the Earth*. Harmondsworth: Penguin Books Ltd.

Wickstead, Helen. 2013. "Between the Lines: Drawing Archaeology." In *the Oxford Handbook of the Archaeology of the Contemporary World*, edited by Paul Graves-Brown, Rodney Harrison, and Angela Piccini, 549–564. Oxford: Oxford University Press.

Witmore, Christopher L. 2007. "Special Reviews Section—Archaeology on the Ground: The Memory Practices of David Webb; Diggers Alternative Archive,

Website, and Photography by David Webb: www.Archdiggers.Co.uk/diggers /frameset.html." *European Journal of Archaeology* 10 (1): 85–89.

Woodall, J. Ned, and Philip J. Perricone. 1981. "The Archaeologist as Cowboy: The Consequence of Professional Stereotype." *Journal of Field Archaeology* 8: 506–508.

Wooten, Cynthia A. 1996. "From Herds of Goats to Herds of Tourists: Negotiating Bedouin Identity under Petra's 'Romantic Gaze.'" MA thesis, American University in Cairo, Egypt.

Wouters, Paul, Katie Vann, Andrea Scharnhorst, Matt Ratto, Iina Hellsten, Jenny Fry, and Anne Beaulieu. 2008. "Messy Shapes of Knowledge—STS Explores Informatization, New Media, and Academic Work." In *The Handbook of Science and Technology Studies*, edited by Edward J. Hackett, Olga Amsterdamska, Michael Lynch and Judy Wajcman, 319–352. 3rd ed. Cambridge: Massachusetts Institute of Technology Press.

Wylie, Alison. 2001. "Doing Social Science as a Feminist: The Engendering of Archaeology." In *Feminism in Twentieth Century Science, Technology, and Medicine*, edited by Angela N.H. Creager, Elizabeth Lunbeck, and Londa Schiebinger, 23–46. Chicago: University of Chicago Press.

Wylie, Alison. 2003. "Why Standpoint Matters." In *Science and Other Cultures: Issues in Philosophies of Science and Technology*, edited by Robert Figueroa and Sandra Harding, 26–48. New York: Routledge.

Wylie, Alison. 2005. "The Promise and Perils of an Ethic of Stewardship." In *Embedding Ethics*, edited by Lynn Meskell and Peter Pels, 47–68. New York: Routledge.

Wynn, L. L. 2007. *Pyramids and Nightclubs: A Travel Ethnography of Arab and Western Imaginations of Egypt, from King Tut and a Colony of Atlantis to Rumors of Sex Orgies, Urban Legends about a Marauding Prince, and Blonde Belly Dancers.* Austin: University of Texas Press.

Wynn, L. L. 2008. "Shape Shifting Lizard People, Israelite Slaves, and Other Theories of Pyramid Building: Notes on Labor, Nationalism, and Archaeology in Egypt." *Journal of Social Archaeology* 8 (2): 272–295.

Yahya, Adel. 2005. "Archaeology and Nationalism in the Holy Land." In *Archaeologies of the Middle East: Critical Perspectives*, edited by Susan Pollock and Reinhard Bernbeck, 66–77. New York: Blackwell.

Zeder, Melinda A. 1997. *The American Archaeologist: A Profile.* Walnut Creek, CA: Altamira.

Zimmerman, Larry J. 2008. "Real People or Reconstructed People? Ethnocritical Archaeology, Ethnography, and Community Building." In *Ethnographic Archaeologies: Reflections on Stakeholders and Archaeological Practices*, edited by Quetzil E. Castañeda and Christopher N. Matthews, 183–204. Lanham, MD: Altamira.

Index

site, *58*; at Temple of the Winged Lions, *47*
archaeological knowledge, 38, 59, 125; comparing workers' knowledge at Çatalhöyük site and Temple of the Winged Lions, 57, 59, 64–65, 67, 90, 100, 109–10; economics of site workers' role, 100, 161; effect of community engagement on at Çatalhöyük site, 57, 89; impact of colonialism on, 119; of local laborers in southern Africa, 119, 121, 122; of Mayan workers, 122; multivocal archaeological knowledge production, 92; reasons for devaluation of expertise in, 33–34; relationships of site workers and archaeologists impacting, 50, 84; use of photography to enhance workers' visible participation in, 131, 150; of women, 27, 102. *See also* knowledge; lucrative non-knowledge
archaeological labor, 13, 20, 34–35, 121, 159, 163, 168n2; compared to factory production, 35; as craft, 33, 35; and Karl Marx's concept of alienation, 35–36, 37; labor models and archaeological interpretation, 127–29; taking advantage of structure of labor relations, 110–11; in Tiwanaku, Bolivia, 123–24. *See also* economics of archaeological labor; labor management; *specific countries and excavations (i.e., Egypt, India, Chichén Itzá)*
archaeological methods, 4, 11, 12, 14, 31, 38; designing field methods that respect community's beliefs and desires, 31; excavation methods, 6, 7, 25–26, 42, 49, 59, 95–96, 97; local and learned methods used, 49–55; network mapping of at Çatalhöyük site based on methods and practices, *60, 61*; network mapping of at Temple of the Winged Lions based on methods and practices, *50*; shift toward reflexivity in archaeology, 13; as a way to undo legacy of lucrative non-knowledge, 126–27. *See also* brushes and brushing; digging tools; research methods; sieves and sieving; soil, handling of from excavations
archaeological research process, 82; and Black African excavation workers, 121; and Community-Based Participatory Research, 8, 31, 88–89; and denial of expertise, 33, 109–10; and ethnography, 37–38; keeping local community site workers from

gaining knowledge of, 33, 53, 68–90, 93, 94, 95; positive role for local community site workers, 4, 12, 59, 67, 136; receiving credit for, 34. *See also* recording strategies that redefine economic dynamics of site worker's role; research methods
Archaeological Survey of India, 118
archaeology, development of in the Middle East, 11; addressing both body and economy affecting site workers, 14; contextualizing, 16–39; financial impact of foreign excavation projects in, 24–25; labor structures in, 12; need for European archaeologists to pose as Arabs, 18; nineteenth-century scientific expeditions and colonialism, 18–22, 154; recent community engagement, 26–29; as a scientific practice, 11; twentieth century continuity and conflicts, 23–26. *See also* archaeological labor; community engagement in archaeology; economics of archaeological labor; labor management
archaeology, outside of the Middle East, 12–13, 114–29, 168n2. *See also specific countries and excavations*
archival records of excavations: at Çatalhöyük, Turkey, 57, 63, 167n12; comparing to oral histories, 11, 39, 69, 76, 83, 85, 148, 152, 157; comparing to site workers' photos, 146–49; contribution of photographic archive to, 151; Goodwin's archives of excavations in southern Africa, 119–20; for Hammond's project, 45–46, 167n4; Wheeler's archives of excavations in India, 118. *See also* diaries recording excavations; notebooks; oral history
Arslan, Numan (interpreter), 167n8
Ashkelon, Israel, excavation in, 21
Assyrian architecture, 16
Atalay, Sonya, 29, 31, 88–89

Baghdad, Iraq, excavation of mounds outside of, 20
Bamboo Spark pens, 137
Barker, Philip, 134
Barley, Stephen, 33, 131
barriers preventing local workers gaining knowledge about archaeology, 12, 13, 68–90; language barriers, 87–88, 93, 133
Bateman, Jonathan, 148, 151

lucrative non-knowledge; Neolithic settlements; recording strategies that redefine economic dynamics of site worker's role

Çatalhöyük Perspectives: Reports from the 1995–99 Seasons (Hodder), 72

Çatalhöyük Research Project (ÇRP), 7; changes in labor management in late 1980s and early 1990s, 156; and community outreach and engagement, 8, 69–70, 157, 158; having goal of community-oriented projects, 11–12; and multivocality, 63, 80, 168n2; site workers knowledge adding to the analysis of finds, 40–67; staff serving as translators for author, 167n8; treatment of site workers at, 66–67. *See also* Çatalhöyük Turkey; expertise; interpretation of archaeological findings; knowledge; lucrative non-knowledge; recording strategies that redefine economic dynamics of site worker's role

CBPR. *See* Community-Based Participatory Research

Çelik, Hatice (worker), **62**, 72

Central America, labor relations at archaeological excavations, 122–23, 125, 159, 168n2

centrality of site workers in network mapping, 49–50, 83–84; eigenvector centrality, 49, 50, 57–58, 83–84

Ceram, Curt W., 22, 128

Cetina, Knorr, 166n5

Chadha, Ashish, 118

Chalcolithic settlements, 4

Chichén Itzá, labor relations at archaeological excavations, 122–23; compared to Temple of the Winged Lions site, 123

children as site workers, 48–49, 65, 93–94

Chrysanthi, Angeliki, 138

Citadel (Amman, Jordan), 23

CLC (American team member), diary of, 56–57

Cloud, use of, 137

colonialism, 112, 115, 119; in Africa, 120, 121; in Central and Latin America, 122, 125, 168n2; colonial authorities enabling *partage*, 19–20, 24–25; colonial model of labor management at archaeological excavations, 11, 12, 21, 110–11, 115–16, 117, 118, 120, 122, 126, 155, 159; colonial powers setting borders in Middle East, 23; "double colonialism," 168n2; and

"global hierarchy of value," 110; in India, 117, 118; legacies of, 14, 22, 110, 111, 120; and lucrative non-knowledge, 12–13; and nineteenth-century scientific expeditions, 18–22; post-colonial countries, 136; setting borders for Middle Eastern countries, 23

community archaeology, 6–7, 12, 29, 31; recommendations for how to engage community, 28–29. *See also* community engagement in archaeology; public archaeology

Community-Based Participatory Research (CBPR), 8, 31, 88–89

community engagement in archaeology, 11–12, 31, 67, 113, 156–57; in Çatalhöyük, Turkey, 8, 29, 31, 88–89, 153, 158; recent community engagement efforts, 26–29; in sub-Saharan Africa, 120; Temple of the Winged Lions Cultural Resource Management as example of, 7; when not a priority, 97–98. *See also* community archaeology; public archaeology

community mapping initiatives, 125

Conkey, Margaret W., 27

Coptos, Egypt (excavations in), 25–26

corvée (conscripted) labor, 116

"craft," as term to describe work of archaeologists, 33, 35

crowdsourcing data in archaeology, 137

ÇRP. *See* Çatalhöyük Research Project

Currusté, Honduras, labor relations at archaeological excavations, 124–25, 126, 136

Dachlallah. *See* al-Faqir, Dachlallah Qublan

Deir el-Bahri, Egypt (excavation in), 20

democratization of stratigraphy, 132

Department of Antiquities (Jordan), 23

diaries recording excavations, 18, 26, 57, 167n11; excavation storytelling, 135–36; praise for site workers, 20, 56, 156. *See also* documentation of archaeological finds

Diggers (collection of photos by Webb), 143

digging tools, 19, 51, 57, 63, 83, 87, 94, 120. *See also* soil, handling of from excavations

Dissard, Laurent, 28

diwan (sitting room), 107, 168n2

documentary recreating Neolithic life, 104

documentation of archaeological finds, 54, 63, 97; drawing as a means of, 133–35; of pottery washing, 52; question of inclusion of site workers, 13, 17, 46, 51, 60, 126, 127, 128–29, 131, 153, 157, 163–64. *See also* archival records of excavations; diaries recording excavations; notebooks; photography

Doing, Park, 33, 34

"double colonialism," 168n2

drawing, involving site workers in to transform economic dynamics, 133–35, 160

Dufton, Andrew, 137

Dumit, Joseph, 33

Dural, Sadrettin (guard), 72–73

Dushara (Nabataean deity), 43, 75, 167n3. *See also al-'uzza* (deity) tablet found in Petra

"eagle in bronze." *See* "bronze eagle"

earthquake in Petra (AD 363), 43

East India Company, 117–18

economics of archaeological labor: economics of site workers' role, 100, 161

economics of archaeological labor, 92, 127; economic dimensions of labor structures, 160; financial impact of foreign excavation projects in, 24–25; redefining economic dynamics of site workers' role, 130–53, 160–61; reward systems in archaeological work in the Middle East, 69, 73; of simplicity in lucrative non-knowledge, 100–105, 108, 110–11. *See also* archaeological labor; lucrative non-knowledge; pay rates

Edgeworth, Matt, 38

Egypt, 16, 117; Burckhardt's travels in, 18; conflicts in, 23; Egyptian independence, 116; Egyptians as site workers, 1, 2, 4, 21, 22; excavations in, 20, 25–26, 28, 116, 136; research center in Cairo, 17; Western civilization as inheritor of Pharaonic Egypt, 20

Egyptology, school of, 20

Eid, Arbayah Juma'a (Spring Friday Christmas), 154, 157

Eid al-Adha. *See* Bayram

eigenvector centrality, 49, 50, 57–58, 83–84

Eken, Ibrahim (worker), **62**

enchantment-led approach to archaeology, 13

English language: use of broken-English as a marketing decision, 108–9; worker hiding ability to speak English, 113

entfremdung. *See* alienation

"epistemic cultures," 166n5

equipment, humans as, 95, 118, 163

Erdoğan, Recep Tayyip, 9

Ertemin, Duygu (interpreter), 167n8

ethical archaeology, 28–29, 38, 79

ethnoarchaeology and ethnoarchaeological projects, 37, 72, 73, 102–3, 158; site workers at Çatalhöyük acting as ethnoarchaeological subjects, 92, 103, 112

ethnography, 17, 33, 34; of archaeology, 37–39, 143; Kalaureia Research Programme archaeological ethnography project, 143; and use of network analysis, 46

Eve, Stuart, 137

excavations by foreign archaeologists, 24; done out of sight of local residents, 96–97; Turkey cutting foreign excavation permits, 166n1. *See also* Çatalhöyük, Turkey; Çatalhöyük Research Project (CRP); Temple of the Winged Lions

excavation storytelling, involving site workers in to transform economic dynamics, 135–36

exclusion of site workers from interpretation: causes and consequences of, 85–90; mapping out, 83–84

expertise, 10, 64–67; archaeologists not respecting Bedouin expertise, 107–8, 113; archaeologists' praise of abilities and expertise of site workers, 154–55; interpretive dialogue as expertise, 80–83; laboratory and laborers, 32–37; and labor management, 64–67; local labor in southern Africa gaining skills and insights, 121; rewarding for downplaying expertise and knowledge, 92, 105–11, 114, 119, 123, 124, 127, 129, 131, 161, 163; in a scientific research context, 33, 166n5; of site workers, 12, 20–22, 40–67, 97, 156–57; site workers having different kind from the archaeologists, 157–58. *See also* lucrative non-knowledge

"Eye-Idol" tablet found in Petra, 43, 74. *See also al-'uzza* (deity) tablet found in Petra

Facebook, 137, 169n1

Faces of Archaeology project (Stephens and Morgan), 143

Fagan, Brian, 18

family members as site workers, 5, 7, 108

faunal remains produced by excavation, 49, 64, 103, 130

feminism and archaeology, 27

Ferahkaya, Haşım (worker), **62**, 68–69
Ferahkaya, Mevlut (worker), **62**
Fergusson, James, 117
Field Methods in Archaeology (Hester, Shafer, and Feder, eds.), 134
Filipowicz, Patrycja, *147*
financial rewards. *See* economics of archaeological labor; lucrative non-knowledge; pay rates for site workers; reward systems in archaeological work in the Middle East
Fisher-Reisner method of excavation, 25–26
flooding problems around Çatalhöyük site, 70
flotation process and equipment, 56, 102, 124, 150, *150*, 158
folklore, learning from, 118
Fotiadis, Michael, 134
Foursquare (networking platform), 137
ful, 39, 166n6

gallayat bendura (stewed tomato dish), 75, 168n1
Garrod, Dorothy, 166n3
gender, treatment of in archaeology, 27; as a category crucial to determining who receives credit, 34
gender identity, 10, 101, 105. *See also* women
genetic descent, 100, 105
Gero, Joan M., 27
Gillot, Laurence, 115–16
Giza, Egypt, excavations at, 116
global hierarchy of value, 110–11
global network of lucrative identities, 113, 114–29, 159
global public archaeology, local labor in, 30–32
GlobalXplorer project, 137
Gomes, Denise Maria Cavalcante, 126, 134–35
Goodwin, John, 119–21
"goofah boy," 95, 163
goofahs (rubber buckets used for moving soil), 51, 167n6
Great Temple (Petra, Jordan), 54, 144–45, *145*
Greenham Common Women's Peace Camp in England, 136
Guatemala, labor relations at archaeological excavations, 125

Hall, Kathryn Elizabeth, 56
Hamilakis, Yannis, 38, *143*
Hamilton, Carolyn, 38

Hammond, Philip C., 5–6, 7, 42, 65–66, 97, 162; archives of, 40, 45–46; on construction of the Temple of the Winged Lions, 73–74, 75; discovery of *al-'uzza* tablet, 43, *44*; excavation dates, 5, 7, 11, 40, 41, 155; headquarters of, 52, 167n7; Sami's memories of, 162–63; treatment of site workers, 5–6, 48–49, 57, 94, 95–96, 155; using children for excavation work, 94; on "workshops" in the Temple of the Winged Lions, 76
Handler, Richard, 38
Harding, Gerald Lancaster, 23
Harris matrices, 57
Haşım. *See* Ferahkaya, Haşım
Hatice Ç. *See* Celik, Hatice
Hatice T. *See* Tokyağsun, Hatice
heart approach to archaeology, 13
heritage management policies, 105; cultural heritage management, 30, 92
Herzfeld, Michael, 110
Hester, Thomas R., 134
Hodder, Ian, 7–8, 11, 42, 71, 88, 104, 156
Hollowell, Julie, 31
Honduras, labor relations at archaeological excavations, 124–25, 126, 159
"House of the Winged Lions" theory, 76

Ibrahim, Hamoudi (worker), 25
Ibrahim ibn Abdulla (Sheikh). *See* Burckhardt, Johann Ludwig
identities, 13, 18, 34, 110, 123, 141; alienation of identity, 125; gender identity, 10, 101, 105; in global archaeological labor, 114–29; as local community members/site workers, 54, 109–10, 113, 115, 116–17, 135, 137; lucrative identities, 113, 114–29, 131; national identity, 24; non-expert identity, 124; traditional identities, 113, 125
İlada, Tunç. *See* Tunç
INAH. *See* Instituto Nacional de Antropología e Historia (INAH)
inclusive recording, 130–53
India, 13; labor relations at archaeological excavations, 117–19, 120; lucrative non-knowledge, 113, 119
Industrial Revolution and devaluation of scientific technicians' roles, 131
Instagram, 137

not being an expert, 105–11; at Çatalhöyük, Turkey, 55–57, 66–67, 76, 156; changes in late 1980s and early 1990s, 156; colonial influences and early archaeological practices, 11, 110, 116–17, 136, 159, 168n2; comparing Çatalhöyük and Temple of the Winged Lions site, 11, 42, 64–67; differing strategies for, 76–77; and expertise, 64–67; a labor model not employing local community members, 127–28; labor models and archaeological interpretation, 127–29; a labor model using locally hired laborers led by foreign project directors, 128–29; linking Çatalhöyük research team members and site workers on topics of analysis, *84*; local labor in global public archaeology, 30–32; reasons archaeologists hire site workers, 124; recent community engagement and treatment of local labor, 26–29; structured by global hierarchies of value, 111; system of inequality created in so workers can't share knowledge, 92, 112, 114, 163, 168n2; treatment of by twentieth century archaeologists, 25–26; treatment of site workers in nineteenth century, 18–22, 20–22, 154; and treatment of workers at Temple of the Winged Lions site, 48, 64–66, 94–96, 108, 111–12, 155, 156; treatment of workers in areas outside of Petra and Çatalhöyük, 114–29; use of in Egyptian excavation, 21–22. *See also* archaeological labor; *specific countries and excavations*
Landow, George P., 136–37, 169n1
Lane, Paul, 120, 121
language barriers preventing local workers gaining knowledge, 87–88, 93, 133
Latin America, labor relations at archaeological excavations, 13, 122–27, 159, 168n2
Law, John, 33
Layard, Austen Henry, 17, 19, 22, 26, 128, 154
Leighton, Mary, 123–24
Lensational program, 138
Leone, Mark P., 39
Lightfoot, Kent G., 31
Lloyd, Seton Howard Frederick, 16
local communities, 16–39; in Africa, 120, 121; at Chichén Itzá, 122; cultural expectations and etiquette in dealing with, 88; disenfranchisement of, 168n2; economic benefits

for, 112, 113; and ethnoarchaeological research projects, 102, 103, 104–5; impact of archaeological practices on, 4; in Latin America, 123–24, 126; relationships with archaeologists, 40–67, 96, 102, 111–12, 115–16, 156, 163–64; and social media, 137; using volunteers instead, 127. *See also* community engagement in archaeology
local labor in global public archaeology, 30–32
London, Treaty of (1946), 23
"lone wolf" concept of the archaeologist, 34
looting, 16, 94, 96–97, 137; nighttime excavations to prevent, 96
Looxcie 2 camcorder, 138
lucrative identities in global archaeological labor, 113, 114–29, 159
lucrative non-knowledge, 12–13, 91–113; and access to interpretation (as seen by both sides), 111–13; behaviors of site workers to maximize benefits from work, 158–59; being a good worker is not being an expert, 105–11; case for memories never made, 93–98; economics of simplicity, 100–105; as a global phenomenon, 113, 114–29, 159; power of not speaking, 98–100; response to concept by archaeologists, 112–13; rewarding expertise rather than non-knowledge, 131

MACHI. *See* Maya Area Cultural Heritage Initiative
Mackenzie, Colin, 118
Madsen, Torsten, 134
Maldonado, Doris Julissa, 124–25, 136
Maler, Teobert, 122
Mandate Palestine, excavations in, 25. *See also* Palestine
Mariette, Auguste, 20, 21
Martin, Louise, 64
Marx, Karl, 26, 32, 35–36, 37, 95, 109–10, 119
Matney, Timothy, 28
Matthews, Wendy, 102–3
Maya Area Cultural Heritage Initiative (MACHI), 125
Mayan site workers, 122–23
McAnany, Patricia, 125
McGuire, Randall H., 30, 35, 168n2
Mellaart, James, 4, 5, 86
MENA. *See* Middle East and North Africa
Meskell, Lynn, 39

methods. *See* archaeological methods; research methods

Methods and Aims in Archaeology (Petrie), 21

Mexico: archaeological research in, 168n2; labor relations at archaeological excavations, 122–23, 125

Mickel, Allison, 7–10; experiments with site workers creating photographs, 13–14, 131, 139–47, *140, 142, 143, 145, 147, 148, 149, 150, 152*, 169n3; interviewing techniques, 9–10, 45, 68, 99, 114–15; languages used in research, 10, 165n5, 167n8; use of names when recording research, 5–6, 20, 119–20, 156, 166n2, 167nn4,5,12. *See also* interviews as a research method

MicroPasts project, 137

Middle East and North Africa (MENA), 115–17; bloody conflicts in Middle East, 23; interactions between archaeologists and local communities, 40–67. *See also individual countries and excavations by name*

mobile broadband connections, 169n2

modularity classes of Çatalhöyük workers, 59–60, **62**; network mapping grouped by modularity classes, 59, *61*, 167–68nn13,14

Mol, Annemarie, 33

Morgan, Colleen, 143

Morgan, Jacques de, 21, 26

Moser, Stephanie, 28–29

Motuk, Elmas (worker), **62**

Mowasa, Darwish Salam (worker), 53–54

Mowasa, Ismail (guard), 75–76

mud brick, 16–17, 73, 103

muhtar (village political leader), 71

multivocality, 92; importance of, 63, 80, 168n2; interviews as key component of, 136; need for, 125, 135, 161; and pro forma sheets, 132

Mutlaq, Musa (worker), 51

Nabataean deities, 3, 43, 167n3; *al-'uzza* (deity) tablet found in excavation at Temple of the Winged Lions, *44*

Nabataean society, 43, 75, 77–79; caves as homes, 105; pottery, 91, 158

National Science Foundation (NSF), 27

Nazal (headquarters of Hammond's excavation project), 52, 167n7

Neolithic settlements, 4, 7, 105; building approximation of a typical Neolithic house,

70–71, 73, 103, 104; efforts to interpret and understand Neolithic society, 69, 70–73, 100–101; Küçükköy residents using Neolithic techniques and materials in own houses, 103; questions on how the people died, 80–81; site workers identifying selves as more than descendants of Neolithic community, 100, 101–2, 110, 112, 121, 158; women participating in a re-creation of Neolithic life, 104

network analysis, 42, 46, 57, 69, 83, 86, 89

network mapping of research team members and site workers, 46–48, 49–50, 83; at Çatalhöyük, Turkey, 57–61, *58, 60, 61, 84*; linking Çatalhöyük research team members and site workers on topics of analysis, *84*; local and learned methods used, 49–55; and modularity at Çatalhöyük, Turkey, 59, **62**, 167–68nn13,14; at Temple of the Winged Lions site, *47, 50*, 57, 85, *85*

Nevada Test Site, 136

New York University, 21

Nicholas, George P., 31

Nigeria, labor relations at archaeological excavations, 120

nighttime excavations, 95–97

Nikon Coolpix P2 used in Çatalhöyük, 169n3

Nimrud, Iraq (excavations in), 20, 128; moving winged lion from to British Museum, 22

Nineveh, Iraq, excavation, 154

North Shelter (Çatalhöyük site), 146

notebooks, 85–86; Allison Mickel's notebooks, 40–41, 45, 68–69, 99; on excavation finds, 41, *41*, 43, 49, 52, 54, 157; on excavation methods and layers, 49, 51, 54, 66; for excavations at Temple of the Winged Lions, 41, *41*, 43, 45–46, 48–49, 74, 167n5; excavation supervisors' notebooks, 48, 157; and network mapping, 46–47; as rigidly structured documents, 85–86; student field notebooks, 6. *See also* archival records of excavations; diaries recording excavations

NSF. *See* National Science Foundation

oral history, 28, 37, 63, 86, 89, 98, 162; comparing site archives to oral histories, 11, 39, 48, 69, 76, 83, 85, 148, 152, 157. *See also* network mapping of research team members and site workers

standardized recording sheets, 132–33, 135. *See also* pro forma

Stanhope, Hester Lucy, 21

Stephen, Jesse W., 143

Stevanović, Mirjana (Mira), 56, 103, 167n10

storytelling, excavation, involving site workers in to transform economic dynamics, 135–36, 160. *See also* diaries recording excavations

Stottman, M. Jay, 30

stratigraphic units, 49, 52, 54, 132; Stratigraphic Unit (SU) 3 (in Petra), 41, *41*, 43; Stratigraphic Unit (SU) 109 (in Petra), 45; Stratigraphic Unit (SU) 151 (in Petra), 45

stratigraphy: stratigraphic excavation, 60; use of pro forma as democratization of, 132–33

STS (science and technology studies), 32, 35

Suez Canal, 21

superiority of Western civilization (to nineteenth century archaeologists), 19–21

Syria, labor relations at archaeological excavations, 115–16, 120

tablet depicting *al-'uzza* found in Petra, 43–45, *44*

Tansey, Elizabeth M., 166n4

Techniques of Archaeological Excavation (Barker), 134

TED-funding for GlobalXplorer, 137

Temple of the Winged Lions (Petra), 4, 137, *140*, *142*, *143*, *145*, 162; 1983 excavation of, 40; *al-'uzza* (deity) tablet found in excavation, *44*; archaeological knowledge of site workers compared to Çatalhöyük site, 57, 59, 64–65, 67, 90, 100, 109–10; "bronze eagle" found in excavation, *41*, 41–42, 43; compared to Chichén Itzá in Mexico, 123; comparisons with Çatalhöyük site, 57–59, 60, 64–67, 83–84, 90, 111–12, 157, 158–59; documenting improper management of resources, 145, *145*; excavation finished by Hammond in 2005, 7; experiments with site workers creating photographs, 13–14, 139–46, *140*, *142*, *143*, *145*, 169n3; finding Roman occupation levels in, 106; high turnover rate for site workers at, 94; "House of the Winged Lions" theory, 76; most site workers having experiences with other sites, 86; negative views on

excavation process, 53–54; network mapping of research team members and site workers, *47*, *50*, 57, 85, *85*; nighttime excavations, 96–97; number of site workers in Petra, 5; predominance of male site workers, 27; site notebooks and final research report, 45–46; site workers disparaging their own archaeological skills, 111; site workers providing differing analysis of finds, 42–49, 73–76, 81–82, 86; Stratigraphic Unit (SU) 3, 41, *41*, 43; Stratigraphic Unit (SU) 109, 45; Stratigraphic Unit (SU) 151, 45; treatment of site workers at, 48–49, 64–66, 94–96, 108, 111–12, 155, 156; TWLCRM starting new project in 2009, 7. *See also* expertise; Hammond, Philip C.; interpretation of archaeological findings; knowledge; lucrative non-knowledge; Nabataean society; network mapping of research team members and site workers; recording strategies that redefine economic dynamics of site worker's role

Temple of the Winged Lions Cultural Resource Management (TWLCRM): beginning new project, 7; as example of community participation in archaeological projects, 7; having goal of community-oriented projects, 11–12; project anthropologist, 8; use of social media by site workers, 137

3D modeling as a potential tool for archaeologists, 57, 137

Through the Eyes of Children program, 138

Tiwanaku, Bolivia, labor relations at archaeological excavations, 123–24

Tokyağsun, Hasan (worker), **62**

Tokyağsun, Hatice (worker), **62**, 72

tools for archaeologists (emergent networks and technologies), 136–37

tools used in excavations: repairing, 56; workers learning the use of, 51. *See also* sieving; washing pottery

tourism, 6, 92, 110; at Çatalhöyük, Turkey, 73, 106; at Chichén Itzá, 123; going to foreign museums, 154–55; as income source for local communities, 37; in Petra, 65, 77, 78, 105–6, 108–9, 133; and self-abjection, 110–11

traditional identity, 13, 103–4